Purgatory Citizenship

Purgatory Citizenship

REENTRY, RACE, AND ABOLITION

Calvin John Smiley

UNIVERSITY OF CALIFORNIA PRESS

University of California Press
Oakland, California

© 2023 by Calvin John Smiley

Library of Congress Cataloging-in-Publication Data

Names: Smiley, CalvinJohn, author.
Title: Purgatory citizenship : reentry, race, and abolition / Calvin John
    Smiley.
Description: Oakland, California : University of California Press, [2023] |
    Includes bibliographical references and index.
Identifiers: LCCN 2022044959 (print) | LCCN 2022044960 (ebook) |
    ISBN 9780520385986 (cloth) | ISBN 9780520385993 (paperback) |
    ISBN 9780520386006 (ebook)
Subjects: LCSH: Prisoners—Deinstitutionalization—United States—
    Social conditions. | Men, Black—United States—Social conditions. |
    Ex-convicts—United States—Social conditions.
Classification: LCC HV9304 .S565 2023 (print) | LCC HV9304 (ebook) |
    DDC 364.60973—dc23/eng/20230130
LC record available at https://lccn.loc.gov/2022044959
LC ebook record available at https://lccn.loc.gov/2022044960

32   31   30   29   28   27   26   25   24   23
10   9   8   7   6   5   4   3   2   1

For my mother, Cheryl Nagel-Smiley, a public school educator who has touched countless lives throughout her lifetime of service.

Contents

Figures

Acknowledgments

Writing a book is hard, but writing an acknowledgments page is harder because there have been so many people who have expressed support and encouragement throughout this process. I am thankful to all those who have touched my life, whether listed or not.

First and foremost, I must thank the people who shared their lives and testimonies to make this project a reality. It is a lot to trust someone to tell your story and I hope I was able to do so within these pages. Over the years, I know that some folks have gone back to prison, had major health issues, and even passed away, not being able to see this work come to fruition. For all, I hope by telling your story, I have done right by you. I also need to express gratitude to the community-based reentry organization and their staff, who opened up to me and allowed me into the world of reentry and "taught me the ropes." Further, I need to thank the city of Newark, a place that has a rich history of resistance and resilience but is often stigmatized; yet I see its beauty.

Next, this book would not be a reality without my tremendous and dedicated graduate school committee, Juan Battle, Lynn Chancer, David C. Brotherton, and the late Jock Young, who all took time to help me cultivate this project by giving both feedback and critique, to help me find my voice and cultivate my arguments and ideas. I also want to extend thanks to my graduate school peers, who read versions of this as a dissertation and continued to support this project when I wanted to turn it into a book: Peter Ikeler, Jan Haldipur, and Jeff London.

I must thank the University of California Press for championing this work about the lived experiences of individuals returning to society postincarceration. Maura Roessner has been an excellent editor, encouraging me and providing guidance throughout this process. Additionally, I need to thank Madison Wetzell, Jeff Anderson, and Sam Warren, who have also been indispensable throughout this process, ensuring all aspects of this project came together by combining our visions of what a final product would look like.

The Newark Public Library became a valued resource for learning about the history of Newark and the July 1967 rebellion, a pivotal moment in the city's history. Additionally, several images used in this book are directly sourced from the Newark Public Library, and I must acknowledge and thank Greg Guderian and Tom Ankner for their assistance in the archives.

Beyond this, I want to extend thanks to Constance Rosenblum, who meticulously read every word of this document to ensure the strongest readability.

I want to acknowledge Hunter College-City University of New York (CUNY), my employer, which has given me unconditional support for this project. More specifically, I need to thank my colleagues in the sociology department, who supported my research by giving professional advice, sharing documents, and reviewing materials: Mike Benediktsson, Erica Chito-Childs, Jessie Daniels, Tom DeGloma, Jess Hardie, Michaela Soyer, and the rest of my colleagues. Beyond this, the school of arts and sciences faculty writing seminar, facilitated by Deans Rob Cowan and Andrew Polsky, gave me early feedback on my project proposal, as well as the Mellon Faculty Fellow of the CUNY Mellon Faculty Diversity Career Enhancement Initiative, facilitated by Arlene Torres and Victoria Stone-Cadena, who read and gave feedback on early chapters of this project. Finally, I need to thank the Roosevelt House Public Policy Institute at Hunter College under the leadership of Harold Holzer, Basil Smikle, and former director of public policy, Shyama Venkateswar, which has given me opportunities to present aspects of this project over the past several years at various public events.

I need to acknowledge two colleagues who have been amazing and help me think through ideas and keep me goal-oriented. First, Keesha M. Middlemass, a mentor, coauthor, and friend, who has helped me grow as a scholar in so many ways over the past decade. Second, Alexandrea Ravenelle, who has become my weekly check-in accountability partner, and with whom I can share good news, ask for professional advice, and complain about all things academic.

Outside of academia, I have been filled with support from friends and family, who have continually asked about progress on the book project and shared in the happiness at each stage of this writing journey: Mario Campo, Jonathan Edwards, Anna Orchard, Garret E. Richardson, and Ahmed Salim.

A special thank you to the Brothers of the Omicron Kappa Chapter of Kappa Alpha Psi, Inc. I could not ask for a better collection of Brothers in my life, who inspire me daily with their personal and professional achievements. I want to shout out Sean Allen, Greg Anderson, Kester Barrow, Karl Brisseaux, Adrian Bruce, Jovan Campbell, Zahir Carrington, Scott Grant, Jamel Haggins, Tennyson Hinds, Curtiss Jones, Kareem M. Lucas, and Shaun Redwood for your support, comic relief, and brotherhood.

I need to thank family. My parents-in-law, Grazyna and Jan Pietruszka, and my wife's siblings and their families for always asking, "How is the writing going?" My father Calvin Smiley Jr., while we have had an unconventional relationship, I still thank you for the love that has never wavered. Without you, I would have not been introduced to the reentry organization that became the basis of this book. Next, I would like to thank my uncle, Udo Hedtmann, and aunt, Karen Nagel-Hedtmann ("Nanny"), as she was instrumental in cultivating my political consciousness. My late grandmother, Mary Nagel, who helped raise me, supported my education, and always encouraged me to read. I have to thank my mother, Cheryl Nagel-Smiley, who has been a best friend. As a public educator for nearly fifty years and who, even in retirement, continues to give of herself to others, she is a daily reminder and inspiration of Muhammad Ali's famous quote, "Service to others is the rent you pay for your room here on Earth," which is something I try to live by every day.

Lastly, I need to thank my wife, Maria Pietruszka-Smiley. This past decade together has had its ups and downs, triumphs and tragedies, good times and bad, but through it all, your support for my work, career, politics, and service has never wavered. The work that you do continues to inspire me to continue to grow as a human and be the best partner that I can be for you. I also want to thank our fur-babies, our cats Stella and Rajah, who always keep us entertained and laughing with their cat antics. Finally, I must honor our beloved Molly, our beagle and my dedicated writing partner, who passed away in May of 2022. Regardless of the time or day, if I was sitting down to write she was always next to me, in her bed, watching and sometimes sleeping, but she was always there. Thank you, Molly monster; I love you always and forever.

Introduction

Melvin[1] was the first person I met at the community-based reentry center[2] in downtown Newark, New Jersey. At the time, he was fifty-one years old, with milk chocolate brown skin, a clean-shaven head, a prominent scar over his left eye, several chipped teeth, and a thin chinstrap beard peppered with gray hairs, and he stood six feet tall. Further, he maintained a well-built physique from a daily routine of push-ups, sit-ups, and pull-ups. Across both forearms he had several "homemade" tattoos, including a brick wall and his name, "Mel," written vertically. He frequently wore a blue T-shirt with purple lettering that read "Made in Newark," signifying pride in his city. Yet it is the same city that determined that more than half of his life would be spent within the New Jersey prison system. In fact, at the time we met, in November 2010, Melvin had been imprisoned for nearly thirty-five years—longer than I had been alive.

On an overcast and gray autumn morning in 2010, Melvin, who had been incarcerated since the early 1980s, was stepping into a world that had profoundly changed around him and, in many ways, left him behind. Technological advances such as cell phones, the internet, and social media were all things he could not fathom and was experiencing for the first time. Everyday items that many of us take for granted were unrecognizable.

During one of our first conversations, Melvin reached into his pocket and pulled out a worn brown leather wallet. "I don't know why I have this," he said. Naively, I began to explain the purpose of a wallet, a response that was received with a smirk and a brief laugh. "What I mean," he said, "is I don't know why *I* have this. I don't have money, credit cards, or family pictures. It just takes up space in my pocket." We both sat for a few minutes in silence, and I reflected on his statement and its profound meaning. I broke the silence by asking if he would share more of his story.

Melvin, who had been born in the summer of 1960, described growing up in Newark—a city that less than a decade later would become a place of urban unrest and uprising in response to decades of social neglect, police misconduct, and economic disparity—and having a normal childhood, playing with friends, going to barbeques, and being a baseball fan. While he could not recall a lot of specific memories from his adolescence, he vividly recollected the 1967 Newark riots.

"I remember it was around my birthday and it was hot in our apartment, and we couldn't go outside," he said.

Raised by a single mother, Melvin had no relationship with his biological father. "He died when I was locked up so we never got a chance to meet, but I heard stories he was a jailbird, so I was always expecting to run into him on the inside." He described his mother, however, as a hard-working Black woman from the South who worked in a hospital during the week and cleaned "rich folks" homes on the weekend. By the time he was ten, his mother had saved enough money to move them out of the projects where they were living and into a house. Two years later, when he was twelve, his mother was murdered.

"She had been dating an older man and they would argue a lot and he use to hit her," he recalled, "but back then you didn't get involved in grown folks' business and wasn't much I could do. She broke up with him because he wasn't coming around. It was a Saturday afternoon, and my mother had sent me to the store around the corner to get milk, eggs, and sugar," he went on. "She was going to make a cake. It's funny, I've never forgotten what she told me to get. While I was gone, he came to the house and shot her. My mother saved my life sending me to the store."

Melvin described this life-altering trauma in a calm and matter-of-fact manner, but it was clearly something he had not spoken about much over the course of his life. While unsure whether his mother's killer was ever charged with her murder, he learned that the man was eventually incarcerated out of state. By the time I met Melvin, his mother's assailant had died, and he described making peace with himself, letting go of the guilt and anger that had consumed him much of his adolescent and young adult life.

Melvin's maternal uncle became his legal guardian, marking the end of his childhood. "My uncle was a gangster," he said, "so I grew up fast under him because I had to earn my keep. He did right by me, but he wasn't really looking to raise a kid."

Although Melvin lacked concrete memories about his childhood, he vividly recalled incidents that occurred while he was under his uncle's care. "I was around thirteen, and he picked me up from school and saw someone who owed him money. He sped up and cut the guy off and ran up and hit him in the head with a pipe." By the time Melvin was fifteen, he was the one with the pipe. "I was always bigger and good with my hands," he said, "so I could fight. If something went wrong or people got out of line I would go, I had a reputation." By age sixteen, Melvin had dropped out of high school, was working full-time for his uncle, and had been arrested in connection with a shooting.

Melvin spent the next four years in a New Jersey prison. During that time, his uncle was murdered, leaving him with no immediate family members. He was on his own. When released, he described going right back to a life defined by criminal activity, particularly armed robbery, as a means of survival. Within months of his release and just shy of his twenty-first birthday, he was back in police custody for robbery and murder.

Melvin discussed committing these crimes with a partner and explained, "This guy and I had done a few jobs together," he said, "and he told me about a bar that had a lot of cash. While we were robbing the place, I thought it was going to be 'business as usual,' but my partner had other plans. Out of nowhere, he starts arguing with someone, but I could tell it wasn't random because they start hollering at each other over some personal shit. Next thing, he shot the guy."

Because Melvin was already on parole, his situation was compounded by these new charges. To add, his partner flipped and became an informant and snitched on Melvin, who was now facing a long prison sentence.

Figure 1. Downtown Newark, New Jersey, 2022. Photo courtesy of the author.

Ultimately, his partner served ten years, and Melvin was given a life sentence.

When I asked Melvin if he had tried to take a plea bargain to reduce his sentence, he responded, "First, I was and still not a snitch. Second, I'm a man and you got to take what's coming to you. Third, even if I wanted to [take a deal], them crackas [White people] wasn't having that. I became an example case, the poster child for the tough-on-crime era."

By this time, Melvin had served a total of thirty-five years in prison. Part of the terms of his conditional release was that he remain on parole forever. In other words, any sort of violation would send him back to prison, as his parole does not end until December 31, 2999.

Embarking on reentry—the transition from imprisonment to community—Melvin has never had a driver's license, opened a bank account, or rented an apartment. He lacked a high school diploma and had never worked in the formal economy. Additionally, he had limited social networks as many extended family members are since dead or fell out of touch with him. He expressed an interest in politics with the election of Barack Obama. Yet he understood that his current condition would prevent him from being able to vote for the rest of his life, as many formerly incarcerated individuals are not allowed to vote in the United States.[3]

In many ways, Melvin's reentry is not a story of second chances but one of initial opportunities. As someone born into a postindustrial society, in a racially segregated, low-income community, and coming of age during the rise of mass incarceration, Melvin faced the daunting task known as reentry, which includes diminished legal rights and amplified social stigmas. For him, and for countless others in similar situations, the reentry process is not linear or clearly outlined but a much more complex and imprecise journey in which individuals must actively participate in *doing reentry*. Ultimately, I argue that reentry is an extension of, not a termination of, the carceral continuum,[4] which exacerbates surveillance, punishment, and restrictions, creating a purgatory citizenship that places individuals in a precarious state of limbo somewhere between confinement and freedom.

REENTRY: A (BLACK) AMERICAN STORY

In the 1980 film *Stir Crazy*, a comedy starring Richard Pryor and Gene Wilder, a pair of city slickers are charged with bank robbery in rural America and sentenced to 125 years in prison for a crime they did not commit. At one point Gene Wilder's character discusses the inhumanity of prison conditions, saying, "I think more Americans should spend a little time behind bars to understand that." His lawyer eerily and prophetically replies, "Well, more Americans probably will."[5]

Since that time, exponential prison growth has expanded the American carceral system, peaking in the late 2000s with over 2.4 million people in jails or prisons.[6] Additionally, more than 7.3 million people are under some sort of criminal legal supervision.[7] Here, Black Americans are disproportionately overrepresented in carceral and surveillance terrain. Remarkably, in 2010, the Bureau of Justice Statistics reported that for the first time since the agency began collecting jurisdictional data in 1977, prison releases *exceeded* prison admissions in the United States.[8] This marked a new era within American punishment and incarceration, which piqued interest in what is more commonly referred to as reentry—the transition out of incarceration.

Today, approximately 650,000 to 700,000 individuals exit prison institutions annually. Unfortunately, the cycle of incarceration remains extraordinarily high, as roughly 67 percent of the people released are rearrested within three years and nearly half of them go back to jail or prison during that time.[9] These numbers underscore the abysmal inability of public policy to create social safety nets for communities as well as the failure of incarceration as a deterrence or rehabilitation.

Yet the story of reentry is not necessarily new but uniquely part of the Black American experience that traces its lineage back to American slavery and the release from bondage, which in turn was replaced by a racist criminal legal system of captivity. Therefore, Black Americans have been in constant flux moving between spaces of confinement and freedom, with liberties and rights simultaneously given and stripped away, making upward mobility a challenging, if not a near impossible, endeavor.

Furthermore, reentry narratives are found in Black history and cultural expression. For instance, human rights activist and Black Muslim leader Malcolm X is one of the most notable examples of reentry. Before becoming a leading spokesperson advocating human rights, he had been incarcerated as a younger man.

Moreover, reentry has been showcased in Black theater, film, television, and music. August Wilson's 1984 play *Joe Turner's Come and Gone* tells the story of Herald Loomis, a Black man, who was forced to work for a White man, Joe Turner, for seven years in the early 1910s, separating him from his wife and daughter, illustrating how the convict leasing system was used to reenslave Black folks after emancipation.

The 2001 film *Prison Song* deals with various themes of race and the criminal legal system, notably highlighting draconian criminal justice policies such as the "three strikes" law, which sends the protagonist's stepfather back to prison for life. In television, the comedy series *The Last OG*, which premiered in 2018, illustrates change and gentrification when the protagonist does not recognize his Brooklyn neighborhood after serving fifteen years in prison. J. Cole's song "4 Your Eyez Only," released in 2016, elucidates legal barriers of reentry such as limited employment opportunities, underscoring many of the current issues within the reentry process.

DOING REENTRY: METHODOLOGICAL OUTLINE

The motivation behind this project is to understand the lived experiences of those returning to society after being incarcerated. Before I began my research in 2010, much of the prominent literature on the subject took a top-down quantitative approach to the topic.[10] In other words, it was very much statistically driven research discussing "what works" in reentry. While this research has its place in the larger scope of criminological inquiry, a major absence in these reports were the lived experiences of those going through this process. Therefore, it was important to take an ethnographic approach to understand reentry, particularly for low-income urban inhabitants of color, the people most affected by the criminal legal system.

Over the past decade, several books have been written that offer insight into the reentry experiences, highlighting many of the difficulties and challenges that face those coming out of incarcerated settings.[11] However, my work differs from these books in several ways.

First, I explore how individuals navigate and negotiate the reentry process by *doing* reentry. In other words, reentry is not simply a static occurrence but rather a fluid mechanism that folks must actively participate and engage in a myriad of ways. If they fail in this regard, they could be subject to both formal and informal penalties.

Second, this work wrestles with the notion of citizenship. A felony conviction interrupts legal status, limiting opportunities for employment, housing, health care, civic engagement, and social relationships. Ultimately, it creates a purgatory status, which builds upon scholarship that engages notions of citizenry.[12] Here, I provide an alternative term, *purgatory citizenship*, to describe how criminal conviction and postimprisonment legal status is altered as individuals are neither fully integrated nor expelled within the American populace, but rather further pushed to the margins without the ability to have a voice or agency, limiting access to power in society, and creating a cyclical perpetual punishment.

Finally, this book differs from others examining reentry because it addresses abolition—the concept of formally ending systems, practices, and institutions of punishment and surveillance, such as jails and prisons—particularly through the lived experiences of those returning to society. Here, notions of abolition are discussed from the perspective of those returning to society in their early days of reentry.

This book is based on three years of ethnographic fieldwork conducted from November 2010 to September 2013 in Newark, New Jersey, primarily within a community-based reentry program that offered social services to recently released men and women living in and around Essex County, New Jersey. Newark was chosen as a place to conduct this research for several reasons. First, Newark is the most populous city in the Garden State, with more than a quarter of a million residents. Second, the city is often associated with criminality, which stems from the 1967 Newark Rebellion and subsequent crime rates. Also, Newark lies within Essex County, which consistently has the highest incarceration rate of commitment by county (15 percent) in the state. Finally, my own family connection to reentry and the city drew me to explore and understand these intricacies in this metropolis.

Drawing upon formal life-history interviews, informal conversations, focus groups, and participatory ethnography with recently released individuals, this book investigates how people navigate and negotiate the reentry process with diminished legal rights and amplified social stigmas. Reentry is often presented as a story of redemption, as it signifies the moment of release back into society, giving the impression of a new beginning. This is often where the headline stops. Yet the story continues. This book seeks to tell the stories of people trying to make the transition back to their community.

In this book, readers are introduced to a myriad of people. The stories told are based on the strictest confidentiality that names, situations, and other potentially identifying characteristics would be modified for discretionary purposes. Many of these narratives do not have the traditional "clean" endings. In some cases, participants ended up back in prison. For example, Melvin has been reincarcerated twice, most recently released in February 2021. As this book illustrates, the reentry experience is often unresolved and a story of incompleteness.

Nevertheless, it is important to note that participants in this research (also referred to as clients by the community reentry center) display perseverance and resilience that is often ignored if a "happy" ending does not occur. Despite the outcomes for these clients, all were processing and trying to "do reentry" in the best way they knew how, which does not always have the fairy-tale ending.

It is also important to acknowledge how capitalism influences and directly impacts these individuals' lives, creating nearly impossible tasks toward the reentry process (such as paying legal fines or securing traditional employment). Finally, while it goes beyond the scope of this book, it is important to recognize the connections that colonialism and postcolonialism have to the global carceral terrain are neither unique nor isolated but impact racialized and indigenous populations around the world.

"THIS IS MY NEPHEW": GETTING INTO THE FIELD

Ethnographic fieldwork can be challenging for researchers, particularly those entering a community in which they are perceived to be outsiders.[13] This is especially the case for research involving those who have been incarcerated, which creates a certain amount of skepticism and paranoia. My entrance into this world of reentry was simultaneously simple yet complex, straightforward but indirect, guarded but also accepted. I attribute this to many factors, including the most obvious: I am a Black man.

On the one hand, my racial background and gender identity as male allowed me to sit in the waiting area or conference room of the reentry center with relative ease as many clients looked like me and this put many of the participants, at least on some level, at ease. On the other hand, I was a person coming into this space with a title and status because of my educational attainment, which could be deemed antagonistic if I was thought to be there only to "study" the clients. Therefore, sincerity and availability became crucial components to this process of gaining access and, by extension, the trust of participants. This meant being in this space and accessible to clients. In other words, immersing myself in this community by spending many days a week at the reentry center for several years.

My being in this space had various meanings for the participants, particularly older Black men, who both challenged and complimented my presence. On the one hand, the purpose of my being in this space was to "teach" the clients as a volunteer, so I was often put to the test of bringing up ideas to get conversations started, such as discussions surrounding the Civil Rights Movement, and having to know prominent figures. On the other hand, many of these participants vocally expressed how proud they were to see a Black man in my position. This duality helped spark discussions surrounding reentry, particularly clarifying and explaining prison terms and lingo. In the end, I was more the student than the teacher.

When entering graduate school in 2009, I did not know that I would focus on the subject of reentry. Yet a pivotal moment in my own life brought me to this work. My parents were divorced when I was two, and I was raised by a single mother. Throughout my childhood I had only sporadic contact with my father, who had a drug addiction and was incarcerated during part of my adolescence. When I was fifteen, he and I had a falling out. We did not speak until I was twenty-three and he reached out to me. At first, I was hesitant to respond, but I realized that speaking to him would ease some of my own life challenges. Ultimately, part of our reconciliation involved discussing his drug use, incarceration, and reentry.

Born and raised in Newark, my father is the eldest child of four. His parents both migrated as teenagers to the city during the Great Migration[14] to escape Jim Crow segregation. A star athlete, he was awarded a football scholarship to a prestigious northeastern private liberal arts college in the early 1970s. Upon graduating, he planned to study law and got a job working for the city of Newark. It was a moment, however, when heroin was ravaging urban Black communities, and he began to dabble in the drug recreationally, which eventually turned into a forty-year addiction, costing him his marriage as well as pursuing a career in law.

In late 2010, we met for the first time in almost a decade, getting together at the famed Sylvia's restaurant in Harlem. During this conversation, we discussed my work in the anti-death-penalty movement and my growing interest in learning more about mass incarceration. He suggested that I speak to his friend, Wadi Darr, the assistant director of a community-based reentry organization in downtown Newark.

Wadi, a year older than my father at age fifty-eight, was also a native son of Newark, and like my grandparents, his parents moved north from the Deep South. However, unlike my father, Wadi was in the streets early in life. Growing up, he was a surrogate older brother to my father, making sure that he went to and stayed in school. It was Wadi who taught my father how to fight, and Wadi who came to his rescue when older boys in the neighborhood began picking on him. By the time Wadi was a teenager, he was the leader of a local crew, hustling and robbing.

Wadi estimated that over the course of his life he had served more than ten years in state prison. At the time we met, he was finishing his last year on parole. Additionally, like my father, Wadi had developed a drug addiction in his younger years but had been clean for more than a decade, attributing his renewed faith in Islam as his path to sobriety.

A few days after my father and I met, my father called and let me know that Wadi was expecting a phone call. Apprehensive, I called, and the phone rang once before a deep and raspy voice answered. I introduced myself and was surprised with the response: "Hey, nephew, I was waiting for your call. Your father was telling me great things about you. When you going to come down here?" Caught off guard, I replied, "When is good for you?" to which he replied, "Tomorrow, be down here ten a.m. sharp, and don't be late."

The reentry center, located in an unassuming dark red brick building in downtown Newark, was a fifteen-minute walk from Newark Penn Station. Upon my arrival, an older Black woman at the front desk greeted me and told me to have a seat. While I was waiting, a young Black man about my age came in wearing a wave cap, a close-fitting silk cloth tied around the head to protect hair.

A few minutes later, I heard that deep raspy voice come through the doorway, accompanied by a six-foot-tall, dark-skinned Black man with a gray goatee, black-rimmed glasses, and low-cut fade hair style who yelled out, "Where Smiley at?" I answered and he responded, "C'mon, you on time, I like that." Before fully turning around, Wadi spotted the young man with the wave cap on and said sharply, "Take that off your head. You know the rules." The young man complied and apologized for the infraction. Stepping through the door, Wadi whispered, "Some of these guys like to test the rules, but I keep them in line," before shooting me a wink with his left eye.

Entering the rear of the building, Wadi took me into his office, a small room with pistachio-colored walls lined with a dry erase board, framed certificates, and a few pictures. Before sitting or exchanging pleasantries, Wadi said, "So what you want to know about reentry. I'm an open book."

At this point, I didn't really have any formal questions and was somewhat unclear what our meeting was even about, but I didn't want to decline his offer from the previous day. I explained that I was a doctoral student at the CUNY Graduate Center in New York City and was interested in learning more about mass incarceration. More specifically, I wanted to examine the connection between slavery, prison, and the 13th Amendment to the U.S. Constitution, made into law shortly after the end of the American Civil War in 1865, which simultaneously freed one population and incapacitated another.

"Oh, you gon' be a doctor?" he replied with excitement. "Come on let me introduce you to some people."

Wadi then introduced me to several other staff members and showed me around the reentry space, which included two conference rooms, a break room, a computer lab, several offices, and a storage room, which among other things was home to donated clothing for clients. When we went back to his office, he spoke more about the organization.

Wadi is what is known as an "OG"[15] in his community, allowing him access to many residents. "I know a lot of people in this city," he said, "so I can go into different neighborhoods and talk to folks. Not everybody can do that, understand what I'm saying? Folks will either know me or know my name, Wadi Darr with the double r, and if they don't I tell them to ask about me and I bet next time I come through they know who I am. That's the kind of person you need in this work, someone who can connect to these guys and get them off the street."

After about half an hour of learning about the organization, I felt our discussion winding down and thought that my day at the reentry center was coming to an end. It was nearly noon, and I was getting hungry. Wadi had other plans. He told me to follow him through the break area into the large conference room where four Black men were seated, including the young man who had been told to take off his wave cap. Putting his large arm around my neck, he said to the group, "Look here, this is my nephew and I mean my kin, my blood. He is getting his doctorate and going to school y'all today on some history. He got a lot of information, and we can all use some knowledge, right?"

The men nodded in agreement. Wadi then turned toward me and quietly said, "I'm going to let you lead this group today, talk to them about the

13th Amendment you were telling me earlier. I'll come check on you in about an hour." With that, he winked at me, smiled, and walked back through the break area. Thus began my journey into the world of reentry.

A NOTE ON CRITICAL REENTRY STUDIES

In 2019 I coedited a book titled *Prisoner Reentry in the 21st Century: Critical Perspectives of Returning Home*, with Keesha M. Middlemass, which was the first critical and intersectional volume on reentry.[16] Here, we argue that critical reentry studies are an attempt to look beyond individual "failure" and "success," and examine structural inequities within reentry policy that impact individuals and communities. More specifically, they scrutinize the complications and contradictions of formal public policy as well as informal social norms that further marginalize, subjugate, and diminish agency for persons reentering society after being incapacitated within state or privately operated institutions of confinement.

Furthermore, we argue, "Critical reentry makes an effort to understand and explain that there is no politically neutral way to apply the law because it is inherently contradictory, and these contradictions are imbedded within its doctrines and systems; when this reality is ignored, the existence of race, gender, class, and 'otherness' is diminished or completely ignored as it pertains to reentry."[17]

Additionally, critical reentry studies make a concerted effort to elevate the voices and experiences, particularly those from racial minority groups and low-income communities, of individuals going through the reentry process. Moreover, they ensure that qualitative research is rigorous as well as taken seriously and viewed as essential as statistically driven quantitative analysis. Often in social science research, preference is given to charts and data sets. Yet lived experiences and narratives are equally important to create cultural competency, transform policy, and pursue paradigms shifts surrounding justice and accountability. In sum, quantitative analysis can speak to the *what* that is happening but often cannot capture the *why* and *how* that qualitative research can expand upon.

Beyond this, critical reentry studies challenge standard practices and thinking surrounding current rubrics and approaches to reentry, which often end with advocating for reform. While certain reforms are needed immediately, such as creating better access of communication for incarcerated individuals and their families or improving food in prison systems, long-term efforts toward abolition are required. Simply put, reform too often reinvents the carceral apparatus, which perpetuates inequality, exploitation, and injustice for already marginalized communities that are plagued with overpolicing, harsher sentencing, and diminished resources. Therefore, advocates of critical reentry studies challenge scholars, policy makers, activists, and other stakeholders to reimagine and rethink assumptions surrounding punishment, particularly postimprisonment and the perpetual sanctions placed on individuals and communities.

The criminal legal system is comprised of various local, state, and federal agencies that include law enforcement, courts, and corrections, creating a complex system of entangled and inconsistent policies. Critical reentry studies look to the genesis of the sociopolitical problems that need to be addressed to uproot systems of inequality and replace them with modalities of care to reduce harm.

Ultimately, critical reentry is invested in putting reentry out of business as we advocate for alternative practices that no longer rely on prisons and invasive surveillance, both in and out of institutions, but rather advocate for investment in communities to avoid the need to "reenter" society at all.

Finally, there are the three Ls: Lingo, Language, and Labels. First, throughout this book, there are terms and phrases that refer directly to incarceration or reentry. For example, clients spoke about their prison sentences in a sort of shorthand, such as a "three flat," which means a three-year sentence. Additionally, the world of nonprofit organizations is riddled with acronyms and abbreviations. For instance, *DUI, IOP,* and *CDS* were all terms I heard repeatedly, along with descriptors such as *DV* and *HUD*.[18] Here, it was important to remember and refer to these terms as they came up frequently in conversations with clients and staff.

Next is the use of language throughout the text. In quoting participants, curse words and other words such as *nigga* are used. The history of the *n-word* is complex and goes beyond the scope of this book.[19] Nevertheless, it is important to contextualize these words. At various points they are meant as terms of endearment and in other places the meaning might be perceived as vague or offensive. I ask readers to both keep an open mind and respect these narratives in their full authenticity.

Lastly is the use of labels. We are living in a moment of changing lexicon, specifically words used to describe identity. Stigmatized terms such as *felon* or *ex-con* are being replaced with *formerly incarcerated* or *justice-impacted*.[20] To that end, I resist using the term *returning citizen* not because I am ideologically opposed to the phrase but because I see the label as misleading in fundamental ways. Throughout this book, I make a concerted effort to highlight the pitfalls, contradictions, and inhumanity in the reentry process by emphasizing how individuals doing reentry are stripped of their political, economic, and social rights. Therefore, not having full citizenship, but rather a sort of liminal status, which I refer to as *purgatory citizenship*, more accurately describes the plight of those coming back to society. I hope this book, along with the work by so many others, will end the postimprisonment perpetual violence that strips people of their rights and that the term *returning citizen* more accurately reflects that reality in a future that moves toward abolition.

COGNITIVE ROAD MAP OF CHAPTER OUTLINE

Chapter 1 introduces Walter Rodney and Manning Marable's concept of *underdevelopment* to interpret the sentiments of clients who feel that government and other institutions failed their community. I frame the context and backdrop of Newark, particularly discussing the 1967 rebellion as a jumping off point to interrogate how participants perceive underdevelopment of their neighborhoods, including (1) removal of leaders, (2) security and surveillance, (3) pretrial detainment, and (4) urban renewal and gentrification.

Chapter 2 investigates the loss of rights because of incarceration and felony convictions, putting forth the concept of *purgatory citizenship*, which argues that people returning to society are in a state of citizenry limbo. In the 21st century, purgatory citizenship presents a complicated status of civic exclusion, creating a confined freedom that is complex, confusing, and imprecise in navigating and negotiating reentry. This chapter explores areas such as loss of voting rights, housing, employment, and familial relationships.

Chapter 3 continues the discussion on *purgatory citizenship* by examining the experiences of participants living in halfway transitional housing, which presents various tasks and rituals that they must engage in to actively do reentry, along with a plethora of contradictory rules they must follow. Furthermore, the expansion of neoliberal policies has privatized many aspects of the criminal legal system that perpetuates inequalities.

Chapter 4 focuses on how prison and reentry change the body because even as a person exits these institutions their experiences and markings stay with them. I argue the body is altered in three different dyads: (1) Invisible & Visible, (2) Mental & Physical, and (3) Abstract & Tangible ways.

Chapter 5 examines the community-based reentry organization and how participants and staff utilize what I call *reentry space*, designated areas of reintegration. Here, I apply Robert Merton's theory of manifest and latent functions, or rather describe the intended and unintended consequences of having this space. While the manifest function is to obtain traditional reentry services such as case management, there is a latent function which is just as important, as this space becomes a way to network and obtain items and services prohibited by the criminal legal system.

Finally, chapter 6 discusses recent criminal legal reforms in New Jersey, but highlights how reforms fall short of creating transformative change. Therefore, I argue that reform must be replaced with abolition. Utilizing clients' interpretations and understanding of abolition, we develop various abolitionist strategies that are meant to be both short- and long-term goals toward dismantling an institution of harm to be replaced by systems of care.

1 Underdevelopment

Elijah had not stood at the intersection of Broad and Market Streets in downtown Newark in over twenty years.

"The last time I was here," he said, looking around in amazement on this sunny June day in 2012, "I was in the back of a van, shackled, leaving the federal courthouse."

For the next two decades, Elijah resided in a federal prison in California. He had been back in his hometown for less than a week, living in a halfway facility when we met. Now forty-seven years old and just shy of five-foot-six, Elijah is a dark-skinned Black man with a pencil-thin mustache and a close-shaved haircut to hide the sprouting gray hairs. Despite his short stature, he is lean and muscular. He typically wears an oversized white T-shirt, baggy jeans, and wheat-colored Timberland boots, attire more reminiscent of earlier hip-hop generations than the slim-fit style of millennials.

Standing at the corner, he continued to look up at the buildings, mumbling, "Wow," under his breath as we waited for the light to change. "Honestly," he finally said, "I never thought I would be here. It's a weird feeling because the city feels the same but different, if that makes sense."

In 1993, when he was twenty-eight years old, Elijah had been convicted of car theft, more commonly known as carjacking, which typically involves the removal of a person from a vehicle in pursuit of the theft. The previous year the federal government had passed the Anti-Car Theft Act, which mandated a fifteen-year-to-life sentence, making this crime a federal rather than a state offense.[1]

Elijah had essentially grown up within the criminal legal system, serving a total of roughly thirty years in federal, state, and local penal institutions. He was first incarcerated as a youth for armed robbery and because of his small stature, his peers and others would attempt to bully him, but he thwarted many advances.

"My first day in juvenile, we lined up in height order and an older boy slapped me in the head," he said. "I had a pencil and let that nigga have it. Nobody messed with me after that, not even guards." From then on, Elijah was a self-proclaimed "street dude" who engaged in criminal behavior. "I stayed in these streets," he said. "That was my whole life." He acknowledged that violence was regrettably an integral part of his life experience as a perpetrator, victim, and witness.

Elijah, who was born in 1965, came of age in the Newark of the 1970s and '80s, during an era of deindustrialization, white flight, and urban decay. It was during this period that Newark, a once thriving city less than twelve miles outside of New York City, lost nearly half of its population (405,200 in 1960 to 275,221 in 1990), which added to the economic and social strain Newark residents faced.[2] According to the 1970 U.S. Census, roughly 88 percent of the city's Black population lived in low-income neighborhoods.[3]

"I saw things no kid should have to see, like guys getting stabbed or shot," Elijah recalled, "but that was the environment, so it was either kill or be killed, no other option." He was the only child of a teenage mother who, Elijah explained, was a young woman who liked to hang around with hustlers. In fact, the first real episode of violence that Elijah distinctively remembers witnessing occurred when he just was six years old.

"My mother always kept different boyfriends," he recalled during a conversation about his childhood. "These were street dudes, and most didn't pay me no mind. But this one guy, everyone called him Breeze, because he was smooth. I really liked him because he would buy me things and showed me love and would do for me like I was his own kin. He was a hustler and made his way on the streets." He continued, "One day we were walking down the hallway of my apartment building, and Breeze was holding my hand. Like I said, he was good like that to me. Anyway, I remember there was this guy walking towards us, and when he got closer, he split us, making Breeze let go of my hand. When that happened, I heard this loud bang and looked up. I saw Breeze sliding down the wall. The guy shot him in the head."

According to Elijah, Breeze's murder was never solved. Elijah acknowledged that he knew who the killer was but never told anyone. "You don't talk to the police," he said. "I was going to get the guy when I was old enough to handle myself, but someone else got him first. That's just how this street shit goes, you put in work yourself."

Even though this event had occurred forty years ago, Elijah upheld what Yale sociologist Elijah Anderson calls the "code of the street" that presents both written and unwritten rules and consequences of street life.[4]

However, over the past twenty years, Elijah had actively worked toward bettering his life and expressed his commitment to continuing that goal now that he was back home.

"I saw things in federal prison that you just can't unsee," he said. "Mexicans and crackas [Whites] don't see Black people as human beings. I saw a dude stab a Black man to death and sit right back down to eat they chow like nothing happened. After all the stuff I seen, I could never hurt another Black person again. You got guys who are never getting out, so taking someone's life is nothing. Shit, I thought I would never get out either."

Despite not knowing his fate, Elijah became a leader of his peers, converted to Islam, and was a gang mediator, who intervened in various disputes in the prison, explaining, "I was only able to do that because I earned that respect." He made it clear that he never became a snitch or worked with correction officers but rather used his status to squash prison beefs and prevent further violence. His model behavior made him eligible for parole after serving fifteen years, but it took another five years of annual hearings for parole to finally be granted.

"I have only been on a plane twice in my life," he said jokingly. "The first time was taking me to federal prison and the second bringing me home."

Like many of the formerly incarcerated individuals who participated in this research and had recently been released from prison, Elijah described a desire to improve the world he lived in. "I want to save my community," he explained. "I was terrorizing Newark when I was younger. That's all I did. I ran around this city and terrorized the entire fucking city for years. I was the problem. I became an example case, and that's why they gave me all this time. But now I need to help change what's happening to the youth in this city so they don't end up spending as much time as I did on the inside because that shit is a wasted life." For so many who are released, this notion of a new opportunity or "second chance" helps motivate this feeling of responsibility to community.

While narratives of personal responsibility were abundant in many of my conversations with formerly incarcerated people, Elijah was also critical of what he saw as structural and systemic problems in Newark and the city's failure to serve its Black residents, quipping, "I can't believe they got a hockey team in Newark, niggas don't like hockey." While said in a jovial manner, Elijah was observant to the fact that ice hockey is not a common sport in urban Black America, as opposed to football or basketball, thus questioning *whom* this facility was designed to attract.

Further, he was critical of the construction of new restaurants, hotels, and loft apartments in the city's downtown, meant to attract young urban professionals, as advertised as only a short mass transit ride from New York City. He pointedly criticized the lack of construction in other parts of the city, where buildings that had been boarded up before he went to prison remained empty for decades, almost frozen in time. He described how the residential buildings in some neighborhoods had been demolished, with nothing to replace them except lots covered with garbage and overgrown weeds.

Yet it was his final comment that struck a chord. "They are not even subtle about not giving a shit about the [Black] people of Newark," he said. "How are you going to put all this money into downtown and leave all the other places undeveloped and fucked up?"

This feeling of Newark being "undeveloped" touched directly on the concept of "underdevelopment" put forth by Guyanese scholar-activist Walter Rodney. In his seminal book *How Europe Underdeveloped Africa*, published in 1972, Rodney argues that the exploitation of Africa by Europe (and the United States) through colonialism and postcolonial policies left Africa without resources, thereby stunting its growth. Rodney states, "Obviously, underdevelopment is not absence of development, because every people have developed in one way or another and to a greater or lesser extent." He continues, "Underdevelopment makes sense only as a means of comparing levels of development."[5]

Rodney expands on this concept, stating, "A second and even more indispensable component of modern underdevelopment is that it expresses a particular relationship of exploitation."[6] Building off this framework, historian Manning Marable expanded on the concept of underdevelopment in his 2000 book *How Capitalism Underdeveloped Black America: Problems in Race, Political Economy, and Society* by linking gender, race, and class as interlocking factors that led to the underdevelopment of Black America. Marable argues, "Development was, more than all other factors combined, the institutionalization of the hegemony of capitalism as a world system," adding, "Underdevelopment was the direct consequence of this process: chattel slavery, sharecropping, peonage, industrial labor at low wages, and cultural chaos."[7]

In this chapter, I posit that underdevelopment perpetuates exploitation of Black low-income urban communities via the criminal legal system, which is exacerbated by the proliferation of mass incarceration in the United States. More importantly, I argue that the Newark rebellion[8] in July 1967, along with other urban uprisings, and Black progressive movements of the mid-twentieth century, were the impetus in shaping criminal legal policies and procedures that overpoliced, criminalized, and removed Black residents from their communities in the name of "law and order" as well as swelled police, courts, and corrections that exploit and ravage Black communities in the name of "public safety." Here I investigate how the concept of underdevelopment unfolds in participants' collective memory, shared experiences, and expressed concerns for their community within the following areas: removal of Black leaders, security and surveillance, pretrial detainment, and urban renewal and gentrification.

THE NEWARK REBELLION USED AS CATALYST FOR UNDERDEVELOPMENT

Newark, a once thriving industrial city during the nineteenth and first half of the twentieth century, has been plagued with crime, political corruption, deindustrialization, white flight, and institutional racism. Mayor Hugh Addonizio, who ran the city from 1962 to 1970, was once reportedly heard saying, "There was no money in being a congressman, whereas you could make a million dollars being the mayor of Newark."[9]

The decline of American manufacturing in urban centers and proliferation of suburban sprawl saw more than 70,000 White Newark residents flee to surrounding communities between 1960 and 1967.[10] According to Douglas Massey and Nancy Denton's book *American Apartheid: Segregation and the Making of the Underclass*, in two decades in the postwar era, institutional housing segregation transformed cities such as Newark into predominately Black metropolises.[11] Yet despite the city's changing racial composition, the overwhelming number of Newark officials in power in the years leading up to the rebellion were White.

Police brutality and unfair treatment of Black residents by law enforcement were a constant in the city. As noted in a report compiled in the aftermath of the rebellion, a survey indicated that 49 percent of Blacks believed the police were too brutal and 80 percent felt that Black complaints to law enforcement were not taken seriously.[12] According to the *Report of the National Advisory Commission on Civil Disorders*, "Although Newark maintained proportionately the largest police force of any major city, its crime rate was among the highest in the Nation."[13]

On the evening of July 12, 1967, a Black cab driver, John Smith, was pulled over, beaten, and arrested by two White police officers. This event was the spark that led to the eruption of the city over the next five days, which in turn brought local and state police as well as New Jersey National Guard troops to the metropolis. By the time the violence had ended, twenty-six people had been killed, all but two of whom were Black, and more than $10 million in property damage had been done, making the Newark rebellion the second most deadly and damaging uprising of the era.[14]

Two government commissions that analyzed the Newark rebellion released reports in February 1968. At the state level, the Lilley Commission produced a document titled *Report for Action: Governor's Select Commission on Civil Disorder, State of New Jersey*. The commission discussed various underlying issues, including inadequacies of Newark city officials, insensitivity toward Black residents, and fractured police-community relations.[15] The report offered ninety-nine recommendations to

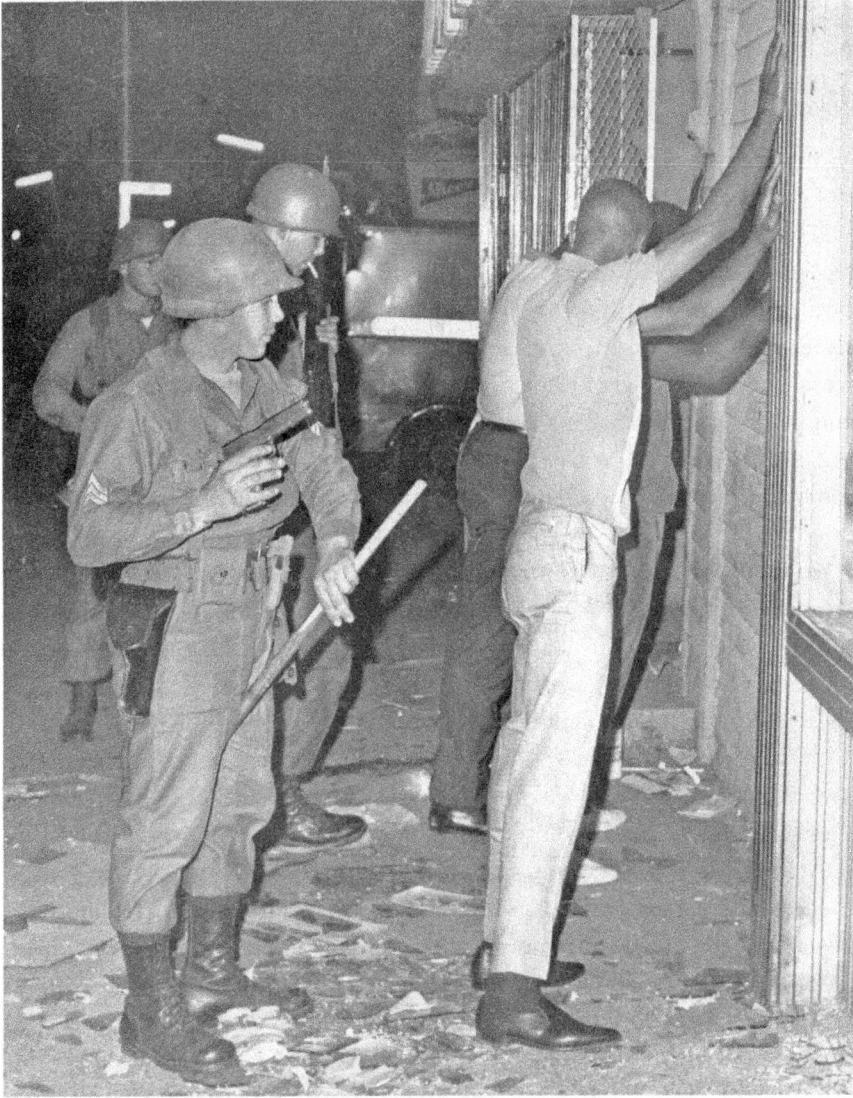

Figure 2. New Jersey National Guard arresting Black men during Newark rebellion, July 1967. Photographer unknown. Courtesy of Newark Public Library.

improve conditions; as of 2014, the vast majority had still not been implemented.[16]

The second report, issued by the federal government, was titled the *Report of the National Advisory Commission on Civil Disorders*, a body commonly known as the Kerner Commission, and examined several "race riots" of the era, including the one in Newark.

This report included several conclusions about the conditions that had produced these uprisings. Most notably it said, "Pervasive discrimination and segregation in unemployment, education, and housing have resulted in the continuing exclusion of a great number of Negroes from the benefit of economic progress."[17] The report also found that Black concentrated poverty and white flight exacerbated urban decay. One of the most profound and troubling statements was this: "Our nation is moving toward two societies, one Black, and one White—separate and unequal."[18]

In sum, the report found that the rebellions in urban Black neighborhoods were the result of frustrations due to systematic racial discrimination. Further, the report recommended massive federal and state investments in housing, education, and social services. Once again, most of these recommendations have not been fulfilled.

Despite these reports, pushing for massive investment in urban low-income communities that had become overwhelmingly comprised of Black residents, many politicians and government officials argued that individual agitators caused urban rebellions. Furthermore, they used these events as a catalyst to usher in the era of "law and order" politics, beginning the period commonly characterized as "mass incarceration."

The Newark rebellion took place during a pivotal moment in the United States. On the one hand, the Civil Rights Movement had succeeded in drawing attention to explicit racist attitudes and overt segregationist policies. On the other hand, the Black Power movement, which was tethered to urban rebellions in the north, pushed for more radical ideologies of liberation premised on self-defense as opposed to nonviolence.

Newark had been a bastion of Black radical politics in the mid-twentieth century. For example, the Nation of Islam, a Black Nationalist group, had a strong presence in the city, establishing Mosque 25 in 1958. Further, the New Jersey chapter of the Black Panthers organized in Newark and

Figure 3. New Jersey State Police patrolling the streets of Newark during Newark rebellion, July 1967. Photo by Al Lowe. Courtesy of Newark Public Library.

Figure 4. Aftermath of Newark rebellion, July 1967. Photo by Al Lowe. Courtesy of Newark Public Library.

neighboring Jersey City. Finally, the city was also home to Amiri Baraka, the famed poet and Black Nationalist, who founded the Black Arts Movement and the Committee for a Unified Newark, which was responsible for helping create organizations such as the Congress of Afrikan People and helped elect the city's first Black mayor, Ken Gibson, in 1970.

Even more traditional civil rights leaders came to Newark. Dr. Martin Luther King Jr. spoke in the city only eight days before his assassination, and his wife, Coretta Scott King, came back to Newark Symphony Hall several years later to fundraise for the King memorial in Atlanta.[19] Finally, only days after the Newark rebellion, the city hosted the Black Power Conference, an event attended by more than eleven hundred delegates, where both organizers and participants shared their sentiments about the direction of Black America. Notably, Floyd B. McKissick, the national director of the Congress of Racial Equality, gave a speech titled "Why the Negro Must Rebel," which criticized civil rights leaders who condemned the "riots."[20]

·   ·   ·   ·   ·

By the late 1960s, White officials began using colorblind language to admonish events such as the Newark rebellion, among other social problems, to advance the need for "moral values" in urban America by expanding the criminal legal system. Moreover, attitudinal surveys on criminal penalties consistently indicated more Whites were in favor of harsher punishments than their Black counterparts.[21] Hence, by focusing on investment in criminal penalty rather than social welfare, politicians were able to appeal to White fears and anxieties stemming from the Civil Rights and Black Power movements as well as to curtail social programs and policies.

Furthermore, many of the so-called "colorblind" policies enacted during this period were clearly targeted efforts aimed at low-income urban Black inhabitants, Black dissidents, and counterculture ideologies, such as Black liberation, creating underdeveloped communities via overpolicing and expanding the use of American jails and prisons in response to social and economic problems.

"LAW AND ORDER": THE RISE OF MASS INCARCERATION

In the mid-1960s, political candidates such as Republican Barry Goldwater began using "law and order" rhetoric. Furthermore, this sort of punitive turn was bipartisan. In fact, Princeton professor Naomi

Murakawa's work highlights Democrat complicity but also active reactionary policies by the party.[22] Yale law professor and historian Elizabeth Hinton writes, "President Johnson saw urban police officers as the 'frontline soldiers' of the War on Crime, and, as such, law enforcement authorities received new military-grade weapons and surveillance technologies, along with new powers in the direction and administration of urban social programs."[23]

Johnson's successor, Richard Nixon, expanded the War on Crime and ushered in the War on Drugs in the early 1970s. While this anecdote is unsubstantiated, a Nixon aide reportedly confirmed that this was a targeted effort at the Left and Black people.[24] At the state level, in 1973, New York Governor Nelson Rockefeller signed what became known as the "Rockefeller Drug Laws," which implemented mandatory minimum prison sentences, legislation that would have devastating impacts in Black and Latinx New York City neighborhoods.

The second half the twentieth century saw an exponential growth in punitive criminal legal policies and procedures. For instance, although capital punishment was deemed unconstitutional in the 1972 United States Supreme Court ruling *Furman v. Georgia*, only four years later, the same court reversed its previous ruling, allowing for the reinstatement of the death penalty in the case of *Gregg v. Georgia*. Furthermore, the rise in retributive punishments spilled over to adolescents. In 1978, under New York Governor Hugh Carey, a Democrat, the New York State Legislature passed the Juvenile Offender Act, which allowed children as young as thirteen to be tried as adults.[25]

The 1980s and '90s continued to witness draconian policies, expanding law enforcement budgets, weaponry, and personnel as well as continuing to increase America's carceral terrain with the construction of jails and prisons during this period. City University of New York geography professor Ruthie Wilson Gilmore's book *Golden Gulag: Prisons, Surplus, Crisis, and Opposition in Globalizing California* highlights California's expansive prison growth.[26] Others have documented the sprawling "prison nation" that the United States created in the twentieth century.[27]

The State of Washington was the first state to implement truth-in-sentencing guidelines and three-strikes laws. In 1984, the truth-in-sentencing guidelines required offenders convicted of violent crimes to serve at least 85 percent of their sentence before becoming eligible for parole. The federal government began using these guidelines in 1994.[28] Further, the three-strikes laws first passed in 1993 prescribed mandatory life sentences for habitual offenders. In 1994, the federal government passed a similar law, and many other states have included three-strikes laws in their criminal justice policy.

In 1995, New Jersey passed its own version of the three-strikes law, officially called the Persistent Offenders Accountability Act, which mandates that anyone convicted of a third violent crime must be imprisoned for life.[29] In addition, in 1994 New Jersey passed Megan's Law, after the high-profile rape and murder of a young girl in an affluent suburban neighborhood. This legislation created a database where people convicted of a sex offense must register, making their whereabouts known to the public. Two years later the federal government, under President Bill Clinton, passed Megan's Law as an amendment to the Jacob Wetterling Act, which required sex offenders to register with local law enforcement.

Beyond legislation, the federal government increased and incentivized local law enforcement and prison growth. For example, during the Reagan Administration, Congress passed both the Comprehensive Crime Control Act of 1984 and the Anti-Drug Abuse Act of 1986. The latter appropriated $1.7 billion for the so-called War on Drugs and created dozens of new mandatory minimum sentences for drug offenses. In 1994, President Clinton signed the federal Violent Crime Control and Law Enforcement Act, which provided funding for one hundred thousand new police officers around the country, $9.7 billion to expand and fund prisons, and $6.1 billion to support prevention programs.

Additionally, civil rights activist Michelle Alexander's seminal work *The New Jim Crow: Mass Incarceration in the Age of Colorblindness* highlights how federal grants and civil forfeiture encouraged local and state law enforcement agencies to make more arrests, which overwhelmingly took place in cities, particularly targeting Black youth. Alexander writes, "In 1997 alone, the Pentagon handed over more than 1.2 million pieces of military equipment to local police departments."[30]

Moving into the twenty-first century, the US carceral system rapidly grew to become the largest prison system, per capita, in the world. After the terrorist attacks of September 11, 2001, President George W. Bush rolled out the "War on Terror," which continued to extend mass surveillance in the name of "public safety." For example, the Patriot Act, passed in 2001, expanded the ability of law enforcement to monitor and tap domestic and international phones, and increased and expanded penalties for acts deemed terrorism, such as treating acts of sabotage carried out by environmental and animal activists as terrorism.[31]

The United States saw its peak growth of jails and prisons in 2008, with roughly 2.4 million residents incarcerated. This resulted in an estimated one in one hundred Americans incarcerated and one in thirty-one under some sort of criminal legal supervision.[32] The vast majority of those incarcerated are disproportionately from low-income urban neighborhoods. Moreover, racial disparities are a hallmark of American prisons, stemming from a much longer history of Black captivity in the United States.[33]

Research has highlighted the fact that Black men, particularly those with less formal education, are at the highest risk of being incarcerated.[34] Furthermore, the expansive presence of law enforcement and increasing size of American jails and prisons has made incarceration seemingly part of the life course of young, low-skilled Black men.[35] Astonishingly, studies report that one in three Black men will be under some sort of criminal legal supervision during his lifetime.[36]

America's obsession with so-called crime control has been at the expense of Black communities, whose residents have for decades been exploited, mistreated, and swept into mass imprisonment.

UNDERDEVELOPMENT AND REENTRY

The Newark rebellion redefined the residents, the city, and Black America. It is one of those events that Newark residents distinctly remember.

My father, a resident of Central Ward who was thirteen when the rebellion broke out, recalled, "My mother kept yelling to get away from the windows every time we tried looking outside. When I got older, I found out that the police were shooting randomly at windows because of rumors of snipers."

For the next several days, my grandmother and her four children were essentially prisoners in their own home while my grandfather was arrested early in the rebellion for allegedly looting. Legend has it that he was caught with a sack of gourmet cheeses.

Many participants who were members of the baby boomer generation divide their own lives into two parts: pre- and postrebellion. Of the former I repeatedly heard narratives that included fond childhood memories despite growing up in poverty. Mack, a Black man in his early fifties, said it best: "My family always made sure we had enough, but struggling is part of being Black in America." Of the latter, the nostalgia faded and was replaced with a more skeptical outlook. "The city was hardened," Mack recalled. "Growing up, we had Italian and Jewish neighbors. My first job was at a Jewish deli sweeping and unpacking boxes, but after the rebellion all that changed and we [Black people] were left with nothing."

The rebellion sparked change in Newark politics, replacing the "old guard" White politicians with a growing number of Black officials representing a range of political ideologies. At the same time, many saw the postrebellion era usher in a new wave of violence, even though Newark had long been a hub for organized crime and home to infamous gangsters, such as Ruggiero "Ritchie the Boot" Boiardo and Abner "Longy" Zwillman, as well as the site of the murder of Dutch Schultz, a Jewish-American New York mobster, in 1935.[37]

Conversely, many members of Generation X and millennials, who were born after the rebellion, heard stories from parents and grandparents, seeing themselves as the children of the rebellion. Simone, a Black woman in her mid-twenties, said, "Growing up, older folks were always talking about the riot—where they were and what they were doing. It's just a part of our history." Yet for the younger generations, the association of Newark and rebellion came with its own set of challenges. Simone added, "Well, maybe Newark is bad 'cause that's what people expect it to be? I moved from Newark to Plainfield when I was in high school, and everyone just assumed I was 'bad' 'cause I was from Newark. So, like, I had to be bad to keep up that image, and that's not fair."

The negative associations of Newark as a "bad" city has plagued generations of Black Newark residents. Yet postrebellion, Newark, particularly Black Newark, has been left with a proverbial "stain" and viewed as a city of dangerous Black criminals by the greater (White) American public.

Often Newark is depicted as a city filled with Black residents who make individual choices to engage in criminal activity and violence. For example, the 1995 crime drama film *New Jersey Drive* sensationalizes the story of young Black men engaging in carjacking for financial gain. The HBO television series *The Sopranos*, which aired between 1999 and 2007, paints the city as a crime- and drug-infested metropolis that used to be a good place to live before the rebellion, particularly for working-class Italian Americans. The NBC sitcom *Friends* (1994 to 2004) offers an underhanded comment about the city when one character asks another if they would like to "hang out" in Newark, after which a character makes a remark about wanting to stay alive. In 1996, *Money* magazine ranked Newark as the "most dangerous city in America."[38] Despite these reductionist views, this section evaluates the ways overpolicing, criminalization, and mass incarceration underdeveloped Black Newark.

Removal of Black Leaders

Many of Newark's Black residents returning home from prison spoke about the plight of the city. Many believed that part of the collapse of their city was due to what they termed the "removal of our leaders." Despite the city gaining majority Black control, participants were more nuanced than simply discussing Newark public officials, instead having a deeper discussion surrounding the assassinations and imprisonment of Black figures, particularly Black radicals. Mustafa and Shaft, both in their sixties, were critical of the government's mistreatment of Black people.

Shaft, who was released after serving just over three years on a drug conviction, spoke about the "good old days" when Black celebrities such as heavyweight-boxing champion Muhammad Ali would come to the city. He described meeting the legendary boxer outside the mosque. "All us kids rushed him, and his bodyguards pushed us away," he recalled, "but Ali stopped them and let us come right up to him. This kid standing next to me said he liked his watch, and Ali gave it to him."

Mustafa, on the other hand, already a young man in the early 1960s, had been a member of the Nation of Islam at this time, and he described hearing Malcolm X preach. "Many [Black] Nationalists came out of Newark or spoke in Newark," he recalled. He went on to say, "I was twenty years old when I joined the Nation of Islam and had already served time in prison. The Nation gave me discipline because I grew up poor, real poor, and had to do what I had to do to survive, but the Nation of Islam showed me a new path. They showed me how to be a man."

Shaft went on to say, "Look what they did to Malcolm, Martin, and a lot of other Black leaders. Whenever a Black person in America challenges this system, they are murdered."

While assassinations of Black leaders were viewed as part of their removal from the community, others saw prison as an alternative mechanism to eliminate dissent. Mustafa received a life sentence and was released after serving thirty-five years. Now, almost seventy, he described his conviction as part of a larger government effort to silence Black dissidents.

"I was a community leader," he said. "I had been in the Nation [of Islam], worked with the [Black] Panthers, and was opening an independent Afrocentric school, but I was charged with murder and sentenced to life in 1976. As a young man, I had been in prison in both New York and New Jersey, and I'll admit I deserved to be punished for those mistakes, but this charge was a setup. They pinned this murder on me to stop the work I was doing. Even witnesses said the person that shot the guy was less than six feet tall, husky, and dark skinned. I am six-three, skinny, and light skinned."

Mustafa continued, "In court, I was made to remove my shirt by the judge because the killer supposedly did not have a shirt on. I was made to stand there half-naked in a courtroom for White people to pass judgment on and they railroaded me. The prosecutor had no evidence linking me to this murder but kept talking about my previous convictions as a young man and saying I was part of a Black extremist militant group. That's all those White jurors had to hear. I have been fighting this case ever since. They didn't want me to open that school, so they took away my freedom," he exclaimed.

Mustafa's claims of being railroaded are not unfounded, particularly in the era and climate in which his case occurred. Federal agents from the FBI's counterintelligence program (COINTELPRO), along with state and local agencies, had infiltrated and disrupted progressive and Black organizations as early as the 1950s. Newark's rich history of Black radical politics was not lost on many of those returning and was a subject that was discussed at length, as was the government's active role in stopping Black liberation.

In addition to Black leftists, reentry participants would occasionally refer to Newark native Wayne "Akbar" Pray, a convicted "drug kingpin" who allegedly ran one of the nation's largest narcotics operations, known as "The Family." As Mack said of Pray's stature as a "hood celebrity," "New York had Nicky Barnes, we had Akbar Pray." Many of those old enough to remember described Pray as a businessman and community leader with a Robin Hood-like demeanor. Pray, who is currently serving a life sentence, has contributed articles to magazines and made recordings titled "Akbar Speaks." He is also the founder of Akbar Pray's Foundation for Change, a nonprofit organization dedicated to changing the lives of at-risk youth.

Interestingly, in tandem with discussions about the removal of leaders were conversations about their replacements. The name Cory Booker repeatedly came up. Booker, the city's thirty-eighth mayor, had been a Stanford all-star athlete, a Rhodes Scholar, and a graduate of Yale Law School. However, unlike his predecessors, he is not a native son but grew up in a more affluent suburb in northern New Jersey. Elected to the city council in 1998, Booker ran for mayor in 2002, challenging the incumbent, Sharpe James. Unlike Booker, James was a lifelong resident of the city and had been educated locally at Montclair State University. During the 2002 mayoral race, James described Booker as a "carpetbagger who was not black enough to understand the city, let alone become its chief executive."[39] Booker challenged him again in 2006 and won after James dropped out of the race.

During his time as a city council member and as mayor, Booker was critical of the open-air drug markets and violence that plagued the city. In 2013, he resigned as mayor after being elected a US senator, becoming only the ninth Black senator in American history. He also was an unsuccessful Democratic candidate for president in 2020. Likened to Barack Obama, Booker was seen as a young, energetic, and progressive face that brought "new blood" to an entrenched political machine and that brought Newark back into a national spotlight, outside of crime talking points.

However, not everyone saw Cory Booker this way. "Booker isn't for Newark," Mustafa said during a group discussion at the reentry center. "I'm not saying someone from the outside can't help, but I see the facade.

He became mayor to help himself, not the people. His Black ass couldn't get elected in White towns, so he came here."

Booker's motives came up on several occasions. In a group discussion, Shaft raised the question, "Is it better to have a corrupt leader who helps out his people or an honest guy who doesn't?" In this question, Shaft was referring to the dichotomy between Sharpe James and Cory Booker. In 2008, James was convicted of fraud and sentenced to twenty-seven months in federal prison. Yet many of the older men had fond memories of the disgraced former mayor. Mack responded to Shaft's inquiry, saying, "Sharpe looked out for Black folks. Guys would come home [return from prison] and get a job doing roadwork, construction, or cleanup. That doesn't happen under Booker. Cory doesn't keep the money in Newark."

Regardless of the accuracy of Mack's memory of the Sharpe James reign, these theoretical exercises and discussions of leadership and the direction of Newark were important to many of the returning residents, particularly older Black men who lived through the rebellion, collapse of industry, and rise of mass incarceration, which they were swept up into because of expanding drug laws and harsher sentencing. For many, the loss of quality Black leaders remains a point of contention, which left their communities underdeveloped, leaving them with perceived less qualified leadership or leaders with alternative motives.

Security and Surveillance

There is always a fervent police presence in downtown Newark, comprised of police cruisers, a motorcycle brigade, and mounted officers patrolling the area. Beyond human authority, there is an abundance of nonhuman security and surveillance in the form of blue-and-white crowd control barriers, mobile police towers, and security cameras. In sum, Newark residents are constantly being monitored by law enforcement. The use of technology for security and surveillance is a popular and growing trend globally. Yet these technologies for surveillance have deep roots in racialized captivity and further marginalize and exploit Black and low-income residents.[40]

Overpolicing, the excessive use of police presence and aggressive responses in mostly low-income neighborhoods comprised of Black and

Figure 5. Newark Police barricades outside Prudential Center, downtown Newark, 2012. Photo courtesy of the author.

Latinx residents, is the norm in Newark. Residents are ten times more likely to be stopped, questioned, and frisked than their New York City counterparts.[41] Research on this tactic in New York found that overwhelmingly Black and Latinx young men represented most of the stops.[42] Ultimately, a New York judge ruled the practice unconstitutional, as data indicated clear racial bias in the five boroughs.[43] Yet, no such ruling was made in Newark.

In 2014, after a three-year investigation, the U.S. Department of Justice issued an order to monitor the Newark Police Department; this was the first time in state history that such an order was handed down, after an investigation revealed a pattern of civil rights violations.[44] In 2016, under the city's fortieth mayor, Ras Baraka, son of the late writer Amiri Baraka, Newark implemented a community complaint review board that is empowered to review police misconduct allegations and administer discipline, even though the Newark Police Union has waged a continuous battle to stifle this oversight.[45]

For many of the younger participants at the reentry center, being under surveillance became a routine aspect of their daily life. Many of them described how this was often their first interaction with police. Wale, a Black man in his early twenties, said his first "real" negative interaction with the police took place when he was sixteen and walking home in the early evening hours.

"I saw this car start to follow me and I ran because I had just been jumped [robbed] a couple of weeks earlier," he said. "I didn't know it was the cops. I thought it was stick-up kids. When they caught me, they slammed me on the ground and beat the shit out of me, telling me they were watching me, had me on surveillance and all this."

Wale was charged with resisting arrest and evading police. No charges were brought against him based on the police's initial reason of "surveillance." At the time we met, Wale was twenty-two and still on probation. Similarly, a weapons charge lodged against the rapper Meek Mill in 2008, when he was twenty-one, was still affecting his life a decade later. His situation did not improve until the billionaires Jay-Z and Robert Kraft became his advocates, and the sentencing judge was eventually removed from the case.[46]

Other young men had more benign but equally malicious initial interactions with police. Malik, a twenty-two-year-old Black man convicted of joyriding and reckless driving, explained that his very first charge was "loitering" and illustrated how this quality-of-life crime can snowball into larger legal battles.

"Honestly, I don't even remember how old I was," Malik recalled, "but I must have been around sixteen and the cops pulled up and started doing their 'tough guy' act, but we weren't sweating them because we wasn't doing anything wrong. My friends and I had just finished playing basketball and hanging out." He continued, "The cops searched all of us, and when they didn't find anything, we all got tickets for 'loitering' and said we were on camera, pointing to the [police] tower. I don't know what happened to that ticket, but I probably saw how much it was for and most likely threw it out."

Yet as Malik explained, throwing out the ticket did not make the issue go away. Several years later he was pulled over for a routine traffic stop, which ended in his arrest after the police officer learned there had been a

Figure 6. Newark Police surveillance tower, Market Street, downtown Newark, 2011. Photo courtesy of the author.

bench warrant stemming from that initial ticket. Malik then spent the weekend in the county jail before he was brought before the judge and remanded until the initial fine and the fees were paid. Malik's experience highlights the economic exploitation of young residents who are targeted by law enforcement and forced to pay fines, which could also have further legal ramifications if unpaid.

In the wake of the deaths of such Black men and boys as Michael Brown, Freddie Gray, and Tamir Rice, among others, in the twenty-first century, the Department of Justice investigated local law enforcement agencies. Even though many police agencies and law enforcement sympathizers attributed the problem of misconduct and harassment to "only a

few bad apples," the Department of Justice found widespread discriminatory practices across local municipalities.[47] Many local law enforcement
agencies in places such as Ferguson, Missouri, were found to disproportionately target Black residents for penalties, such as fines and fees.
Northwestern University African American studies professor Keeanga-
Yamahtta Taylor calls this a "black tax."[48]

After the video-recorded death of George Floyd in Minneapolis,
Minnesota, in May 2020, along with the deaths of Breonna Taylor and
Ahmaud Arbery in Kentucky and Georgia earlier that year by law enforcement agents and White vigilantes, respectively, a renewed critical lens on
law enforcement expenditures and the increasingly exorbitant budgets
given out to police has been met with calls to "defund the police" and rein-
vest resources in other sectors. So far Newark has redirected $15 million
from its annual budget from the police department into alternative programs, such as closing the 1st Precinct, the site where the 1967 rebellion
began, and converting the building into a museum.[49]

Despite this response by city government, the overall public safety
budget for Newark in 2020 was $229 million. This represents a $24 million increase from 2019, an 11 percent increase for police pensions, and
the hiring of two hundred additional officers.[50]

Ironically, the continued expansion of police personnel along with
investment in equipment and technology to monitor and surveil residents
serve to create more barriers and friction between government agencies
and Newark denizens. The continued underdevelopment by not reinvest-
ing in other aspects of society exacerbates social and economic problems.
Clearly, law enforcement cannot be the catchall for solving every societal
issue. A new orientation and investment in universal health care and basic
income as well as social services such as hiring mental health counselors,
social workers, crisis interventionists, credible messengers, violence inter-
rupters, and other community organizations is needed.

The overpolicing of communities occurs in neighborhoods deemed
"unsafe," which are then inundated with constant forms of securitization
such as closed-circuit television cameras, curfews, checkpoints, and massive floodlights. This surveillance not only makes it hard to live but is also
symbolic, indicating who needs to be "watched." Sociologist Loïc Wacquant
has argued that the hyperincarceration of young Black men from urban

neighborhoods has created a phenomenon he calls a "deadly symbiosis," where urban ghettos and prisons have merged and meshed to look identical.[51] As Malik said in summing up his experience with Newark police, "Shit, I don't get harassed as much when I'm locked up."

Pretrial Detainment

Pretrial detainment has devastating effects on community cohesion and contributes to underdevelopment of communities. Often people who cannot afford bail or who are denied bail must remain imprisoned before trial. In New York City, 85 percent of the people in jail in 2016 were pretrial detainees, serving on average 273 days each.[52] In New Jersey, roughly 73 percent of all people in jail are pretrial detainees.[53] This waiting period affects family relationships, employment, housing, and other economic stressors such as accumulating bills, and contributes to day-to-day problems.

Arguably, the most infamous case of pretrial detainment in the modern era is the incarceration of Kalief Browder in New York City. Arrested in 2010, at the age of sixteen, Browder spent a little more than three years on Rikers Island, New York City's jail, awaiting trial as prosecutors continually pushed back the trial date. In part, this tactic is used to force defendants to take a plea agreement. In total, more than 95 percent of criminal cases in the United States end in some sort of plea deal.[54]

Yet Browder, who knew he was innocent, would not concede. During those three years he was the victim of abuse by both staff and fellow prisoners, and spent most of his time in solitary confinement.[55] Because of the lack of evidence, the case was dismissed, and all charges were dropped. Unfortunately, the emotional and physical trauma Browder faced culminated in him taking his own life in 2015. The state failed Kalief Browder. He should not have had a reentry story.

Many reentry participants had their own experiences being held pretrial. Furqan, a thirty-year-old Black man with a beard and a prominent tattoo on the front of his neck, had just been released after spending nearly ten months in Essex County Jail. I met Furqan when he came to the reentry office to inquire about employment opportunities. While describing his experience, he admitted that this was not his first time at county jail but his first instance facing time in state prison. However, this was the longest stint. He said, "I been to county before. Few days here, few days there. I think the most I was in at one time was like two weeks on some bullshit, but this time, I was there almost a full year."

Charged with a series of violent crimes, including aggravated assault causing serious bodily injury, Furqan knew he was going to state prison. What he did not know at this point was for how long. During his time in the county jail, he described turning thirty and initially not wanting to take a plea agreement. But as time went on, he saw no other option. He eventually made a deal and was now awaiting his sentencing. Three months later he was sentenced and remanded to state prison to serve a sixteen-year sentence, not eligible for release until 2028.

Gerry, a Black man in his mid-thirties with long dreadlocks, served just over six years for robbery. He believed that his pretrial detainment, prior to his court date, caused bias in the presiding judge. He described going to and from court as an all-day event that requires intrusive security and body searches. He also described the difference in presentation between someone who arrives at court on his or her own versus someone being escorted from jail. "When you go to court from county [jail], you got on this dark green prison jumpsuit, and you are handcuffed behind your back holding all your paperwork."

Beyond the jail uniform, Gerry described feeling unclean, as he did not have a proper haircut or beard trim to be presentable. "The judge took one look at me and never looked up at me again," he said. "I think it's easier for them to give out all that time when they don't see us as men." Gerry's opinion about court bias is not unfounded. Research has indicated that judges, prosecutors, and juries favor and sympathize with certain defendants on a range of factors, including race, age, gender, and class.[56]

Finally, Rudolph, a Black man in his late forties, had been arrested for narcotics. He was initially charged with intent of distribution, but the charges were later dropped to simple possession. Admitting that he had relapsed, Rudolph said he had been arrested multiple times for possession. Rudolph described being transferred while in the county jail because of overcrowding. "I thought I was getting out after a couple of days, but I was put across the street to Delaney Hall."

Now an Immigration and Customs Enforcement migration detention center, Delaney Hall was one of the largest halfway house facilities in New

Jersey. Operated by the now defunct Community Education Centers, Delaney Hall could house upward of twelve hundred residents. However, Rudolph, who believed that his simple possession would have him back on the streets in less than forty-eight hours, ended up spending a full month inside a halfway house waiting to see a judge because he simply got "lost" in the system.

"My family didn't know where I was at," he explained, "because when I called them I was at the jail, but when they went to see me I had been moved. It was a whole mess." For Rudolph, the loss of this month was a strain not only for him but also for his family who had to take off from work to visit him, crowd-source the money for his release, and subsequently attend court with him. Additionally, his family had to retrieve his pet cat, which had been without food or water in his apartment for the first several days. He explained, "I was worried about my cat, and I know my sister is allergic, but I needed them to take her in. She [the cat] shouldn't have to suffer because of me." All these things placed an added burden on an already fractured relationship, highlighting the fact that pretrial detainment is both socially and economically exploitative.

In the end, Rudolph was not sentenced to prison but given a fine. However, he still struggled with sobriety. "I can't believe they [the court] didn't make me do a piss test," he said, "because I don't think I would have passed." In this case, the courts were more interested in financial penalties than treatment for a person with a history of substance abuse.

Pretrial detainment only serves to alienate and harm individuals before any sort of due process, making a person effectively "guilty until proven innocent" as opposed to innocent until proven guilty.

Urban Renewal and Gentrification

Communities such as Newark are often underdeveloped because of disinvestment in infrastructure, education, and social programs. This lack of investment allows communities to be deemed blighted, and "urban renewal" becomes the race-neutral term for reinvention. Beginning in the early 1970s, the "new" Newark campaign, which started with the construction of the Gateway Center, a set of interconnected above-ground tunnels and buildings, sought to bring businesses and consumers to the downtown area.[57] While much of the latter half of the twentieth century saw the city falter in attempts to build up the local economy, former mayor Sharpe James successfully oversaw the construction and completion of the New Jersey Performing Arts Center in 1997 and fought fervently to have the Prudential Center built in downtown Newark.

Downtown Newark has shifted dramatically. In the past two decades, major construction projects, including restaurants and hotels, have been completed. Nevertheless, the downtown Newark skyline is still riddled with dilapidated buildings and rusting billboards. For example, the historic Paramount Theatre, which opened in 1886 and closed its doors in 1986, has remained empty on Market Street.[58] Pedestrians can still see the vertical "Paramount" sign and the marquee bearing the word "Newark," reminding passersby of the theater's earlier prominence and subsequent neglect.

If you stand at the intersection of Broad and Market Streets, you can see two different cities. Near the bus stop on the northwest corner, you can observe various individuals clearly suffering from mental health and substance abuse problems idling about. Street vendors selling everything from African oils and street food to CDs and clothing line the sidewalk. However, the further one walks toward the flagship Prudential Financial building, the more the environment begins to look like Wall Street without "public characters."[59] In addition to Newark police, private security officers monitor this area.

Many people utilizing the reentry center believed that downtown Newark was gentrified only to serve White folks who didn't come from the city. Research has shown correlations between higher rates of police contact and gentrification, particularly police making more arrests as White residents move into a neighborhood.[60] Furthermore, my own ethnographic work focusing on Newark Penn Station suggests that the Gateway Center was created as a place that tries to keep certain people in and other people out.[61]

Returning to Elijah's earlier comments about the New Jersey Devil's hockey team, he commented, "They brought the hockey team here to 'Whiten' Newark's complexion. I never saw this many White people downtown before. Back in the day, only White people downtown after five p.m. was cops and junkies."

On the opposite side of the Prudential Center, Elijah and I stopped in one of the new cafés located on Lafayette Street. As we approached, Elijah stopped short as he stared at the name of the place. Looking at me with bewilderment, he said, "Stop playing. They really named this place Brick City?" The full name of the café was the Brick City Coffee Company. Upon entering, Elijah turned to me and said, "They got some fancy shit in here." After we ordered our meal and sat at a table near the window, I asked Elijah about his reaction to the café's name.

"It's just funny to me," he replied, "because 'Brick City' has always been the name used to put Newark down. Brick City is the name people use to describe gangs, drugs, and violence in Newark. When someone from Newark says, 'I'm from the bricks,' that means they are tough. A brick is hard, it ain't coffee beans. But that's what happens. Even though the name 'Brick City' has been associated with people like me, it's now 'hip' to use the name to sell coffee and sandwiches."

Elijah's point about it being "hip" to repurpose Newark's nickname elucidates the argument of how gentrification can be a way of exploiting both culture and history. To encourage the participation of outsiders, old ways are diluted and whitewashed, yet parts of the past are kept for a certain edginess that is safe. For instance, seeing city-commissioned murals erected in gentrifying urban areas such as Bushwick, Brooklyn, where individuals can take "graffiti tours" but Michael Stewart was killed by New York police in 1983 for spray-painting graffiti on the walls of the First Avenue subway station, highlights the often complex, bizarre, and mind-boggling way that gentrification operates.

In a group discussion about gentrification, Shaft commented, "Black folks think they own this city. We never owned Newark. It's always been White people's town and they want it back." Shaft's point about ownership is not far off from the truth. According to Newark advocate and historian Robert Curvin, only about 25 percent of Newark families own their home, which is one of the lowest rates of any city in the country.[62] The lack of home ownership further highlights a form of community underdevelopment as Newark residents have greater housing insecurity and are at the mercy of landlords, building management companies, and corporations that purchase properties for development projects.

Moreover, participants in the group discussion talked about not feeling totally welcomed or comfortable going to many of these new establishments. Shaft described feeling unsafe when he walked past an Irish pub next to the Prudential Center. Multiple inebriated White patrons stumbled out laughing and cursing loudly, yet the police in the area continued to keep their eyes affixed on Shaft. "It didn't seem like any Black people were in that place," he said. "I don't know if I would go in there. It didn't feel like a place that I should go."

Surrounded by Irish flags, White hockey fans from out of town, and a vigilant police presence, Shaft innately understood what Yale sociologist Elijah Anderson describes as "white space."[63] While they did not articulate it in the same manner, many participants recognized that their race, class, gender, and criminal status did not afford them the same privileges as their White counterparts.

In recounting a similar experience, Mack described entering a Whole Foods supermarket on Broad Street. "I was excited when they opened," he said, "but I really haven't shopped there much. I'm used to bodegas, not all these aisles. I'm simple, but that's not even the main reason. It's just expensive." Clearly, affordability also explains why certain Newark residents feel excluded from these new places.

While participants were critical of gentrification occurring downtown, they were equally critical of their neighborhood neglect. In fact, like Flint, Michigan, Newark also found itself in the middle of a water crisis. In 2016–2017, testing of Newark water, particularly in schools, found higher than acceptable levels of lead in the drinking supply.[64] The city has addressed these issues, yet the findings highlight the fact that public officials were not investing in the city, along with the fact that when it comes to maintaining public works, lack of oversight and accountability is part of a longer, and often tragic, history of underdevelopment and neglect of the city.

SUMMARY

Overall, this chapter gives a brief context to the community of Newark. While residents are resilient, that does not come without struggle. Participants understood and articulated living in an underdeveloped community.

As Mustafa expressed, "Do you think the cops could get away with doing the stuff they do to us in some of these other towns around here?

Hell no. They can harass us because we are Black and in Newark. The city's got its problems but locking every Black person up isn't going to solve them. I bet they don't go downtown and start harassing those White boys. They probably got more drugs in those offices than we got up on South Orange Avenue."

To reiterate Walter Rodney, "Underdevelopment makes sense only as a means of comparing levels of development." Mustafa, Shaft, Elijah, and others recognized the disproportionate treatment, particularly of Black Newark. Therefore, the underdevelopment of Newark, like many urban communities of color, has been systemic and deliberate, to stunt community growth and cohesion. In sum, Black Newark has been underdeveloped by the proliferation of criminalization, overpolicing, and mass incarceration of Black residents.

2 Purgatory

November 6, 2012, was a chilly Election Day in northern New Jersey. But the sun shined bright, reflecting the atmosphere in downtown Newark as President Barack Obama, the incumbent, earned 78 percent of the votes cast in Essex County.[1]

That morning, the city was jubilant as residents celebrated *their* president. On the corner of Broad and Market Streets, storefronts displayed large posters of Barack and Michelle Obama. Street vendors were selling Obama T-shirts, hats, and buttons and playing his speeches through large speakers. Canvassers were encouraging passersby to "get out and vote," and residents were proudly showing off their "I voted" stickers.

Walking to the reentry center to facilitate group with participants that morning, I had mixed emotions. On the one hand, I had felt inspired by Obama's presidency and was hopeful that he would be reelected. Yet a feeling of anxiety came over me, knowing that I was walking into a place where most clients were barred from participating in the political process.

Every state except Maine and Vermont has some sort of voter disenfranchisement law, which limits participation in the electoral process.[2] Scholars have pointed out that many voter disenfranchisement laws were enacted around the time of the Civil War, particularly in the years after

Figure 7. Image of Barack Obama on T-shirt in storefront window, Election Day 2012, downtown Newark. Photo courtesy of the author.

Black Americans gained the right to vote under the 15th Amendment.[3] Disenfranchisement laws were enacted in New Jersey in 1844, and for the next 175 years the state constitution, which barred anyone under criminal justice supervision from voting, remained virtually unchanged.[4]

When I arrived, the group of clients had already assembled for our weekly discussion on reentry, and I was thinking about how I would open the conversation about what the right to vote means. Before I could take off my jacket, Stuart asked, "Smiley, did you vote?" Thus began our conversation about the intersection of race, reentry, and disenfranchisement.

"N——R WON"

Stuart was a clean-shaven, fifty-two-year-old Black man with brown skin and an athletic build who, as he put it, "got out" of Newark. He explained that his parents, both migrants from the Deep South, had worked hard to put him and his siblings through college and owned their home, something rare for Blacks who were members of the Silent Generation.

"I come from a political family that would debate politics," Stuart told me. "From an early age, I knew what it meant to be Black and proud. My parents were community leaders, organizing on our block and championing civil rights."

After high school, Stuart was awarded an academic scholarship to a prestigious university in the Midwest, where he pursued a degree in communications. However, unlike his siblings, he did not complete his undergraduate studies but instead landed a dream job in television broadcasting, becoming the first Black male investigative journalist at the station in the early 1980s.

He described having a good life that afforded him the opportunity to travel abroad and buy a multibedroom home, a luxury car, and designer clothing. But despite his successful career, Stuart's world came crashing down in the early 2000s when the police came knocking at his door.

"There had been rumors I was going to be arrested," he explained, "but I didn't want to panic or draw more attention to the allegations. Eventually they came for me. It was early in the morning, and I was in my kitchen making coffee, and I saw the blue and red lights reflecting off the trees. It just felt surreal, like a dream, and I was thinking, 'It's all over.'"

Stuart continued, "Then I heard them knocking on the front door, and that's when I freaked out. I ran upstairs and grabbed my suitcase and started packing clothing, money, and whatever else I could. And then I realized I was trapped and went into the bathroom and slit my wrists."

Stuart survived. But he was subsequently charged with and convicted of multiple sex offenses involving a group of male teenage minors whom he had met through a mentorship program. Because Stuart was a prominent figure, his case created a local frenzy. And as for the clarification?

"I'm gay," Stuart explained. "I don't think I ever really admitted that to myself and did not admit it to anyone else. I was in relationships with women trying to do the traditional thing, but deep down, I always knew I was attracted to men. I'm not saying this to excuse my actions. I know what I did was wrong, but I think if I was honest with myself, I could have avoided all of this. I was just unhappy and depressed and made a horribly stupid mistake, and because I was an investigative journalist that covered police brutality, the cops really went after me."

Stuart ended up taking a plea agreement and served a little more than five years in prison. Because of the nature of his crime and the cause célèbre that his case became, Stuart served most of his time in a segregated housing unit (SHU). It was during this time that Barack Obama was first running for president. Stuart vividly described the exact moment he learned of Obama's victory.

"I was in the SHU," he recalled, "and the guard, this fat White racist piece of shit, knew I was following the election closely, and some time in the late evening while making his rounds he whispered into my cell, 'The nigger won.' He said it that way to try and get me angry, but I remember crying out of joy and then regret, because millions of Black people were out in the streets celebrating this moment and my Black ass was in prison. I felt ashamed because I thought about my parents and grandparents who sacrificed so much, who never got the opportunity to vote. I didn't just let myself down but generations of Black people."

While Stuart understood that he was disenfranchised because of his criminal penalty, he argued, "Voting holds government accountable. I had really bought into the democratic process, but how can this be a democracy when lots of people, particularly people locked up, cannot vote? It's not just wrong but outright contradicts democratic values."

Stuart's words underscored the notion that individuals returning to society who have a criminal record, specifically those with felony convictions, risk losing social, economic, and political rights. In the process they create a distinctive form of citizenry that is unique to people experiencing the reentry process. I call this *purgatory citizenship*.

In purgatory citizenship, individuals are neither a fully integrated in-group nor a totally excluded out-group but rather stuck in a limbo status between "citizen" and "other." Typically, citizens with a felony conviction do not enjoy the same rights and privileges as those without a criminal conviction. Conversely, unlike noncitizens, formerly incarcerated citizens are not deported or removed from the country.[5] This unique status creates a complicated, complex, and fragile relationship between individuals and the state.

More specifically, purgatory citizenship highlights the various ways individuals *doing* reentry navigate and negotiate their identity and freedom with amplified social stigmas and diminished legal rights. Further, highlighting reentry is neither linear nor straightforward, but often precarious and imprecise as individuals' lives are at the mercy of various actors, both private and public individuals and institutions, which creates and results in raised fear, anxiety, and mistrust in the system. In sum, purgatory citizenship creates more barriers than opportunities.

PURGATORY CITIZENSHIP

The notion of citizenship, specifically the right to inclusion, is foundational to democratic societies.[6] The United States was founded as a "peculiar institution" that embraced concepts of both individual liberty and institutional bondage, based on social constructions of race and inferior status affirmed by ethnocentric ideas on ethnicity, culture, tradition, and language.[7] The peculiar institution has continued to expand into the criminal legal system.[8]

This chapter builds upon various concepts that have been used to discuss the relationship between citizenry and criminal status, highlighting that simply transitioning out of prison does not make an individual free. For example, Michelle Alexander and Bruce Western have both highlighted the various legal ways felony convictions recreate second-class status.[9] Further, Amy Lerman and Vesla Weaver discuss their concept of "custodial citizenship," which emphasizes criminal legal involvement dictating, specifically to low-income Black Americans, experiences of citizenry.[10]

Conversely, Reuben Miller and Forest Stuart argue that "carceral citizenship" has benefits as well as no difference from traditional citizenship, but is simply an alternate legal reality.[11] Here, I push back on this assertion as their argument undermines the struggle to obtain full citizenry by downplaying the severity of these losses. Finally, Susan Sered argues a "diminished citizenship," which considers both criminalization and other forms of marginalization as failures of the state rather than the individual.[12]

Purgatory is often imagined as a physical place where souls go to atone for sins. Reentry, the process of return, is a purgatory status that extends, not ends, punishment. When it comes to the criminal legal system, a myriad of factors including conviction, supervision status, and place of residence dictate limitations and allowances in the reentry process, creating both confusion and frustration for those making this transition. Just as the concept of purgatory leaves an individual's soul stuck in limbo, reentry mimics this process by keeping a person's citizenship status in flux.

Simply put, reentry creates a confined freedom, limiting a person's ability to move past a criminal conviction. It also continues to marginalize individuals through perpetual punishments that rely on numerous rituals and rites of passage to gain inclusion back into society, which is never guaranteed.

The best summation of this limbo status, highlighting purgatory citizenship, was offered by Sharif, a Black man in his early fifties, who was completing a thirty-year sentence for murder. "It's like dangling a carrot in front of a rabbit. That's how I feel," he explained. "We can see freedom and maybe even taste it, but they are never going to give it to us. It's like I have one foot in and one foot out and must straddle that line [snaps fingers] because in an instance it can all be taken away, just like that, no matter how well we do. When you come home you must be perfect."

Sharif, who stood six-four and weighed almost 250 pounds, was a soft-spoken, dark-skinned man, and was bald and had a long beard that came to a gray point. During his three decades in state prison, Sharif became both a jailhouse lawyer and a mentor.

Despite being incarcerated for thirty years, longer than I had been alive at the time, Sharif arrived at the reentry center each week with a warm smile. When I asked him what made him happy, he responded, "You have to be able to laugh, otherwise, you lose your humanity." He then explained what had led to his lengthy imprisonment. He had joined the army at eighteen, and engaged in drugs, alcohol, and the party scene of the late 1970s. To keep up this lifestyle, Sharif described needing fast money, and devising various robbery schemes to get it.

"My cousin was a homosexual," he recalled. "Back at that time, a lot of people didn't want to be around gay people because AIDS was just discovered, but his sexuality never bothered me. He did what he did and respected me and vice versa. He had been turning tricks [sex work], so I came up with the idea that we would work together to hustle."

According to Sharif, his cousin would engage in illicit sex work and after he got picked up, he would wait nearby and rob both parties, making it look like a random theft. Afterward, he and his cousin would split the spoils.

After a few successful robberies of unsuspecting motorists, their luck ran out as Sharif recalled, "When I approached the vehicle, a Mercedes, I saw two White men. One was holding a knife, and the other was holding my cousin. The older guy jumped out, and we fought for the knife. My size and military training gave me the edge. I later learned it was a father and son. This guy was cruising with his own child."

Instead of taking a plea agreement, Sharif decided to stand trial, arguing that he killed the man in self-defense. In court he learned that the deceased man was a wealthy and prominent local figure from a nearby suburb. When asked about his sentence, Sharif believed that in hindsight he should have taken a deal, but doing so was also not an option as his cousin turned state's witness and testified against him in return for a reduced sentence.

While Sharif acknowledged his crime, he also asserted that race and class played an important role in his case, pondering whether, if the positions were reversed and he had been killed during the altercation, would the White man have been sentenced to thirty years. "Being Black in America is a crime," he said, "and I have never been truly free."

.   .   .   .   .

When I began this research on reentry, one of the questions I routinely asked was "What does the term *democracy* mean to you?" The question was almost always met with a long pause. For some, it was an admission of not knowing or understanding the word. For others, it was because the word was reserved for White America.

Being Black in America has granted a unique perspective of constantly feeling that one does not belong and is treated as a stranger, outsider, and other. In sum, as Loïc Wacquant says, to be Black is "the living antithesis to the 'model American.'"[13]

At the core of the notion of race is the problematic issue of being the *wrong* race. In his 1903 seminal work *The Souls of Black Folk: Essays and Sketches*, sociologist and historian W. E. B. Du Bois begins with a fundamental question: "Why did God make me an outcast and stranger in mine own house?"[14] Du Bois is referring to the dichotomy of being both "Black" and "American" in a system that finds the conflation at odds. This feeling of being left out, or rather excluded, is conveyed through Du Bois's idea of "double-consciousness"—having the ability to see the world through one's own identity but also forced to see life through the dominant culture (i.e., white supremacy), or rather having the feeling of "two-ness."[15]

Ralph Ellison's 1952 novel *Invisible Man* highlights the paradox of being Black in America. He writes, "Well, I was and yet I was invisible, that was the fundamental contradiction. I was and yet I was unseen."[16] In other words, to be invisible and unseen shapes Black life in America. This perspective is supported by John Langston Gwaltney's 1980 work *Drylongso: A Self-Portrait of Black America*, in which a Black woman states, "Now, to White people your colored person is always a stranger. Not only that, we are supposed to be dumb strangers, so we can't tell them anything!"[17]

In the twenty-first century, Black Americans are still challenging the American system for racial inclusion. Jay-Z raps in "F.U.T.W," "Feelin' like a stranger in my own land,"[18] showcasing how Black Americans are still wrestling with the fundamental notion of obtaining racial belonging.

Furthermore, as the carceral state has become routinized and part of the Black experience in modern urban America, criminal status (i.e., felony) is superimposed on top of race.[19] This concept is synthesized best by James Davis III, a student at Wesleyan University's Center for Prison Education, who writes, "Convicted of a crime, he must grapple with his criminality, but being perceived as a criminal was his reality before committing any criminal act. He was born guilty of possessing black skin and was later convicted of being a black man. *Double-double consciousness* is the prisoner's response to his oppression, but also an affirmation of his own humanity."[20]

Therefore, Black Americans who have a criminal conviction have a distinctive perspective and relationship to American democracy. In sum, the "double-double consciousness" highlights the uniqueness of purgatory citizenship.

·   ·   ·   ·   ·

The "social contract" is a collective effort contributing toward the greater purpose of all.[21] As sociologist John Torpey writes, "This consideration is especially important in a world of states understood as nation-states that is, as comprising members conceived, at least from the outside, as *citizens*."[22] Therefore, citizenship grants individuals' rights as well as organizes groups around collective identities. For example, passports are both symbolic and physical representations of identity and residency.

However, more important to the concept of citizenship is the notion of *belonging*. As ethnic studies professor Evelyn Nakano Glenn writes, "Citizenship is not just a matter of formal legal status; it is a matter of *belonging*, which requires *recognition* by other members of the community. Community members participate in drawing the boundaries of citizenship and defining who is entitled to civil, political, and social rights by granting or withholding recognition."[23]

In other words, rights are granted or taken away based on constructed membership of citizenry, particularly for non-Whites, in the United States where variation and progression of citizenship differs by group.[24] In the case of Black Americans, there are clear, established historical points of exclusion.[25] Furthermore, mass incarceration has become a new iteration of economic, social, and political exclusion. Michelle Alexander articulates this by arguing that the vast and disproportionate imprisonment of Black Americans has created a "racial undercaste," which in turn stymies future decisions and life course upon reentry,[26] hence, resulting in purgatory citizenship.

"'CAUSE OF DOGS"

Research on reentry indicates that an important marker of stability is housing.[27] Yet in many instances, stable housing is either not an option or comes with complications. For example, Jennifer Gonnerman's 2005 book *Life on the Outside: The Prison Odyssey of Elaine Bartlett* describes the life of Harlem resident Elaine Bartlett, who was sentenced to life imprisonment under New York's Rockefeller drug laws.[28] Bartlett served sixteen years and struggled to mend familial relationships, find work, and obtain housing. Often, individuals with a felony conviction, particularly if they are on parole or probation, are denied access to public housing and can be barred from housing in the private sector.[29] Because of housing restrictions, individuals returning to society are stuck in limbo, literally.

Many clients of the reentry center had housing issues, with many of them living in one of several halfway houses scattered throughout Newark. Yet securing housing was a crucial aspect of maintaining freedom as was stipulated in their release.[30]

Some individuals had concrete ideas of where they were going to live after the halfway house, in other words, a setting that included a spouse, partner, relative, or friend. Others had more abstract notions of housing, not being able to give a specific location or name individuals they would reside with. In many cases, individuals who left the halfway houses would move to a shelter for houseless people, places that were typically described as filthy and dangerous. In 2010, there was a bedbug outbreak in the metropolitan area, and clients had to keep their belongings in garbage bags and sleep, fully clothed, on top of the sheets to avoid bug bites.

Jamal, a twenty-six-year-old who had been released from state prison after serving three years for drug distribution, exemplified the precarity of securing housing after release. After he had lived in a halfway facility for less than six months, his aunt agreed to let him move in with her and her two sons. Jamal said that his mother had died some years earlier and his father had a drug problem, fracturing their relationship. Jamal did not graduate from high school and, being on his own after his mother's death, was frequently homeless or stayed with friends.

After the first two weeks of living with his aunt, in Newark's West Ward, a primarily Black section of the city, he described the difficulties of this transition. Among other things, his aunt took issue with how long he spent in the bathroom. "I like long hot showers because it calms me down," he said. "In prison, most you get is a short cold shower. She told me that I was running up her water bill. She put me on a shower time limit."

Jamal described having his own room, jokingly calling it his "cell," and had access to television, a family computer, and video games. During the day, Jamal began looking for employment and came to the reentry center for case management, which helped him secure hard and soft employment skills.

After a month, Jamal was still struggling to find a job, and his parole officer, a Black man of West Indian descent in his early forties, was dissatisfied with his effort. This is when Jamal's housing issues began.

After a random inspection of her home, the parole officer gave his aunt a list of needed modifications. For instance, his aunt's cell phone was considered insufficient to keep tabs on Jamal, and she had to add a landline phone, with a cord, that did not have call forwarding, three-way calling, or caller ID, or the ability to put a person on hold. While this type of phone was not expensive, it took some effort to find a phone without any of these amenities. The cost, however, involved installation fees and monthly telephone bills, which were now charged to his aunt. As this example indicates, the financial cost of reentry can be burdensome, not just for those going through this process but tangentially for those around them.

By the end of the second month, Jamal was on edge and agitated, explaining that his and his aunt's relationship was being strained because of parole, which conducted two more inspections of the home. The first occurred in the early evening and the officers began searching the home and forcefully explained that they could come at any time, day or night, despite the fact that the aunt protested the intrusion on the family's dinner.

Yet it was the second inspection that truly violated the family. As Jamal explained, "They showed up at fucking three a.m. They banged on the door so hard we thought they broke it down and made us all sit with our hands on our knees and our heads facing down. The entire time, saying unnecessary things to my aunt and her sons. They try and get you mad so if you say something back, they will arrest you. You got to just sit and take that shit."

Showing signs of physical distress while recounting the events, he went on, "They tore her house apart, overturned the furniture, emptied out all drawers, and 'accidently' broke the phone. They were there for over an hour, and after they left, my aunt had to calm her sons down. We all had to spend the next day cleaning the house. The boys didn't go to school, and she called out of work."

Because of Jamal's status as a felon who was still under criminal legal supervision, the same rights that many believe apply to all citizens do not exist here.

Despite this traumatic event, Jamal's aunt bought a new landline telephone and continued to let him stay at her residence. A few days later, Jamal informed me that he had gotten a part-time job at a local cheese manufacturer. It was the holiday season, and the factory hired him on a temporary basis, with the possibility for a permanent position.

At the end of the third month, Jamal's parole officer was no longer allowing him to stay at his aunt's home. When I asked why, he responded, "'Cause of [the] dogs." Jamal's aunt had two pit bull terriers. Up until this point, Jamal had barely mentioned the dogs. But when he had met with his parole officer the previous week, he was told that he was in violation of his parole if the dogs remained in the home. The parole officer claimed that these types of dogs are used in the drug trade and not suitable for his living conditions. (In recent years, pit bulls have been stigmatized and racialized as both "bad" and "Black" dogs.)[31]

Jamal was distraught. "I don't even have a violent crime," he said, "and this guy just wants to see me fail. I'm not going to make my aunt choose between her dogs and me. She loves those dogs, so I got to leave."

For the next two weeks, Jamal did not show up to weekly group sessions at the reentry center. When he finally returned, he explained, "I started back at the shelter but left after a few days. It's a lot of sick [mentally ill] people and it was fucking with my mental." Jamal eventually ended up living with his grandmother at a senior living building; he had become friendly with the overnight female security guard, who allowed him to come during her shift if he left before she went off duty.

When I asked Jamal if he was afraid of being caught by his parole officer, he defiantly replied, "Fuck him." At this point Jamal was trying to get a new parole officer, and his aunt had filed a complaint about the second search of her home.

The experiences of Jamal, who was unofficially "living" with his grandmother, highlighted one of the many ways that people going through reentry had to constantly navigate and negotiate this process. Jamal attempted to *navigate* his parole by finding stable housing, making modifications to his aunt's home, and trying to fulfill stipulations such as gainful employment. However, his parole officer made this process essentially impossible. Therefore, Jamal began *negotiating* his freedom.

In this case, his aunt's home became prohibited, and he refused to live in unsafe and unsanitary conditions at a shelter. His grandmother's residence provided him a modicum of safety and stability, and so he slept there a few hours each night. His predicament underscores the way reentry becomes incredibly complicated and complex. The guard at the senior residence, understanding or at least sympathizing with his plight, looked the other way, which in turn put both her job and his freedom at risk. Unfortunately, Jamal was violated, breaking a condition of release, and sent back to prison several weeks later.

"STUCK": SOCIAL IMMOBILITY

The concept of *stuck* was common in many reentry stories. In several cases, individuals were either unaware or unclear about what they could or could not do upon returning to society. However, being "stuck" was not simply a metaphor for their new status but highlighted how individuals were unable to move around freely or legally.

Rickey, who served twenty years in institutions in New York and New Jersey for multiple robberies, spoke candidly about being stuck. A short, stocky man, he is half-Irish and half-Puerto Rican, growing up between Manhattan's Hell's Kitchen and Newark's North Ward. When we met, he was still under Department of Corrections supervision, awaiting release to parole and living in a halfway house. One aspect of his personality was trying to find the best in people; as an example, he described a chance encounter on his first day in state prison, when he accidently ate lunch with the "Son of Sam," a convicted serial killer in New York City in the 1970s. "I would have never thought someone like him would be that friendly," Rickey said. "You got to get to know people before you judge them."

Yet Rickey was struggling in his reentry, particularly suffering from anxiety, and having panic attacks. He came late to group one day, sweating profusely. Afterward, he was apologetic and explained that while boarding the bus to come downtown, his bus pass card was not working properly. He panicked and stepped away, saying, "I just felt everyone on the bus staring at me. It was too much pressure and too many people. I felt my chest tightening, and so I just got off and ran over here as fast I could."

Rickey also admitted to having issues with anger, something that had gotten him in trouble in prison. After starting a prison pen pal relationship with a woman who eventually became his fiancée, he began practicing daily meditation. Yet he described apprehension and feeling stuck, not knowing if his practices would translate in his new environment.

"My anger always got the best of me," he said, "and I'm scared that when I come out, I might ruin our relationship. Plus, she got an eight-year-old son, so I got to make sure I'm good for them." His rocky past relationships made him wonder if he could be in a healthy cohabitating space postincarceration. Research surrounding carceral relationships highlights that stress, particularly surrounding release, can be daunting.[32]

Finally, Rickey was candid about feeling stuck in another respect. "I know guys won't admit this," he said, "but I'm scared to have sex, it's been over twenty years. When you are in this environment for so long, you don't think about it the same way."

Rickey's honesty and hesitation underscored ways in which imprisonment and reentry create obstacles. While he expressed an eagerness to be with his fiancée, he also realized that his current environment was not preparing him for a stable lifestyle with a woman and child. In prison, Rickey operated in "survivor" mode, a skill that becomes not only unproductive but also dangerous in society.

Beyond personal relationships, social immobility of feeling "stuck" occurs via legal barriers in the reentry process. For example, Stuart and another Black man, Sheldon, were both in similar situations. Sheldon, in his mid-fifties, convicted of sexual assault and child endangerment, was sentenced to ten years in state prison. His situation was somewhat unusual, as he said, "Before I was convicted, I was a corrections officer. So, I have a lot against me."

Both Stuart and Sheldon were registered on the state and national sex registration databases. Yet research surrounding sex registries has shown that they have little to no impact on keeping communities safe while at the same time costing taxpayers millions of dollars each year.[33] Additionally, both men were on the highest tier of sex offender list, creating situations where both men felt stuck because they lacked social mobility.

Sheldon explained that going out was an arduous process and that he avoided crowds as much as possible. He specifically recalled a situation at a movie theater when students on a school trip arrived, and he decided to simply leave the theater to avoid any potential problems.

Stuart described how complicated a simple night out in the city could be, commenting, "I have a lot of friends who live in the city [New York].

It's a group of gay guys, and they all know my situation." He continued, "When I want to go see them, I must notify Newark police and tell them exactly where I am going and how long I plan to be out. If I want to stay at a friend's house overnight, that's a whole other issue because I must call the local precinct in New York and do the same thing."

In the end, Stuart expressed frustration with this network of calls and check-ins, saying, "It's all bullshit. Honestly, I don't even know how they would know where I go. I don't have an ankle monitor or anything, so I probably could get away without telling them. But if anything was to happen and my location isn't known, I'll be going right back to prison, and that is something I will avoid at all costs."

Because of Stuart's status as a sex offender, he will never be able to come off the registration list, a status that ultimately led to a less active lifestyle. "I really don't leave my parents' house," he said. "It became too much trying to coordinate. It takes both the excitement and happiness out of seeing people. So now, I stay inside and am fortunate to have a place to stay."

Sheldon did not have the same safety net. He was struggling to find a job and lived in a single-room occupancy building. While not ideal, it was a step up from the shelter, and he paid a manageable rent. Yet he expressed feelings of being stuck. His wife and children had cut ties with him after his conviction, an action that stemmed from him having an affair with an underage girl, which prompted his incarceration.

Both men expressed being in a perpetual state of punishment and purgatory status under current policies that shape sex offense guidelines.

"F IS FOR FELONY"

A main purpose of the reentry center is to assist in finding employment opportunities for clients. Like that on housing, existing scholarship on reentry is hyperfocused on employment.[34] Many people believe that a job is sort of a catchall problem solver. I found that for many clients of the reentry organization, the initial impetus to use the place was to help them find a job. Many, however, had more pressing concerns.

A growing discourse surrounding employment and felony status deals with policy issues such as employers being able to use a person's criminal history as grounds to discriminate. To combat this, campaigns such as "Ban the Box" have proposed legislation to remove language on job applications asking about a person's criminal history. New Jersey has a version of the "Ban the Box," known as the New Jersey Opportunity to Compete Act, which limits the amount of information an employer can request from a potential employee.[35]

On the surface, these types of policies are attempts to circumvent the discriminatory policies that make reentry harder. Yet, without an intersectional lens, these types of protocols exacerbate rather than mitigate these problems. For example, Devah Pager's book *Marked: Race, Crime, and Finding Work in an Era of Mass Incarceration* shows that felony job discrimination is still second to racial discrimination, as White job applicants with a felony conviction had the same or higher rate of job callbacks than their Black counterparts without a felony conviction.[36]

In other words, race still undergirds many facets of our society. Without more critical and nuanced approaches, we could replicate systematic discriminatory practices as Pager's work alludes to the fact that racial stereotypes surrounding myths of Black criminality could supersede actual criminal pasts.[37] In sum, American society believes that Blacks (and other minorities) are simply more prone to criminality and treats them accordingly.

Additionally, there is the issue of reentry versus reintegration. Criminologist Douglas Thompkins makes a clear distinction between the two, explaining that reentry is not reintegration, arguing that reintegration does not begin until an individual is no longer under criminal supervision.[38] Furthermore, it is important to differentiate between *reintegration* and *integration*. Often, reentry is positioned as a return to something a person has already had in their lives. Yet returning to society does not necessarily mean an opportunity at a "second chance" but an initial possibility.

When I met David at the reentry center, we were both the same age, twenty-four, having a birthday only weeks apart. Yet a decade earlier our lives had taken dramatically different turns. While I had graduated from high school, completed my undergraduate studies, earned a master's degree, and was in my second year of a doctoral program, David had been incarcerated at age fourteen for manslaughter and sentenced to ten years in prison. He was remanded at a youth facility until he turned twenty-one and then transferred to an adult prison.

Born in Newark to an Ecuadorian mother and a Puerto Rican father, David had a slim frame, a short Caesar-style haircut, and a chinstrap beard, and wore oversized white T-shirts. On his forearms were multiple tattoos, highlighting his allegiance to a Latino street gang.

During a workshop on résumé writing, clients began brainstorming the most effective way to summarize their education, skills, and previous employment. For many of the older men in the room, trying to create explanations and fill gaps between various employments became their main task. David sat quietly twirling his pen between his fingers. When I approached him and asked what was wrong, he shrugged half-heartedly. "Just put down all the jobs you have worked," I responded. He looked up at me and with a half smirk said, "Smiley, you don't get it. I been locked up since I was fourteen years old for a body [killing someone]. I ain't had no job."

This response took me by surprise. Naively, I hadn't realized that educational attainment, employment histories, and other marketable skill sets were not readily available to all people returning from prison. While most youth are garnering social skills and cultivating bonds in their teenage and young adult years, David was imprisoned. Therefore, his reentry experience was not one of reintegration but of *integration* into the formal economy. David was embarrassed about his current life condition and said he earned a certain level of respect from his peers in prison because of his gang ties and criminal conviction. Unfortunately, those credentials do not transfer in society. As he summed up his situation, "All I done with my life is fuck up and do time."

Along with not having any previous employment history or formal job skills, David also lacked official documents that indicated his existence other than his prison identification card. David never had a driver's license or official state identification, he lacked a passport, and he did not have a birth certificate or Social Security card. Before he could even begin the process of applying for jobs, he needed to obtain these credentials. In sum, the only verification that proved his existence was his state bureau identification number from prison. What made matters more difficult was that he was listed under two different names within the Department of Corrections, creating confusion as to which was his legal name.

Many clients discussed the difficulties of moving forward because of the loss of formal identification, other documents, and personal possessions. Jerry, a fifty-nine-year-old Black man, seemed like an anomaly at the reentry center. Born and raised in neighboring Jersey City, he had in the early 1970s attended a prominent university in the Northeast where he played Division I basketball and joined a historically Black fraternity. Upon graduating, Jerry married, had a daughter, and worked in the airline industry for over twenty-five years.

"Playing basketball allowed me to travel all over the country and see places I never thought I could," he said, "and once I graduated, I found a job in the airline industry and that took me all over the globe."

As an airline steward, Jerry described traveling the world, highlighting trips to Rome and San Paulo. He described meeting people of various cultural backgrounds and supported these claims with a variety of vintage photographs. During this time, he began freebasing cocaine. Over the next three decades, Jerry went from using cocaine recreationally to occasionally to frequently.

"I found myself doing it on a weeknight or after work, before work, and eventually doing it all the time," he said. "I am an addict, and the addiction consumed my life, taking over and costing me everything." His addiction, he said, ruined his marriage, made him estranged from his daughter, and eventually got him fired from his job.

Jerry's addiction also put him in debt with a local drug crew because he was consuming more than he could afford. To repay his debt, he struck a deal with his suppliers, allowing them to use his home as a stash house. The drug crew would use women to pick up narcotics, and this practice eventually attracted the attention of law enforcement.

Since the drugs were in Jerry's home, he was charged with distribution and possession. As a first-time offender, he was sentenced to what's called "a two with a ten," which meant that he was sentenced to ten years and had to serve two years before being eligible for parole. When asked about his arrest, he responded, "It was my day of reckoning, a moment of clarity, and a blessing in disguise, because I would have either overdosed or they [the drug crew] would have killed me if they ever figured out I was ripping them off."

Jerry did not understand the prison environment when he was arrested, but he had the ability to connect with others, especially younger men who were involved with the criminal legal system. He struck up a friendship with David at the reentry center, whom he began to tutor. For several weeks, these two men from opposite worlds brought together through the reentry process would meet an hour before group. David's reading comprehension was deficient, and Jerry showed patience, helping him sound out words and explaining their meaning. It was clear that a proxy father-son relationship was forming.

Unfortunately, David began skipping weekly groups and eventually stopped showing up altogether. Jerry was upset but understood that things in life happen and was more concerned about David's well-being.

Several weeks later, in downtown Newark, a young Latino man approached me, saying, "Hey, Smiley." It was David. He was almost unrecognizable. His short hair had grown out, his pristine chin-strap line up was now scruffy with various patches in his unkempt beard, and the large bags under his bloodshot eyes gave him a lethargic look. He was with another man who hung back while we spoke.

I noticed that under David's soiled white T-shirt were several beaded necklaces, indicating his gang affiliation, something he hadn't been wearing previously. I asked how he was doing and if he was OK. Without making eye contact, he said that he had been released from the halfway house and was doing "all right." Before we parted, he told me that he was going to come back to group. This was the last time I saw or heard from him.

The following week, I told Jerry and members of the larger group, who had gotten to know David, that I had seen him and that in my opinion he did not look well. It was at this point that Melvin, who also had gotten friendly with David, said candidly, "That young man still has more time in him."

"Everything stacked against him, and he will most likely go back to prison," he elaborated. "He wasn't prepared for all this [reentry and release]. He was trying but some forces are just too strong, you feel me? I bet he will be a different person in ten years and really be ready to do this right. I know from experience. If they had let me out when I was his age, without anything I would have gone right back too. It's that simple. The boy just got more time in him."

Around the same time that David had disappeared, Jerry was released from the halfway house, living in a shelter, and mending the relationship with his daughter who had moved out of state years earlier and was raising her own daughter, while putting herself through graduate school. Eventually, she sent him an iPhone so they could communicate more frequently rather than relying on a pay phone. However, the iPhone was stolen a few weeks later. This incident galvanized Jerry's effort to move closer to his daughter.

"There is nothing left for me," he said. "Everything I had is gone. It is not worth trying to start over in New Jersey. My daughter said I could come live with her. I am not going to waste this opportunity," he explained.

It took Jerry approximately one year to get his parole transferred to the state of his daughter's residence and he had to abide by both states' parole restrictions, which were confusing and contradictory. "They don't make sense," he said. "One state says I am not allowed to travel outside the state. The other is saying I can. Which one is it?"

Upon moving in with his daughter, Jerry was able to get a job in the cafeteria at a local community college and was overjoyed by the ability to continue to be around young folks and share his experience. "So many students are shocked to learn I have a college degree and now do what I do," he said, "so I hope it helps them make better life decisions."

In 2016, Jerry suffered a severe stroke, leaving him partially paralyzed and without the ability to fully communicate. He could no longer work and needed care, which is provided by his daughter and granddaughter. I visited him in June of 2018. When I arrived, he looked at me strangely and admitted that he could not remember me but offered me his left hand. We sat for several hours watching television. Before I left, he turned and looked at me and in a slurred speech said, "Newark." It was an indication that the man I had met years earlier still had some recognition of his former life.

· · · · ·

Many of the men who were over the age of forty-five were unhappy with the job options provided. As Ray, a sixty-two-year-old Black man who had just completed three years of an eight-year sentence for drug distribution, said bluntly, "I'm sick of lifting heavy boxes all day." He complained about having bad knees, a sore back, and developing arthritis in his hands because his current employer did not provide safety equipment such as a back brace.

"I'm sure there is work I can do that doesn't have to be dangerous and unhealthy for a man my age," he said. "But *F is for felony*. They don't care if I get sick or hurt."

Ray begrudgingly took this job to satisfy his parole requirement, but he would rather spend time with his wife. In fact, he was looking beyond employment altogether. He spoke often and fondly of his two grandsons, both all-star football athletes. One was already playing Division I college football, and the other was being recruited by top-tier universities.

"If I had my way," he said, "I wouldn't have a job. I'm in my golden years. I want to spend what little time I have on this earth with my wife, my kids, and watching my grandkids play ball. They got an opportunity to go to the league [National Football League]. I want to go to the games, sit in the stands, eat a hot dog, and cheer them on. I want to work with the younger one before he goes to college. I don't need a job. I worked all my life, some in the streets and some not, it's time for me to relax and once I'm off parole, I'm quitting."

Other reentry participants agreed that employment options were limiting. JR, a sixty-year-old Black man, gave an example about how unfair he felt employment opportunities were for people caught up in the legal system. Before he went to prison in 1999, for robbery and possession of narcotics, he was a commercial truck driver, married to his wife of thirty-two years, and father of two adult children, both of whom had graduated from college. Yet because of his conviction he lost his commercial driver's license and feared he would not be able to get it again. He also felt that a decade in prison was a harsh punishment after a thirty-year career with an unblemished record except for a single charge dating back to 1969. "All of this was brought up in court," he said, "but all they saw was a criminal, not a father, husband, or businessman."

Often, women spoke about discrepancies and unfairness when it came to certain types of employment, among them Charlotte, a dark-skinned Black woman in her mid-forties who had been arrested and jailed, based on her own count, "at least a dozen times" for engaging in illicit sex work.

"I'm not ashamed 'cause I use condoms and can make money," she said in a conversation about trying to find a more conventional job. "It's not like they give life sentences for having sex. The job process is slow, but in the streets, I can make more and do less." Engaging in sex work was an outlet that Charlotte used as an opportunity to generate income and sustain her substance abuse. While sex work is not considered actual "work" in the conventional sense, there is an abundance of literature that examines the role of sex work in the underground as well as the formal economy.[39] In other words, sex work *is* work.

Because Charlotte was in and out of jail, her life was understandably unstable. When we spoke, she was living in a women's shelter. But this arrangement was not ideal because it required sobriety and residents needed conventional employment. Charlotte had been kicked out of the shelter twice before, and she understood that her chemical dependence would put her at risk of being removed a third time.

While prostitution is typically considered a misdemeanor, Charlotte's frequent arrests, along with a drug charge on her record, labeled her a convicted felon. This resulted in a vicious cycle. She would be arrested for sex work, jailed, released with limited opportunities, and revert to sex work. In her eyes, this pattern represented a double standard.

"I don't see what I do as wrong," she said. "Everybody has sex, and if a nigga going to pay me for it, so what? Ain't that what porn is? Am I supposed to believe all these cops, lawyers, and judges never watch porn? The police know me, and when I get picked up, they usually let the guy go. This one time the cop had the nerve to apologize to that nigga, like they were inconveniencing his night. I won't apologize for what I do. If the system really wanted to help me, they would get me off these drugs instead of putting me in lockup."

Regina, a light-skinned Black woman with freckles and a prominent keloid scar on her forearm, also engaged in sex work as a teenager. She said she had a violent upbringing and refused to talk about her life before the age of thirteen. She ran away from home and was frequently homeless before being placed under the care of the State Division of Youth and Family Services.[40] Now in her early twenties, Regina described overcoming an addiction to prescription drugs and being recently released from state prison after serving slightly less than two years on weapons charges.

As a young mother, she was actively trying to gain custody of her son, who was four years old and in foster care. At the time, she had supervised visits with him on the weekend, a time when she and he played games. "I am going to get him back as soon as I get a job and an apartment," she said. "It was so cute, last weekend we fell asleep next to each other watching a movie. When I'm with him I feel my best."

Growing up, Regina became affiliated with a gang, and the gang became her family during some of her toughest times as a juvenile. The father of her son is also a member of the gang. He was arrested at the same time as Regina and is now serving a twenty-five-years-to-life sentence on both state and federal charges.

Regina discussed employment struggles and how they related to her physical size. "Why is every job that I can apply made for a man?" she asked. "I'm five-foot-three and a hundred and forty pounds. I can't lift heavy boxes, and I don't want to do that type of work." While Regina did not have a high school diploma, she believed that she had employable skills, such as hair braiding. "I learned when I was younger," she explained. "I can do all types of designs and styles. It was a way to get boys' attention. They would be sitting between my legs for hours while I did their hair."

However, because of her felony conviction, along with the cost of cosmetology school, doing this type of work in the short term was not a legal option for her. "Yeah, I wish I could work [doing hair] 'cause I think it would make me an overall better person," she said. "You know, like a better mother to provide for my son."

After several months of living in a halfway house, Regina found housing in a private residence that worked specifically with women and victims of substance abuse. With the help of a caseworker, she was able to secure work in the fast-food industry. While it was not her long-term vision for employment, she needed the job to help her get her son back. Finally, after several more months of working, Regina did secure her parenting rights, moved into an apartment with her new boyfriend, and planned to pursue cosmetology school with the hope that she would be granted a state license to do hair.

"BUT THESE ARE MY KIDS"

Regina's story ended with a positive outcome. Not all women were so fortunate. Parenting was an identity, particularly for the women. While some of the men spoke about being a parent, women clearly felt that because of their gender they were judged differently upon reentry. As Jamie said, "It's different for men. A man can go back and forth and still get a woman 'cause he a 'thug.' But for me, being a female, I don't get that many tries. When I walk down the street, guys holler at me, but I bet if a lot of them knew I been locked up they would turn the other way. It's the same for a job. I bet all these guys in here could get a job before me because they are men, and it looks worse for women who go to prison than a man."

The gender difference within the reentry process was apparent in many of the stories I heard. Women talked about the impact of imprisonment on their familial ties. Furthermore, research indicates that while mothers typically take on the role of parent when a father is incarcerated, when a mother is incarcerated, the parenting responsibilities typically fall on extended family members, such as grandparents.[41]

Jamie was the only White woman who was part of this project, which made her perspective unique. Now in her mid-thirties, Jamie was born and raised in Newark and was, as she put it, "the only White girl from her neighborhood." Unlike most White Newark residents, who fled to the suburbs, her family remained. She spoke about her experience as a racial minority in a minority-majority city. "My family is White trash," she said. "All my uncles, brothers, and cousins been locked up, and I got into fights as a kid because I was 'ugly' and as an adult because I was getting attention from the Black guys."

Jamie was a mother of two children, a girl, six, and a boy, two. She was arrested in connection with crimes committed years earlier, when she sold drugs with her children's father, who was Afro-Puerto Rican. "I was young and stupid," she said. "He was handsome, and I always knew he was in the streets, but I didn't care so started hustling with him. The shitty part is that I was the one that got locked up."

She was tied to a larger conspiracy case that stretched across the State of New Jersey. Despite no longer being involved, she was named in the indictment and arrested. She took a plea deal and was sentenced to three years in state prison, serving just over one year before being released to a halfway house. Her incarceration put strain on her romantic relationship, and she noted that her children's father was an unfaithful partner and did not "step up" and take on a more prominent role after her arrest. In her absence, her mother became the children's legal guardian to prevent them from being sent to other families as foster children.

"My daughter is upset because she is starting to understand," Jamie said, "and my son cries for his 'mommy' and wants my mom. That's hard to hear."

While Jamie is grateful that her mother stepped into the role of guardian, she spoke candidly about frustrations and conflicts with her mother, particularly surrounding issues involving visitation. "She gets on my last freakin' nerve," Jamie said. "I know I messed up, but she always reminds me, but doesn't see her own contradictions. I'm the only woman in my family that has been to prison, but when my uncles and brothers got locked up, she never complained. She would drive down to South Jersey to visit them every week when I was a kid. Meanwhile, I plead with her to come so I could see my kids. I call every night, so they know my voice, but some nights my mom won't pick up the phone."

Jamie also discussed her children's racial identity and her mother's denial of the children's heritage. "My mom is racist," she said. "I know she loves her grandkids, but she is a racist woman. You would think, growing up and living around Black people her whole life she wouldn't think like this. My son has a Spanish name, but my mother gave him a nickname. My daughter has darker skin than her brother, and my mother comments about not liking when she plays outside because she gets 'too dark.'"

Jamie began the legal process of trying to regain custody of her children. Because of her status as a felon, she was finding it hard to make any headway. However, she was granted extended visiting hours, and her mother was obligated to bring the children to see her on a biweekly basis.

This story highlighted the feeling of being "stuck" in a purgatory status. In the end, Jamie found herself in a precarious situation, one that would not be legally resolved until she had completely left the criminal legal system.

·   ·   ·   ·   ·

Unlike Jamie, Gwen had no chance of regaining custody of her child. A tall, thin-framed Muslim Black woman, Gwen was in her late forties and wore a head wrap that concealed her hair. Convicted of drug trafficking and released a year before our meeting, she served twenty years in federal prison and was no longer on any form of criminal supervision but was using the reentry center to find employment. In time, I learned that for her finding a job was a means to the end of reconnecting with her son.

"I was pregnant when I was arrested," she explained. "I didn't know it at the time, but when I was waiting for my trial, they gave me a pregnancy test, and that's how I found out."

Gwen described how hard it was to be incarcerated while pregnant but was fortunate that older Black women smuggled in special food and vitamins to keep the unborn baby healthy. When she went into labor, she was not allowed to have an epidural and was shackled to the hospital bed, as is the case across the country, despite the medical risks to both mother and child.[42] "Every time I pushed, I felt the cuffs on my wrists getting tighter and tighter," she said. "That was the hardest thing I ever had to do, but I gave birth to a healthy baby boy."

Prior to the birth of her son, Gwen had already decided to give him up for adoption. She had been influenced by the prison social worker, who had inquired about her plans for the child and had suggested adoption as the best option. "She manipulated me," Gwen said. "I was looking at twenty years and knew I wasn't going to be able to raise him. When he was born, I only got to hold him for a few minutes before they took him away." After the birth, Gwen sunk into a depression and stopped eating. She contemplated suicide. But the same group of elder Black women who had supported her earlier did so during this time.

Soon thereafter, Gwen tried to reverse her decision about adoption but was told that it was too late; her son already had adoptive parents, and there was "nothing that could be done." Eventually she was able to find out that her son had been adopted by a Black couple out of state and her son's adoptive parents were open to Gwen writing him, which she did for several years. "I was so nervous the first time I wrote him," she recalled. "I must have gone through an entire legal pad rewriting my letter. I just had so much to tell him and didn't know how to say it."

Over the years, Gwen received letters and pictures depicting various milestones in her son's life. But she admitted that she was not the best at keeping up communication, and their correspondence ended. Upon her release, however, with the help of social media, she found her son and learned that he was a father to a baby girl. After completing parole in 2011, she traveled out of state and met her son for the first time since his birth in 1991. "I had never been more scared in my life," she said. "I think he was too. When he opened the door, I just lost my breath. I hugged him and squeezed tight and just kept whispering, 'I'm sorry.' He kept saying, 'I know, Ma, I know.' He has a job and a girlfriend, and my granddaughter looks just like me as a baby."

SUMMARY

Reentry does not restore individuals back into society because mechanisms and policies are implemented to keep the carceral apparatus cycling individuals in and out of the legal system. In other words, reentry is an extension—not termination—of the criminal legal system. The next chapter exhibits how the carceral system operates within halfway house facilities, where many clients were sent upon exiting prison facilities and prior to being fully released into society, exacerbating purgatory citizenship through various rites and rituals.

3   Halfway

Saladin was a burly, forty-two-year-old Black man with a thick beard who was completing a seven-year sentence for drug distribution and manufacturing. A quiet individual, Saladin would sit in the back of the conference room at the reentry center rather than at the table. Eventually, after a few weeks, he raised his hand and asked if he could speak at the end of our group meeting.

Before making his point, Saladin took a deep breath and preemptively apologized for what he was about to say. Then he recounted an incident that had taken place at the halfway house where he was residing the previous evening. "The supervisor put his hands through my food," he said. "I get my food special from the outside because I'm a Muslim and I don't like eating what they serve. I've been doing this for a while now, but last night this man put his fingers all through it claiming he needed to search it for contraband."

Saladin became physically distressed while describing this event. He said he had tried to talk to the supervisor about the incident, but no one would tell him why his food had been singled out and searched in this particular manner. "I'm telling you, I just finished up all this time," he said of his years in prison, "but I was ready to go back last night."

When Saladin finished describing what had happened, other participants thanked him for sharing his experiences, as others had had similar
negative interactions with staff at halfway facilities. Some said how proud
they were of Saladin for not "taking matters into his own hands," as they
put it, noting that these facilities often encourage criminal behavior rather
than stop it.

This episode sparked a discussion about various issues surrounding
halfway houses, which are temporary transitional housing for many exiting either a state or federal prison facility. In the end, Saladin thanked the
group for allowing him to "get that off my chest." He explained that he had
been brooding about the incident all night, had not slept much, and had
contemplated not attending group but was happy that he did.

Issues and problems related to halfway houses were not the exception
but the rule for many individuals doing reentry. Often, clients complained
about unpleasant exchanges with staff, supervisors, and other residents.
In this way I learned about the complex, complicated, and politically connected institutions within the New Jersey halfway house system.

This chapter explores and centers the experiences of participants in
halfway transitional housing in the state of New Jersey, as many clients
were either currently or formerly residents. First, I give a brief overview of
the history of halfway transitional housing through to the present in what
is considered the "prison reentry industry" (PRI).[1] Second, I investigate
the narratives of those living in these facilities and how they interpret
their experiences and interactions. Next, I discuss how participants perceive *doing reentry* as a ritual, having to participate in programs and
events as a form of atonement and rite of passage. Finally, I explain how
neoliberalism via privatization, austerity, and deregulation of state agencies into the private and nonprofit sector has created systems that put
revenue over humanity and cost-efficiency above reintegration, highlighting the conflict of interest in reentry services.

HALFWAY HOUSES AND THE PRISON REENTRY INDUSTRY

In 2012 the *New York Times* published a three-part investigative series
titled "Unlocked," by Sam Dolnick. The ten-month inquiry focused on

New Jersey's halfway house system, exposing such alarming issues as violence, escapes, drug use, and lack of responsible supervision within these facilities.[2] The journalist asserts that while New Jersey has been praised for its criminal justice reform efforts, many of these efforts were focused not on rehabilitation of those incarcerated and reducing harm in the community but on cutting budgets and saving money. Dolnick also highlights the various political connections that New Jersey's largest operator of halfway houses, Community Education Centers (CEC), has within the state, which created strange bedfellows and conflict of interest.

In the 1990s, halfway house facilities began to reemerge in the state, led by CEC under its leader, John J. Clancy. By the end of the 2010s, CEC and its nonprofit entity, Education and Health Centers of America (EHCA), controlled six different halfway house facilities, including the Albert M. "Bo" Robinson Assessment & Treatment Center. The purpose of EHCA was to skirt New Jersey's policy that only nonprofit organizations could operate halfway facilities within the state.[3] Additionally, former Republican governor Chris Christie had professional and personal links to the company.[4] At its height, CEC operated more than a hundred correctional treatment programs in twenty-two states and Bermuda and employed more than four thousand people.[5]

In New Jersey, incarcerated individuals sent to halfway houses are first directed to "Bo" Robinson for assessment and then distributed among the various facilities operated by private nonprofit organizations, including facilities run by CEC, creating a conflict of interest. In other words, CEC receives a per diem payment from the state when individuals are sent to "Bo" Robinson for assessment and an additional per diem when the person is sent to a CEC facility—in effect getting paid twice for the same person.

Nevertheless, many of the halfway facilities operated by CEC and other large transitional housing organizations resemble human warehouses far more than traditional halfway facilities. For example, Delany Hall, operated by CEC, had a capacity of 1,196 occupants according to the CEC website.[6] Moreover, unlike traditional prisons with trained correctional officers, steel bars, restrictive movement, and two-person cells, many halfway facilities employ staff, otherwise known as "counselors," have auditorium-style sleeping areas, and allow more movement within the facilities, giving many participants mixed feelings about these places.

Figure 8. Delany Hall, Newark, a former halfway house operated by Community Education Center, now owned by GEO Group, 2022. Photo courtesy of the author.

In the spring of 2016, the organization's founder and CEO, John J. Clancy, died. The following year the Geo Group, a private for-profit prison company, bought CEC for $360 million, integrating the organization into the company's existing business units, known as the GEO Corrections & Detention and GEO Care companies.[7]

·   ·   ·   ·   ·

Halfway house facilities have been drastically transformed in the United States since their inception in the mid-nineteenth century. In 1845, an abolitionist, schoolteacher, and social welfare activist named Abigail Hopper Gibbons, along with her abolitionist father, Isaac T. Hopper, founded the Women's Prison Association, an organization that focused on improving jails and creating separate facilities for women.[8] In 1847, the association started the Hopper Home in New York City, which is considered the first halfway house in the United States.[9] In 1896, Maude Ballington Booth, a cofounder of the Volunteers of America, opened the first privately run halfway house, known as Hope Hall No. 1, which was established to help people find jobs and get health care.[10]

In the early twentieth century, halfway house facilities remained focused on rehabilitation. By the mid-twentieth century, innovations in treatment such as the use of "medical" models focused on mental health as well as substance abuse as causes of crime.[11] However, by the mid-1970s, many of the innovative, progressive, and rehabilitative efforts in the criminal justice field had disappeared.[12] Notably, sociologist Robert Martinson's 1974 article "What Works? Questions and Answers about Prison Reform," published in *The Public Interest*, described the generally accepted approach followed by conservatives and other reactionary stakeholders, who highlighted his controversial, and later redacted, stance that "nothing works" when it comes to rehabilitation.[13]

The 1980s saw a resurgence of halfway facilities that shifted to a more punitive position, mirroring the emergence of the "tough on crime" era, which implemented mandatory minimum or maximum stays. By 2009, 2.4 million Americans were behind bars, highlighting a nearly four-decade expansion of incarceration, which had become an utter failure, particularly when it came to state budgets.[14] It turned out that locking up enormous numbers of people did not actually deter crime but was quite costly, and states such as New Jersey began looking for ways to curtail its prison spending. In this landscape, privately operated halfway facilities began to flourish. As Dolnick writes, "Community Education [CEC] charges government agencies roughly $70 a day per inmate, about half the cost of a spot in state prison."[15]

Therefore, change began not because lawmakers or other stakeholders had a vested interest in a paradigm shift away from punitive measures, but rather to save money. Unfortunately, this line of thinking has given rise to what criminologist Doug Thompkins calls the prison reentry industry.

According to Thompkins, the prison reentry industry is part of a larger tool of social control to continue to monitor a person postincarceration. Thompkins, Curtis, and Wendel write, "These [PRI] are the systems charged with overseeing the release of prisoners—to post-prison supervision (dubbed 'reentry')—and with policing the behavior of the former prisoner during periods of quasi-incarceration, while supposedly at the same time helping to prepare them for reintegration back into the community. . . .

[T]he PRI now parallels the prison system itself in its political-economic spread. Charged with social control responsibilities and given unique tools of surveillance and interference in the daily lives of former prisoners and their families, these institutions exercise a kind of super-authority, allowing for the continued recommitment of released prisoners to the custody of the prison industry and/or continued post-prison supervision."[16]

Furthermore, criminologists Jennifer Ortiz and Hayley Jackey posit that the PRI is a form of intentional state violence, which continues to penalize formerly incarcerated persons through psychological, social, and economic ways such as underfunded programming, postrelease supervision, and fees.[17]

Thus, the prison reentry industry is the counterpart to the prison industrial complex (PIC), which Eric Schlosser describes as "a set of bureaucratic, political, and economic interests that encourage increased spending on imprisonment, regardless of actual need."[18] Along with other scholars such as Angela Davis, Schlosser also argues that the prison industrial complex perpetuates institutional violence as a state of mind that becomes a driving force for economic and political power.[19] Ultimately, the PRI is designed in the same fashion. However, unlike the PIC, which is devoted to *bringing people in*, the PRI is invested in *not letting people out*.

Over the past quarter century, many prominent scholars, activists, and prisoner rights advocates have argued that the prison industrial complex has determined and dictated policy and strategy surrounding the prison industry, placing profit over humanity. A primary example is the private prison industry.[20] Yet it has been accurately pointed out that private prisons only account for roughly 8 percent of all prison institutions.[21]

Nevertheless, public institutions still exploit prison labor through third-party organizations. In other cases, the state directly benefits from subjugated prison labor, such as California prisoners who "volunteer" as firefighters.[22] Finally, regional geography has spurred debate surrounding prison institution need and a disruption of the prison industrial complex.

In New York, fifteen correctional institutions were shuttered under Governor Andrew Cuomo, who said, "These new closures are another step toward reversing the era of mass incarceration and recognizing that there are more effective alternatives to lengthy imprisonment."[23] Yet many upstate New York communities and correctional officer unions see these closures not as victories for reform but as economic suicide for remote rural regions because these institutions are major local employers.[24]

Similarly, the prison reentry industry, particularly large corporate-style transitional housing services, are invested in filling their units. This is typically done through the number of available beds per night at a facility. Halfway houses receive a per diem payment from the state per person each night, incentivizing full capacity. Ultimately, the PRI is reminiscent of the lodging industry, and companies such as CEC blur the line between rehabilitation and profiteering.

I posit that neoliberalism and capitalism, along with CEC's close ties to state politics, the conflict of interest of operating both assessment facilities and transitional housing, and the lack of oversight into daily operations, has created and allowed a system that privileges earnings over care and investment to shareholders over community.

Interestingly, while the PIC and PRI are perceived as late twentieth- and early twenty-first-century phenomena, the history of the Black American experience is tethered to human captivity and bondage. W. E. B. Du Bois's seminal 1935 work *Black Reconstruction in America: 1860–1880* discusses the proliferation of prisons, prison labor, and the overhaul of the criminal legal system in the American South after the Civil War.

As Du Bois writes, "I confess I am more and more suspicious about the criminal justice of these Southern states. In Georgia there is no regular penitentiary at all, but an organized system of letting out the prisoners for profit. Some people here have got up a company for the purpose of hiring convicts."[25] He goes on to state, "In some states where convict labor is sold to the highest bidder the cruel treatment of the helpless human chattel in the hands of guards is such as no tongue can tell nor pen picture. Prison inspectors find convicts herded together . . . packed almost as closely as sardines in a box."[26]

Du Bois is describing the convict lease system, which used prison labor for public and private profit woven through a corrupt and racist legal system enhanced by Jim Crow–era policies.[27] Most eerily of all rhetoric on the penal system is the description of a Southern prison that outlines the foundation of the prison industrial complex and by extension the prison reentry industry.

Du Bois writes, "This penitentiary system began to characterize the whole South. In Georgia, at the outbreak of the Civil War, there were about 200 white felons confined at Milledgeville [prison]. . . . The white convicts were released to fight in the Confederate armies. The whole criminal justice system came to be used as a method of keeping Negroes at work and intimidating them. Consequently, *there began to be a demand for jails and penitentiaries beyond the natural demand* due to the rise of crime."[28]

"I RATHER MAX OUT"

Discussions about life at the halfway facilities focused on the problems, such as the fact that these institutions created stress and anxiety. Sociologist Alison McKim's work on community-based drug treatment programs highlights how women are often left feeling discouraged by contemporary penal treatments centers, creating additional complications in their reentry process.[29]

Clients at the reentry center who were also residents of these halfway facilities believed that these institutions were nothing more than a form of warehousing. As Jerry remarked, "I saw more fights in the halfway house than I witnessed my entire time in state prison." Malik said, "Everybody in my unit [at the halfway house] got some sort of mental issue, and nobody is getting medicine like in prison." Melvin added, "They just send anyone to these places [halfway houses]. A lot of times guys who are nuisances in prison are sent to the halfway house for a while to break up the monotony."

Overall, clients claimed that individuals who should not have qualified for halfway facilities were sent regardless. "I can't figure out the 'assessment,'" Jerry said. "When I got to 'Bo' Robinson, I saw guys who were constantly getting shots [violations], guys I avoided, and now was sleeping in the bed next to me."

One of the most vocal critics of the halfway system was a White man named Alex, an intimidating figure who stood six feet tall and weighed nearly 240 pounds. Alex had long, slicked-back brown hair, and his entire upper body, including chest, back, arms, hands, and neck, were covered with tattoos. Alex, who was in his early forties, had been sent to a halfway house to complete the final year of a five-year prison sentence for burglary, theft, and aggravated assault.

Growing up in a nearby suburb of Newark, Alex loved cars and music. During his junior year of high school, he formed a thrash metal rock band. "Those were the best days of my life," he recalled. "We would drink, smoke weed, write songs, and play music all day. We had long hair, wore makeup, and had these awesome leather armbands with spikes. We were badass!"

It was also during this time that Alex developed a drinking habit. "I would wake up and pound a six-pack before school, and then drink hard liquor all day," he said. By the time he graduated, his band had achieved local fame in central New Jersey, playing at celebrated venues such as The Stone Pony in Asbury Park and was an opening act at the legendary CBGB club in New York City.

Yet before the band released their debut album in the late 1980s, Alex left. By the early 1990s he had joined an outlaw motorcycle club, which only fueled a lifestyle dominated by drugs and alcohol.

Alex has been arrested more times than he can count and served three separate sentences in state prisons. "I'm an angry drunk," he admitted, "laughing and joking one moment, then the next get pissed off and looking for a fight." According to Alex, his current sentence is a direct result of a daylong drinking binge that ended with an altercation with his neighbor.

"I was loaded [drunk] and my neighbor was accusing my son of stealing from him," he recalled. "This guy was a crackhead and would sell his shit [property], then accuse people of stealing it. I saw him push my kid, and I went ballistic. I really beat the shit out the guy. They claimed I robbed him because he had a tape player, and I threw it down the street. I got more time for destroying a CD player than putting my fist through his face."

In prison Alex began taking steps toward sobriety and decided to go the route of halfway transitional housing. "After my first two times in prison I maxed out," he said, "but I figured that didn't really help, so I signed up to go to the halfway house." The phrase "max out" refers to completing an entire jail or prison sentence to be free from further criminal supervision such as parole. However, Alex regretted his latest decision.

"If I knew what I know now I would rather max out from prison again. This place is fucked up. It's worse than prison. I'm constantly on edge in that building, and it really impacts my sobriety." Other reentry participants confirmed Alex's sentiments regarding the lack of guidance and overall chaos of these facilities. "These places have no stability because there is constant turnover," said Sharif. "There is so much movement, it creates disruption to routines. You might have a different guy sleeping next to you every night. That's a lot to process."

Reentry center clients described state prison as having more predictability than halfway houses and while prison was often boring it maintained a certain level of order. Political scientist David Skarbek's work suggests that the rise of organized prison gangs has helped create social order in penal institutions.[30]

Many of the clients felt that the halfway facilities were less safe than state prison, arguing that folks who would never be jailed together, such as rival gang members, were forced to cohabitate in halfway facilities. "I haven't had a good night sleep," Alex said, "going from living with one guy in a cell to a large gym with bunk beds. Every morning, guys have busted lips or black eyes. These places are stress factories."

Beyond fights and other violence, men spoke about the uncleanliness and disorganization of these facilities. Jerry described his time in a halfway house as "hell on earth. The place smelled awful. A mixture of cigarette smoke, urine, and bleach." And the noise was earsplitting. "All night guys would just scream," he said. "Some complaining and others, probably mentally ill, just constantly moaning."

.   .   .   .   .

Part of the disorder many clients of these facilities complained about had to do with the abundance of rules and contradictions of those guidelines. As James, who went by the nickname Conscious, said of one halfway house, "This place has so many hidden rules. I know how to jail, what the rules are, and what I can and cannot do, but this place is just constantly looking to violate me."

Conscious has light-brown skin and wiry, shoulder-length dreadlocks. His moniker is derived from his self-proclaimed consciousness as a righteous Black man, deriving much of his verboseness from the Five Percent Nation of Islam, more commonly known as the Five Percenters.[31] He was deeply critical of the halfway house conditions, particularly limitations on mobility.

"These facilities have no intention of helping us out," he said. "They give a time limit on how long it should take for us to get from the halfway house to wherever we got to go, and you got walk with blinders on. It doesn't matter if I see an old lady being assaulted. If I intervene, instead of being called a 'hero,' I would be violated for not being where I was supposed to be. That's not rehabilitation. That's indoctrination."

Habitually, clients from halfway houses had to make check-in and checkout phone calls from preapproved landlines in the reentry center. These calls, which lasted no more than a few seconds to a minute, required clients to state their name, ID number, and location.

The stress of having to make these superfluous phone calls added to the clients' disdain for halfway houses. According to clients, the halfway facilities contradict their own rules when it comes to resident mobility. Conscious pointed out that the calls were a form of "babysitting," saying, "They can't stop me from leaving the halfway house, so I'm allowed to leave, but if I'm not back by the time they want me, I'll be violated. It doesn't make sense."

Eventually, Conscious was violated, explaining, "I was late [getting to the reentry center] because of bus delays." He continued, "I was frustrated and irritated because it messed up my day. Instead of leaving to go back to the house, I went to my sister's place to eat dinner with my family. I planned on going back later in the day, but they already sent the bulls [law enforcement] out looking for me because I was labeled an 'escapee.'"

For the next two days, Conscious hid out, staying with various friends and family, but he finally decided it was best to go back to the halfway house. To his surprise, he was sent to "Bo" Robinson for a reassessment and ultimately went back to the same halfway house two weeks later.

"I couldn't believe it," he said. "I thought I was going back to state prison, but I overheard staff talking about my case. I only got three months left on my sentence, so sending me back to prison is more expensive, but sending me back to the halfway house, they continue getting paid. These places rather get the money than bad publicity. In my situation, nobody got hurt and didn't make the news. They downgraded my charge. It's like it didn't even happen."

Finally, clients believed that halfway houses undermined their own efforts to find gainful employment. Clients complained about work restrictions, describing how facilities encouraged clients to apply only for certain jobs. Lemon, a Black man in his early thirties who was finishing a three-year sentence in connection with weapons charges, was skeptical of the employment process. "It's all bullshit. I peeped game [understood the con]. The counselors only push for us to apply to certain places. I thought it was funny, so I told them I applied to a different job, and they told me I couldn't work there saying it was too far from the halfway house, but it's closer to the house than the reentry center."

In other cases, clients complained of halfway house counselors sabotaging jobs. Shawn, a twenty-seven-year-old Black man who had served eight years of a ten-year sentence for robbery, got a job working for a demolition company, hoping to stay long enough to earn his union card. However, by the time I met Shawn, he had been let go.

"The halfway house didn't like that I had the job," Shawn told me. "The supervisor [at the halfway facility] kept calling my manager every fifteen minutes needing to check up on me. My manager knew my history, and half the guys working the job had been on the inside [prison], so it wasn't nothing, but all the badgering, my manager had to let me go. The calls were fucking up the job. My manager told me when I get out to come back and see if there is an opening. This place [halfway house] puts too many fucking restrictions, and now I'm sitting up in this place going into debt 'cause they still charging me."

In halfway house facilities, residents are responsible for paying various fees.[32] Upward of 25 percent of any gross income could be garnished and paid directly to the facility.[33] Sharif expressed his frustration with this system, saying, "We are encouraged to work but that is only so the halfway house can make profit. I've asked where this money goes, but no one has answered that question. Until then, I won't work."

Upon completing his stay at the halfway house, Sharif and his wife moved south, and he regained his driver's license and began working as a ride-share operator, seeing himself as an entrepreneur within the gig economy.[34] "It's a nice business venture," he said, "because I control my hours, choose which rides I accept or decline, and the prison system doesn't make a dime off me now."

"I'M ALL GROUPED OUT"

When Freddy began attending group, he wore an expression of contempt and annoyance. A forty-three-year-old Black man standing six feet tall, he had recently arrived at a halfway house after being in state prison for twenty-one years.

The first time Freddy was arrested was at age seventeen on assault charges, and he was imprisoned for the next two years. Upon release, he was rearrested for a parole violation and remained in prison until he was twenty-one. Nine months after his release, he was back in police custody in connection with robbery, aggravated assault, and weapons charges. Since he was still on parole stemming from the initial charge and was already a parole violator, Freddy was now deemed a predicate felon, a term used to describe repeat offenders, and he was given a fifty-year sentence for the robbery. "The judge threw the book at me," he said. "It was the same judge in all my cases. I guess he was done seeing me, and he gave me all that time."

According to Freddy, the first ten years of this sentence were a blur. The days, weeks, and months blended, which helps explain why individuals returning to society have trouble with the concept of time.[35] For some, linear time becomes unclear because of the cyclical nature of incarceration.

"I was a monster," Freddy recalled. "I was twenty-two facing fifty years. I couldn't think that far ahead. I was going to make them guards earn their checks." Studies on life without the possibility of parole, long-term sentencing, and other forms of extremely punitive treatments, such as administrative segregation, show an increase rather than decrease in violent behaviors in prison settings.[36]

In the early 2000s, reforms to the New Jersey criminal justice system made Freddy optimistic that he could one day become a free man, as his sentence was reduced from fifty years to twenty with the possibility of parole. "It gave me hope," he said. "I was in over a decade, so I started to get my act together, stopped fighting, respecting the officers, and doing programs because I wanted to get out."

After he served twenty-one years, Freddy's wish came true, and he was granted parole. Eventually, he became a fixture at the reentry center and a peer leader among the participants. Yet it was in those early weeks that

Freddy made a statement that encapsulated what many clients were feeling and experiencing. During a group discussion about reentry issues, Freddy raised his hand and announced, "I'm all grouped out." When I urged him to elaborate on this statement so I could more fully understand what he meant, he responded, "These groups are always the same, teaching us the same shit."

He went on, "In prison they got groups, at the halfway house they got us in groups, and here they got me in groups. Everywhere I'm sent I've done group, every type of group they got, but nothing changes. They all say the same thing—'people, places, and things,' 'change my attitude,' and 'modify behaviors.' It's all talk and a check mark so the counselors can get paid."

He finished his statement by saying, "I know you don't get paid, Smiley, and I like this group, but none of these groups giving me something new or different, it's the same repetition going through the motions-type stuff."

While I believe that Freddy was trying to spare my feelings in that moment, he tapped into another layer of the reentry process. Freddy's description of "going through the motions" highlights how individuals must actively *do reentry*. Similar to work on "doing gender"[37] or "doing difference,"[38] "doing reentry," I argue, is both social and political.

Here, part of the return process is interactional, and individuals must both actively participate in and complete various rituals for praise of accomplishment from the greater society. In sum, "doing reentry" becomes part of a larger amalgamation of the reentry process that is fulfilled by taking part in rituals that are deemed acceptable and compulsory. Thus, the process creates an environment where individuals must atone for their past via these ceremonies, such as programming, groups, and reentry services, despite the overall outcome. With nearly two-thirds of individuals released in the United States being rearrested within three years, a critical analysis of contemporary reentry services should be undertaken to understand these institutional failures.[39]

According to the French sociologist Émile Durkheim, rituals play an important role in life. They create a profound form of interconnectedness among participants and even have a transformative nature.[40] Furthermore, according to interpretations of Durkheim, it is noted, "The most important effect of punishment . . . is neither expiation nor deterrence, but rather the reaffirmation in the minds of the innocent of the rules defining social reality. . . . This they do by means of ritual and especially through the *agency of ceremonial gatherings*."[41]

While Durkheim's analysis of rituals is often portrayed and described as having positive outcomes in society, others have pushed back. Notably, Mary Daly's work articulates that rituals can create experiences that are meaningless, exploitative, and methodical.[42] In this tradition, Freddy was ultimately describing Daly's interpretations of rituals that were repetitive and did not add an overall value to his reentry process but instead reinforced notions of paternalism, othering, and stigma.

In sum, using programs and groups, reentry can continue to marginalize individuals in the return process by relegating them away from the greater population. Therefore, instead of perpetuating current models of reentry, a paradigm shift that is inclusive of abolitionism must become the focus that will ultimately eliminate the need for reentry.

.   .   .   .   .

Despite grievances, clients such as Freddy wanted and recognized the need for programs, adding to the complexity of this predicament. Clients expressed complaints with the way many reentry rituals were carried out. Often, many of the groups that clients participated in were short-lived, disrupted, or facilitated by individuals ill equipped for their jobs.

The theme of consistency became interwoven into the weekly group sessions as clients expressed admiration for the regularity of these events. As Larry, a fifty-nine-year-old Black man, said, "The fact that this group meets every week is very important to me." Released from prison after serving thirty-years of a life sentence for various robbery charges and a manslaughter charge, Larry said he enjoyed the consistency of groups because in prison his life operated in the same manner. He explained that he needed to have order to, as he put it, "keep everything together." He complained that he had signed up for a group at the halfway house and was still waiting for it to start because the facilitator had not shown up. "It's been three months," Larry said. "I asked the supervisor, why don't you get a replacement for this guy, he is robbing you, but that comment ain't make it too far."

Other clients described programs that were abruptly discontinued or developing feelings of insecurity in such spaces. "I don't feel comfortable talking in the halfway house because the counselors are snitches," said Regina. "They take information and use it against you, so I just be quiet in those groups."

Finally, many participants were critical of counselors at the halfway facilities, claiming that many of them lacked the proper qualifications. Conscious noted that many of the counselors were also formerly incarcerated individuals who were "boot lickers," a reference associated with individuals perceived to be sucking up to their oppressor, who could not be fully trusted.

Conversations about counselors ranged from acknowledgment that some were genuinely invested in reentry but "in over their head," to finding others problematic or worse. Jerry described an incident where he witnessed a fight in the halfway facility and a counselor joined the melee. "I thought he jumped in to break it up," Jerry said, "but he started swinging at the guy, and it became a two-on-one fight. This guy was acting like he was locked up with us."

Many critiques about programming revolved around substance abuse treatment. As Mack, who is completing a six-year sentence for robbery, weapons, and unlawful taking, put it, "Everybody coming out of jail addicted to something. They might sell coke but sniff heroin or sell weed but pop pills. Other guys can't go without drinking or smoking. A lot of times guys don't want to admit they have a problem. I used to be like that. I thought I was maintaining but was just lying to myself."

Groups such as Alcoholics Anonymous (AA) and Narcotics Anonymous (NA) are ritual organizations in which many of the clients participated. This was overtly expressed in their narratives or covertly shared through language and phrases, such as "people, places, and things," "let go and let God," "one day at a time," and "this too shall pass," used as coping mechanisms. Andrea Leverentz's scholarship focusing on formerly incarcerated women highlights the complexity of the relationship people going through reentry have with substance abuse and their self-efficacy and agency.[43]

Mack's commitment to sobriety was expressed by not letting himself be distracted by negative situations. "It's a lot of jokesters but a lot of them are just young," he said. "I'm older and trying to get home. I don't have time for games. I'm learning a lot and trying to get something out of these groups." In other words, while some people were merely going through the motions of reentry, he was actively doing reentry.

Although this was Mack's third and longest prison term, he was optimistic about his reentry, partly since he was not in a CEC facility but in a much smaller halfway house that was home to only forty men. But despite the smaller and more intimate setting, Mack said this facility came with other challenges, including a language barrier. "I'm one of three Black guys in my building," he said. "Everybody else is Hispanic." Mack found it difficult to participate at house group meetings as the conversations were predominately in Spanish. "I had to ask one of the guys if he could translate for me," he said, "because I didn't know what was going on."

Over time, Mack reached an agreement with his Hispanic cohabitants. They would slow down the group dialogues and speak a modified "Spanglish" to include him, and he in turn would help residents with their paperwork, becoming a de facto secretary for the halfway house.

"I have been a hustler my whole life," he explained, "so I can really get along with anybody. Guys asked me to help with their paperwork. Even the counselors come to me if they have a question about something." Part of Mack's enthusiasm for the rituals of programs, groups, and paperwork had to do with a feeling that his reentry was being part of something larger than himself, something that included his son.

"He is nineteen and dabbling in the streets," Mack said, "got to show him other ways and actively encourage him to pursue other paths because if I came out of prison angry and negative, he is going to respond to my energy the same way. I want my son to do better. He already doing better than me because he finished high school, I didn't do that, but I'm doing my GED so I can get my diploma. Shit, maybe we will both go to college together."

Others described the negative relationship they had with Narcotics and Alcoholic Anonymous programs because of bureaucratic red tape. For example, Alex described not being allowed to attend these groups at his halfway facility because the charges against him were not directly related to drug offenses, even though, he said, "I told them I have a pattern of using, and I had been attending sobriety circles in prison."

As it turned out, the reason Alex was not immediately allowed to attend the groups was because there was a waiting list. Clients described these groups at the halfway facilities as the most coveted, explaining that upon conclusion of a program cycle, residents receive a certificate of completion that helped reduce an individual's overall sentence and release date.

Ironically, Freddy was able to use Narcotics Anonymous as a sort of loophole to get himself moved out of state prison and into a halfway house. "They told me if I told them I had a drug problem they would send me to the halfway house, so I told them I had a drug habit." Freddy had never done a drug in his life, he said, and had a beer only once as a young man because he didn't like the taste. Here, Freddy saw an opportunity to be released and exploited that option. Conversely, Alex, who openly acknowledged his struggles with alcohol and narcotics, was barely afforded this chance.

Ultimately, Alex felt that these programs failed him, and he began opting out of the rituals of doing reentry at the halfway facility altogether. In time, Alex admitted to drinking, saying, "I have had a few beers since being out the halfway house but none of the hard stuff."

Programs and groups are part of the ritual and rites of passage in doing reentry. First, individuals must seek out, sign up for, and attend such events, which is viewed as expending time, energy, and initiative. Second, individuals must prove attendance through sign-in sheets, participation, and in some cases finding a sponsor. Finally, the end goal is finishing, which is conferred through certifications of completion in the form of diplomas or other documents, as well as ritual ceremonies such as a graduation.

"THEY JUST NOT GONNA SEND US BACK"

The proliferation of mass incarceration occurred at the same time as the rise of neoliberalism, which gained widespread attention in the 1970s and 1980s as a direct response to earlier global recessions.[44] Accordingly, neoliberal principles favor fiscal austerity, privatization, and deregulation of state control over industries as well as dismantling organized labor, shrinking public services, eradicating welfare programs, and criminalizing the urban poor.[45] At its core, neoliberalism projects the idea that all aspects of society should operate as a business and humanity is nothing more than a value of capital, making some lives more "disposable" than others.[46] Sociologist Nicole Kaufman's work critiques various nongovernmental organizations' roles in incarceration and postprison life.[47]

Furthermore, corrections and reentry have been exploited by neoliberalism. Mark Yates and Richard Lakes highlight how neoliberal policies have shaped governance over corrections, such as eliminating Pell grants for incarcerated individuals.[48] Justice studies professor Alessandro De Giorgi discusses how these policies have manifested into twenty-first-century reentry, describing what he calls "neoliberal neglect."[49] In this case, neoliberalism has created a climate that understands reentry at the individual rather than institutional level. He writes, "At every turn in their trajectories through the carceral state, from arrest to reentry, criminalized people are taught that success or failure is entirely dependent upon their own efforts. . . . [T]he the neoliberal ideology of personal responsibility, market competition, and self-help ultimately pervades every aspect of the reentry process as it is presently framed."[50]

Therefore, men and women returning to society are perpetually targeted through a myriad of red tape, fines, fees, and other expenditures that impede them and create situations that make a linear process of reentry unmanageable. In sum, neoliberal reentry is invested in profit that is accumulated from an individual's circumstances within the criminal legal system.

·   ·   ·   ·   ·

One of the most egregious findings that clients discussed in detail surrounded the penalties, fines, and fees that were associated with living in halfway facilities. Individuals are often penalized for breaking various rules and given penalty fines, which accumulate over time. However, most shocking was what clients said about what are called "bed fees."

As Saladin explained, "They make us pay to stay at the halfway house. You might have a dozen guys paying for one bed. If I'm supposed to be there a year but either I want to leave early or the house says I can leave early, they will write up the paperwork and let you leave. But you still got to pay for that bed for the entire length of your stay. That's on the paperwork, and you might have six months of rent on that bed. You start seeing all this turnover, and in one month you might see three different guys sleeping in the same bed and even though the first two not there anymore, best believe they still paying for it."

Other clients had other things to say about the bed fees, among them Sharif, who refused to leave the halfway facility early, arguing, "After a few months my counselor was urging me to leave complimenting I was a model inmate, and I could be with my wife. They were trying to manipulate my situation to free up my bed. I refused to leave. I wouldn't give them the satisfaction. If I'm paying for the bed, I'm sleeping in the bed."

Sharif further explained, "My wife and I been together twenty-four years, I been locked up for thirty years, we never slept in the bed together before, I can wait a few more months. For these institutions it's all about that turnover, and the more bodies they get passing through the more profit they make. Every day they are releasing guys, some who don't have any business getting let out early because they don't have the necessary skills to survive. Then they end up getting arrested, going back through the system, and end up right back at the halfway facility a year or two later."

This explanation of the vicious cycle of incarceration highlights many of the problems associated with reentry, especially in New Jersey. While the Garden State is considered a leader in decarceration, many of its residents are being cycled through the process of reentry.

Mandated programs and testing forced residents to pay fees, such as for drug testing and supervision costs. One person who was swept into the reentry cycle was a forty-five-year-old Black man named Bobby. A stocky individual with a stern look, Bobby had spent the past thirteen years in prison for manslaughter. While he did not participate as often as other clients, he attended group weekly and spoke openly during our one-on-one conversations.

Bobby admitted that during his time in prison he developed a drug habit. While he said he wanted to stop, his closest confidante, Freddy, described the situation differently. "I've known him a long time," Freddy said. "He not ready to stop using that stuff. He thinks I don't notice when we are back at the halfway house, and he go off with those other guys. I know what they are doing." Soon enough, Freddy told me that Bobby had been sent back to "Bo" Robinson for reassessment after failing a drug test.

A few weeks later Bobby returned to group with a new outlook and a positive attitude. Yet, Bobby found himself going back to "Bo" Robinson twice more for reassessment. At one point, he described the challenges of sobriety, saying, "It's like I know what I'm doing is wrong, but I'm so used to doing things one way, it's hard to stop, especially in this environment. The problem is that I got caught with dirty piss, and the halfway house staff know that anytime they want to send me back, all they got to do is take a urine."

After Bobby's third time being sent to "Bo" Robinson, he was sent back to state prison. Freddy summed up this cycle of reentry clearly: "The halfway house got all they could out of him. He went back and forth three times. That's three different payments on him. Each time the clock starts over. They not just going to send us back. They squeezed him dry and got all the money they could out him. And watch, next year, they going to send him back to the halfway house. It's all a scam. The prison system is the biggest hustlers out here. We small time compared to them."

Clients also complained about the fact that they were obligated to pay for their own medical care in halfway facilities.[51] Jose, a forty-eight-year-old Puerto Rican man, described what happened when he needed dental care. "I was going down to the infirmary for months complaining about my tooth," he recalled. "I know the routine—the dentist comes and just pulls the tooth. It is what it is. But for whatever reason this guy was refusing to see me. I was filling out the slips, submitting them, I would get sent down, and sit there all day, and nothing. It's like I needed flames coming out my mouth. I must have gone down to him about six times and now I'm here [halfway house] and I got to figure this stuff out on my own."

Rubbing the side of his mouth, Jose continued, "A dentist is expensive, and I don't have any insurance. Even if I find someone and they pull it out, it's still going to run me a few hundred dollars. I don't know what I'm going to do, but my mouth is killing me, I lost a few pounds because the tooth is infected and hurts to eat."

Terry, like some others, believed that she was sent to a halfway house to silence her after she threatened to take legal action in connection with her medical treatment.

A slender, thin-framed Black woman in her mid-forties, Terry wore a silk scarf around her head and a beige wrist brace on her left hand. She had previously served time within the state system and was currently completing a ten-year sentence in connection with federal drug trafficking charges. According to Terry, state prison was "not so bad" in comparison to her experience in the federal system. "Feds is another word for slavery because it's run like a plantation," she said. "In there you can only make twelve cents an hour." She described working in the kitchen and cooking in the dining hall for prison staff.

It was working in this unit that led to an accident that left Terry with three years of medical issues affecting her ability to use her left arm. After a cleaning crew left large puddles of water in the kitchen area, Terry slipped on the floor while carrying a tray of food, smashing her left elbow. "I was hoping I had just dislocated my arm," she said, "but the X-rays showed that I shattered my elbow."

The prison brought in an orthopedist to perform surgery. After the procedure, the doctor came to check on her progress but could not find her original X-rays. Despite Terry's complaints of feeling a "pinching" in her arm, the doctor dismissed her concerns. Yet the pain continued to increase. "I don't have any feeling in my first three fingers, my forearm tingles like pins and needles, and I can't fully extend my arm," she said. "I also can't squeeze anything in my left hand."

Terry's continued complaints were dismissed for the next two years. During that period, she documented each time she asked to see the doctor and the various excuses prison officials made when turning down her request. Eventually, she was granted an appointment and a new set of X-rays was taken, indicating that her arm was still broken and had not been set correctly during the first operation.

The orthopedist tried to reassure Terry that her arm would get better in time. By this point, she had documented almost three years of interactions between herself, prison staff, and the orthopedist, and she announced her intention to bring legal action. "I told them I mean business," she said. "I got all my paperwork, copies of my slip requests, and medical records. I'm going after everyone."

After her threat of legal action, she met with the orthopedist once more, and he agreed to perform another surgery to correct the problems. However, like Jose, she was transferred to the federal halfway facility with a year left on her sentence and has not had the corrective surgery.

"The feds know what they are doing," she said. "They think if they send me here, they can shut me up. I wasn't thrilled with that doctor, but he was planning to do the surgery again. I mean I rather find my own doctor now that I'm back in Newark, but that's a lot to do and I'm going to have to pay out of pocket for this surgery. I don't have that kind of money. I have some saving, but now I'm paying for this halfway house. I'm probably not even going to be able to get this surgery until I'm released."

In the interim, Terry said, she had been self-medicating with a combination of over-the-counter painkillers and cough syrup to ease the constant discomfort in her arm.

Stories such as the ones recalled by Jose and Terry underscore the ways neoliberalism in conjunction with a callous culture of dismissal turn problems that should be resolvable into issues that are seemingly impossible. Terry will never again have full use of her left arm and a legal proceeding against the federal prison system is more of a scare tactic.

The austerity that neoliberalism has created allows reentry via halfway houses to remain economically and politically strategic for various politicians and stakeholders. On the one hand, privatization fills voids left by the public sector and is presented to save taxpayers money. By outsourcing corrections and rehabilitation, state agencies can divert state budgets into other areas. On the other hand, the use of these private facilities still maintains a "tough on crime" image, as individuals are not simply released back into society. Through deregulation practices, individuals residing in halfway houses are in a precarious halfway situation: a state of limbo in which they are not fully free and not fully incapacitated, creating confusion and adding complexity to an already fragile situation. In other words, reentry becomes a vortex that pulls individuals reentering society into a category that is unique unto itself, insofar that this population is not completely imprisoned but not completely free.

SUMMARY

This chapter highlights the various ways individuals utilizing halfway transitional housing think about these institutions. Overall, many of the clients understand and yearn for programs that are comprehensive, inclusive, and overall can help reintegrate them back into society. However, the vast majority feel as if these programs pay nothing more than lip service and exploit their condition for purposes of profit through fees and fines.

The next chapter picks up where Terry's story ends. Many of those coming out of institutions of incarceration leave with various visible and invisible, physical and emotional, tangible and abstract blemishes. I explore the ways incarceration is inscribed on the body, mind, and soul. Just because a person leaves a specific location does not mean all the experiences, traumas, and issues remain behind. In fact, many of these issues persist and shape a person beyond the prison walls.

4 Body

In early 2011, about six weeks after I began facilitating weekly reentry center group sessions, I began bringing Dunkin' Donuts Munchkins, as these two-hour meetings were often held in a small, windowless conference room with poor ventilation, which encouraged a lethargic atmosphere. From my time as a graduate student, I knew that food was incentivizing and could bolster participation.

Accompanied by a cup of coffee or a glass of water, the small pastries were successful in inspiring conversation. However, I noticed various subtleties in the different ways clients interacted with the food. First, participants only took three doughnuts per session, encouraging a sense of community. Second, folks would ensure a certain level of hygiene such as by announcing that they were going to wash their hands before touching the doughnut box as well as using a tissue to grab their respective doughnuts. Finally, a large roll of brown paper towels became the de facto doughnut napkins used as makeshift plates so that clients would not have to hold their doughnuts in their hands or put them directly on the table.

Yet, as always when there are rules, there were outliers. Freddy would eat about six doughnuts before group began and then take three to eat during the session. By contrast, Jerry would take three doughnuts and not touch them until group ended. Louis would never take a doughnut.

Louis, a clean-shaven, dark-skinned man who was completing a seven-year sentence for robbery, was short in stature, standing about five feet three inches, and tipped the scale at two hundred pounds. After a few weeks of observing the "doughnut politics," I finally asked Louis if he wanted a doughnut, as there were several remaining after the session. He politely declined, and because of our rapport I said naively, "You don't like free food?"

"It's not that," he replied, "but I have diabetes, and these are full of sugar. I can't eat them." Louis, who was fifty-one years old, went on to discuss his health, explaining that he had had weight issues since childhood and had developed type II diabetes as a young adult. For Louis, incarceration exacerbated these issues: "I developed hypertension and have high cholesterol since my time in prison."

Interestingly, Louis mentioned that while incarcerated his diabetes remained relatively under control. "I was always able to get my shot," he said of the regular injections of insulin he needed. "They had to give it to me every day." However, this was no longer the case in the halfway facility. "Since being here I have gone into diabetic shock twice," he said. "The last time my sugar went over three hundred. I should be dead."

I then asked Jerry why he would not eat his doughnuts during group. After the session he explained, "I'm missing three of my front teeth. It's embarrassing to chew in front of people, and so I just wait until I'm alone." Louis and Jerry, along with other clients, began to discuss their health and other health-related issues during group sessions. More specifically, they discussed the disparities in health care they were now confronting in the face of reentry.

Imprisonment has a broad and profound impact on a human being's health. While reentry is often positioned as leaving the past behind, many of the events that take place during an individual's sentence are not so easily left behind just because the person is living outside the prison walls. Here, I unpack the various ways the prison experience is inscribed on the body, mind, and soul. First, I conduct a brief examination of health and incarceration-related issues, as these institutions often exacerbate morbidity. Second, I explore the historical ways racialized bodies were used and transformed under conditions of captivity, namely enslavement and convict leasing, both tethered to modern mass incarceration. Finally, I examine how the body shifts from "citizen to con to ex-con"[1] as individuals are released from incarceration settings and move through the rituals of the criminal legal system, culminating in doing reentry that is marked by visible and invisible, physical and emotional, and tangible and abstract modifications.

HEALTH, INCARCERATION, AND REENTRY

There is a growing amount of literature and research that investigates the relationship between health and incarceration. Unsurprisingly, scholarship highlights the fact that jails and prisons are a determinant of poor health as well as incubators for communicable diseases.[2] In fact, according to the U.S. Department of Justice, almost half of all incarcerated individuals have a chronic illness and are more likely than the public to report having a chronic condition or an infectious disease.[3]

Additionally, more than half of all persons in jail or prison settings have reported or meet the criteria for having a drug dependence or abuse issue, whereas only 5 percent of the general public meets this condition.[4] Finally, nearly a third of all persons confined to a prison setting have at least one known disability and more than half of these people have one or more concurrent chronic conditions.[5] In sum, data suggests that the population I describe in this book is afflicted with multiple health-related problems. Therefore, health concerns need to be front and center rather than marginalized in the process of doing reentry, especially because discussions of mental and physical health are often stigmatized in society.

The existing literature about incarceration and health has expanded beyond focusing on the individual person in prison to incorporate a discussion of how carceral settings negatively impact familial and community health. For instance, mental health is disrupted when a family member is incarcerated, creating issues such as elevated levels of psychological distress and depression.[6] Furthermore, research has found physical ailments develop when a family member is incarcerated, among them a higher likelihood of stroke, heart attack, obesity, hypertension, and diabetes.[7] Sadly, the risk of greater mental and physical health-related issues increases among Black women who have a family member incarcerated.[8] This type of strain on one's physical health is typified in the case of Kalief Browder, who was held at New York City's Rikers Island Jail for nearly three years. A year after Browder's untimely death by suicide, his mother, Venida, died after suffering complications of a heart attack.[9]

Beyond this, research highlights the fact that children of incarcerated parents suffer from various issues, including behavior problems such as increased aggression and childhood trauma.[10] In addition, research that examines children witnessing parental arrest indicates increased predictive posttraumatic symptoms.[11] Moreover, while limited in scope, research suggests links between parental incarcerations and elevated levels of C-reactive protein, primarily among adolescent girls.[12] Finally, Black children are at greatest risk of parental incarceration and must strive to overcome these obstacles through resilient attitudes.[13]

At the community level, research suggests that people who live in neighborhoods with higher rates of interaction with law enforcement have worse health outcomes.[14] Erin Kerrison and Alyasah Sewell found associations between local law enforcement use of "stop, question, and frisk" practices and chronic health issues, signifying neighborhoods that are overpoliced have higher rates of public health issues, which need to be addressed.[15]

The Black Lives Matter movement has given increasing visibility to patterns of racial injustice via law enforcement and overaggressive tactics in neighborhoods that have been historically disadvantaged. Interestingly, while scholars find higher rates of morbidity among individuals incarcerated, sociologist Evelyn Patterson has found lower rates of mortality among Black men incarcerated compared to their nonincarcerated Black male counterparts.[16] Her findings suggest that prison has an opposite impact on Black men by creating an environment with less mortality than their neighborhoods. Ultimately, this emphasizes the abysmal public policies and social services available to young Black men in the United States.

Finally, research looking at reentry underlines the various disadvantages and health-related experiences of those being released. Notably, physicians such as Emily Wang and colleagues found that formerly incarcerated young adults (aged eighteen to thirty) had increased associations with future hypertension and left ventricular hypertrophy, which contribute to higher rates of cardiovascular disease.[17] Furthermore, sociologist Bruce Western and his coauthors found that older formerly incarcerated individuals, particularly those with histories of mental illness, were least likely to be socially integrated into society and had weak family relationships as well as unstable housing and diminished levels of employment.[18] Moreover, this research indicates that stress and anxiety related to material insecurity negatively impacts the transition from incarceration to community.

Therefore, this chapter continues this important discussion surrounding health within the reentry process, focusing on the body holistically to understand how individuals returning to society participate in the reentry process with various health-related issues. A significant point in the transition back to society is the ability to engage in the physical, mental, emotional, and spiritual components of doing reentry. Here, we see how individuals coming back must alter, modify, and confront their reentry with various health-related issues that impact their corporeal and mental state. In sum, exiting a penal environment does not mean that all the experiences, traumas, and ailments are forgotten, but rather that these issues persist and can be exacerbated postincarceration.

"WE ARE MARKED"

Three institutions of captivity tether the Black American experience in the United States: slavery, the convict lease system, and mass incarceration. Sociologist Loïc Wacquant articulates how various "peculiar institutions" have shaped social exclusion of Black people, culminating in hyperincarceration that has created a "deadly symbiosis."[19] This overlap of history and experience of captivity was not lost on participants at the reentry center.

Mustafa readily discussed the interrelatedness between slavery and incarceration. When I asked, "Do you feel included or excluded in the United States?" he responded, "When independence was won in Africa in the 1950s and early '60s, colonialism was replaced with neocolonialism. The same thing happened in America. Slavery was replaced with neoslavery through a combination of capitalism, imperialism, and colonialism."

He added, "I feel like I'm eternally colonized here and not part of this system because there has never been an equal playing field. I don't consider myself American. I'm an African in America. In fact, we [Black people] are marked, physically and mentally. The scars of slavery still exist today."

Mustafa's statement about being "marked" and "scarred" is important to the larger discussion surrounding the social construct of race, crime, and punishment, particularly inscribed on Black and racialized bodies.

·   ·   ·   ·   ·

During the Enlightenment period between the seventeenth and nineteenth centuries in Europe, modern ideas surrounding race and racial differences developed. As the philosopher Emmanuel Chukwudi Eze writes, "Enlightenment philosophy was instrumental in codifying and institutionalizing both the scientific and popular European perceptions of the human race . . . articulating Europe's sense not only of its cultural but also *racial* superiority."[20]

Notably, one of the founding fathers and third president of the United States, Thomas Jefferson, contributed to this concept in his book *Notes on the State of Virginia*, written in the late eighteenth century, which argues that color is the first difference between the races, marking Black people as inferior in both mind and body.[21] Since the colonial period, the Black body in Western civilization has been categorized, archived, and studied to continue to make claims of racial inferiority.[22] For example, in the eighteenth century policies such as "lantern laws" required Black, mixed race, and indigenous populations to carry candles after dark when not in the company of White people as a way to police and monitor the Black body.[23]

In the 1850s, the biologist Louis Agassiz produced the earliest known images of Black slaves on daguerreotypes focusing on body shape, such as hands and posture, to justify claims of Black racial inferiority. Today technologies impose implicit racial bias.[24] For example, in 2019, Nijeer Parks of New Jersey was arrested based on faulty facial recognition software, placing his body at the scene of a crime, when in fact he was not there.[25] Police mug shots illustrate the Black body, particularly the face and profile, in disparaging manners that negatively link race to criminalization.[26]

The premise of racial inferiority was used as a justification for slavery and was enforced through psychological and physical torment. The whip became a tool of punishment that is synonymous with this institution.[27] One of the most striking images of the antebellum South is a photograph of a Black man known as Gordon, a runaway slave, whose back was covered in keloids, a raised scarring, as a result from being whipped. This torture left permanent marks across Gordon's back as a physical reminder of the agony endured.[28]

Moreover, numerous slave narratives describe the use of the whip as a means of discipline and punishment for rules infractions. The abolitionist and former slave Frederick Douglass describes being whipped by an exceptionally brutish slave driver known as Mr. Covey, who had a reputation for breaking slaves in body and mind.[29] Angela Davis, a professor and activist, describes how whipping was gendered as pregnant enslaved women were made to lay face down with their stomachs in a hole to protect future slave labor from punishment.[30] Theodore Dwight Weld's 1839 book *American Slavery As It Is* highlights various whipping scenes, showcasing the barbarity of this practice.[31]

The exploitation of the Black body within the confines of enslavement was all encompassing, including but not limited to labor, entertainment, and sexual gratification. Typically, slavery has been viewed as an economic creation, based on the need to cultivate raw materials.[32] While this was the impetus, the institution metastasized into its own unique phenomenon. In other words, enslaved Africans were prisoners to their enslavers, having to concede to various demands, particularly beyond labor. For example, historian Sergio Lussana outlines how "prizefighting" was part of American slavery as a form of entertainment among slave plantation owners.[33] Furthermore, enslavement took on various forms of sexual assault. Often portrayed in literature and cinema as only being heteronormative (e.g., White man and Black woman), Vincent Woodward's book *The Delectable Negro: Human Consumption and Homoeroticism within U.S. Slave Culture* counters the cisgender narrative, highlighting homoeroticism as well as male rape on slave plantations. Furthermore, Woodward's work unearths documentation that the scope of slave consumption included cannibalism.[34] In other words, the Black body became a literal cuisine of white supremacy.

The American Civil War and the passage of the 13th Amendment in 1865 officially ended the formal institution of slavery. Yet this legislation created a "captivity loophole," as it is written, "Neither slavery nor involuntary servitude, except as a punishment for crime whereof the party shall have been duly convicted, shall exist within the United States, or any place subject to their jurisdiction."[35] While this amendment frees a population from bondage, it simultaneously allows and reinforces the captivity of another group, which ultimately kept Black people incapacitated but changed the title from "slave" to "convict."

Beginning as early as the 1840s, the convict lease system began in the United States. Premised on a system of outsourcing incarcerated individuals to companies for profit, this industry quickly rose in popularity following the Civil War's end in 1865. Within a decade, various states, particularly former Confederate states, began to pass legislation that impacted former enslaved people. For example, sociologists Christopher Uggen, Jeff Manza, and Angela Behrens trace the history of disenfranchisement laws between the 1840s and the 1870s, showing a significant uptick in legislation directly following the Civil War.[36] Additionally, vagrancy laws, otherwise known as Black Codes, which racially profiled Black Americans, were passed to limit mobility.[37] These codes disproportionately impacted Black life in the second half of the nineteenth and first half of the twentieth centuries, sending Black people into the criminal legal system.

Pulitzer Prize–winning journalist Douglas Blackmon's book *Slavery by Another Name: The Re-Enslavement of Black Americans from the Civil War to World War II* traces the history and highlights the corrupt, profit-driven, racial degradation that was the convict lease system. Individuals were placed in bondage, labeled as criminals, and leased out to private companies to be used as workers. Imprisoned men and women were confronted with unsanitary living circumstances, unsafe work conditions, and brutal violence as a means of punishment. Blackmon recounts many instances where whipping was the default punishment, writing, "a recaptured black escapee to lie 'on the ground and the dogs were biting him' . . . took a stirrup strap, doubled it and wet it, stripped him naked, bucked him, and whipped him—unmercifully whipped him, over half an hour."[38]

The continued use of the whip, particularly in a postslavery era, was not unique to the American South. In the North, prisons incorporated the whip into their repertoire of punishment. In the editor's introduction of Austin Reed's 1858 autobiography, *The Life and the Adventures of a Haunted Convict*, Caleb Smith provides an illustration titled "The-Cat-o'-Nine-Tails" and a description stating, "An officer administers stripes to an immobilized prisoner while a keeper looks on."[39] Reed's memoir is the earliest known text of a Black prisoner, and he describes being punished by whip frequently. Furthermore, Smith highlights that similarly to convict leasing in the South, northern institutions also exploited prison labor. He writes, "From the start, though, the society hired out the boys and girls to private contractors, who set up manufacturing in the shops. The inmates made shoes, rope mats, brooms, and other simple commodities."[40]

Beyond the bounds of the formal criminal legal system, extrajudicial violence, in the form of lynching, was inscribed on the Black body. While the precise number of lynching occurrences is unknown, nearly seven thousand transpired between Reconstruction and passage of the 1964 Civil Rights Act.[41] Historical records highlight the fact that lynching occurred throughout the United States and indicate that White mobs justified these killings by arguing that these individuals were criminals who broke the law.

In many instances, the ritual of killing presented opportunities to capture and control the Black body beyond death. Pieces of the anatomy were removed and kept as relics by participants and onlookers. Professor of law Barbara Holden-Smith recounts the 1904 murder of a Black couple in Mississippi, writing, "They were forced to hold out their hands while one finger at a time was chopped off. The fingers were distributed as souvenirs."[42] In another instance, the knuckles of a man named Sam Hose were put on display at a butcher shop in Atlanta.[43]

These grotesque and barbaric forms of violence were intended to have physical and emotional consequences. The former inflicted profound pain on the individual(s) who was (were) being killed. The latter implemented mental trauma as a warning to others. In sum, lynch mobs are a culmination of white supremacy in the United States that maintain control over racialized bodies via accusation of crime and exacting punishment.

.   .   .   .   .

Today, captivity takes the form of jails and prisons, with Black Americans disproportionately incapacitated. According to The Sentencing Project, Black men are six times more likely to be incarcerated than White men. Astonishingly, roughly one in every twelve Black men in their thirties is in jail or prison on any given day.[44]

While the formal use of the whip no longer persists, other institutional mechanisms are used against those imprisoned to achieve obedience and conformity of the body and mind. The rise of the American "supermax" prisons, which provide long-term segregated housing, highlights the increased sadism that has been incorporated into punishment rubrics. In 2013, incarcerated individuals in California's prison system housed in long-term solitary confinement went on a hunger strike to call national attention to these unlivable conditions.[45]

Remnants of slavery and convict leasing continue today. Several prison institutions are former slave plantations, among them the Ramsey Unit in Texas, the Cummins Unit in Arkansas, and the notorious Louisiana State Prison, more commonly referred to as "Angola Farm." Today, Angola continues agricultural production and holds an annual prison rodeo.[46] Similarly, institutions from the convict leasing era remain. David Oshinsky's book *Worse Than Slavery: Parchman Farm and the Ordeal of Jim Crow Justice* traces the history of Parchman Farm, also known as Mississippi State Prison, back to the convict leasing era.[47] Further, in the American Southwest, former sheriff of Maricopa County, Arizona, Joe Arpaio infamously used chain gangs, dressed incarcerated persons in pink jumpsuits, and forced individuals to sleep in tents to not only punish but humiliate in the twenty-first century.[48]

Because of the punishments endured while incarcerated, the body experiences change postrelease. Sociologist Lucia Trimbur's ethnographic work with formerly incarcerated boxers illustrates various struggles upon return.[49] Critical theorist Albert de la Tierra finds that for some Black urban men, continuing an exercise routine postincarceration, known as "carceral calisthenics," helps maintain normalcy.[50] The work of both Trimbur and de la Tierra on reentry deals directly with (re)shaping the body. Ironically, "prison style" fitness classes, which commercialize carceral exercises, have become popularized and are a mixture of genuine and exploitative fetishizing of imprisonment.[51]

Geographer Dominique Moran discusses how prison is inscribed on the body in various ways, including prerelease anxieties surrounding emancipation, social stigma felt because of criminal conviction, and physical reminders of incarceration, such as dental hygiene or lack thereof.[52] Furthermore, numerous justice-impacted individuals have written about the lasting impacts of incarceration. For example, Mika'il DeVeaux writes about the various emotional and physical traumas witnessed while incarcerated that continue to inform and plague his reentry.[53] Formerly incarcerated activist Five Mualimm-ak writes of his experiences, "But solitary doesn't just confine your body; it kills your soul."[54]

"FROM CITIZEN TO CON TO EX-CON"

Learning about the lived experiences of participants underscored and reinforced the notion of the body moving through various rituals and transitions within the criminal legal system, which changed their body, mindset, and attitude at various stages of their incarceration and reentry. This was succinctly said best by Darren: "We go through this process of being a 'citizen' to 'con' to 'ex-con' in our lives. For the people in this room, we are all 'ex-cons' and fighting against that label, trying to shake it off our backs."

Darren, who often showed up for group wearing a collared shirt and necktie, was a brown-skinned man with facial stubble, stood five-foot-eight, and was living in a halfway facility after serving fifteen years for charges including robbery, assault, and escape from prison.

Darren, who was born in the early 1970s, described coming of age in the "crack era" and the violence he witnessed in his Newark community. When asked about his first interactions with the criminal legal system, he responded, "Are you asking about the first time I was arrested or first time I got my ass beat by the cops?"

Explaining the difference, he continued, "My first arrest was when I was seventeen, but the first time a cop beat my ass I was about fourteen. Some neighborhood kids and I stole some bicycles, not for any reason but to just ride around and this older Italian cop caught us and beat us up, calling us animals. He put us in handcuffs and one by one slammed us against the wall, patted us down, and then threw us on the ground. I hit my head and left this mark [points to upper right side of forehead]. Then he took the cuffs off and said, 'Every time I see you out here, expect the same shit,' and he kept his promise. For probably the next two years, if he saw me, it was the same thing, and I just remember he had what seemed like giant hands when he used to grab me." According to Darren, this cop assaulted him at least six times over the next two years.

Darren's description of institutional and systematic violence at the hands of a law enforcement officer was shocking. When I asked how this experience shaped his outlook on police, he responded, "It marked the end of my childhood. I wasn't an angel growing up, but those beatings made me grow up quick because I was embarrassed that I couldn't defend myself." Darren eventually dropped out of high school and drifted between licit and illicit occupations.

In 1990, he was arrested on a weapons charge and spent the next several years in prison. Upon his release, he described 1995 as a transformative year, stating, "When I was locked up, I was using drugs and fighting, I was out of control, but I always watched the Nation [of Islam] and the Five Percenters and how they conducted themselves. I was curious but never sought them out in prison."

He continued, "When I got out, my cousin, who was dabbling in spirituality, encouraged me to go to the Million Man March in Washington, DC. All I can say is that I was overwhelmed seeing so many beautiful brothers and sisters in unity. I had never cried in public before, and I remember just standing at the National Mall weeping. When I got back to Newark, first thing I did was join the local mosque."

Although Darren described having a renewed sense of self after joining the Nation of Islam, his legal troubles did not end. In early 1996, he was arrested and sent back to prison. While he admitted to committing the crimes he was charged for, he was adamant that the amount of time given to him was unfair, stating, "I got thirty years, which was crazy. I didn't kill or harm anyone." Without giving many details, Darren revealed that within the first year of his three-decade sentence, he escaped. "It wasn't anything like in the movies," he said. "Just had an opportunity and took it." But without money or any other options, he turned himself in after a few weeks.

He explained, "While I was on the run, I connected with someone from the mosque, and they encouraged me to go back to prison. They told me that if I wanted to be a man, I needed to confront my obstacles, children run away from problems. Following the teaching of the Honorable Elijah Muhammad, I would get through this stage of my life."

After his arrest for his escape, Darren was once again subject to abuse by law enforcement, as he described, "I've gotten beat up by every level of the criminal justice system—cops, bailiffs, and corrections officers. When you are charged with escape the level of security goes up because you are considered high risk. When they brought me back to court, extra security was brought in. They chained my hands to my waist, shackled my feet, and put four guards around me."

Darren's story reminds us that the criminal legal system operates on a level that enforces discipline through punishment, which is carried out in public view. Professor of comparative and foreign law James Whitman's work suggests that degradation plays an integral role in how societies punish and discipline.[55] Theorist Michel Foucault's theory on biopolitics illustrates how state power over the physical and political bodies within a population operates to achieve control.[56] And sociologist and law professor Dorothy Roberts's scholarship proposes that race and biopolitics reinforce racial categories and inequality. She writes, "The acceptance of torture of enemy combatants not only helps to normalize the abuse of incarcerated black citizens; it also threatens to support mass incarceration itself, along with other forms of institutionalized racism, and to contain organized resistance against it."[57] Ultimately, Darren's body was put on display by the criminal legal system.

First, the police officer who physically assaulted him as an adolescent showcased Darren as a public spectacle that community residents witnessed and could not intervene in. This is the case with many of the recorded videos of law enforcement killing Black residents. The most shocking example is the murder of George Floyd in May of 2020 in Minneapolis, Minnesota. The officer knelt on Floyd's neck for nearly nine minutes as onlookers pleaded with the cop to remove his leg. Yet no one interfered because it was understood that there would be reprisal by officers ready to inflict deadly violence.

Second, Darren experienced being part of public theater as his body was presented in a courtroom in a distinct prison jumpsuit and shackled.

Figure 9. Market Street, downtown Newark, 2012. Photo courtesy of the author.

Additionally, his personal information, such as height, weight, race, and criminal penalties, was made known for spectators to find listed on the New Jersey Department of Corrections' Offender Search Form. Finally, Darren's imprisonment placed him in a state-operated public prison.

In all three instances Darren described being assaulted. While in custody awaiting his various trials, he described being beaten by court bailiffs, recalling the shackles being squeezed as tightly as possible, and punched about his abdomen. Moreover, in state prison he experienced the trauma of having to defend himself from other incarcerated men as well as correctional officers.

He described being incarcerated in various state institutions in North and South Jersey, the latter being a culture shock. He recalled, "When I was little, I remember going down south to visit family and seeing how different everything was than in Newark, so when I went to Bayside [State Prison] I was stunned because it felt just like when I was a kid. The COs are a bunch of racist White boys that call the Black guys all types of racist names. They are supposed to address you by your last name or number, but they'll just say, 'nigger such and such.' This one cop was vicious and would beat the shit out of Black guys for looking him in the eye. He had this large Confederate flag tattooed on his arm."

As it would turn out, however, in the wake of the George Floyd murder, a senior corrections officer at Bayside Prison was fired after participating in a reenactment of Floyd's death during a counterprotest at a march against police brutality.[58]

Darren's body is marked by various scars, which retell his criminal legal involvement. Besides the mark on the upper right side of his head, he revealed blemishes around his wrists from tight handcuffs as well as various scars on his shoulders and arms from prison fights, mostly at the hands of corrections officers. When I asked if he ever fought back or made formal complaints, he responded, "It's a tough position, because if you fight back, they come back ten times harder. They go get their boys and do an 'extraction' with riot gear and pull you out of your cell. That's a difficult fight because you are punching armor, so you end up hurting yourself more than them." He went on to explain, "Complaining makes you look weak. The guards are a gang, and they protect each other. If you want to make a formal complaint that process starts with going to a CO, so that doesn't usually go far. When there is an investigation what usually happens is either the guard is moved to a different unit, or you get transferred to another facility. The best advice I can give anyone going to prison is just survive, tell your story, and prevent someone else from going."

Survival was something that Darren had been doing much of his life. He was optimistic that now in his early forties the days of fighting were behind him. Yet he acknowledged that his criminal legal involvement changed him and he had to have a plan moving forward in doing reentry. He explained, "Physically, I'll have these scars for the rest of my life as a reminder, but it's all the unseen things that happen to a person in that environment. Now, I can joke around, laugh, smile, but you can't do that inside. You become hard and numb and doing that for so many years, I can't just undo that all at once, it's going to take time for me to fully let my guard down, think before I react, and trust people. I'm confident I'll get there but right now it's baby steps."

So many of the participants had Darren's perspective, which was cautious optimism about reentry, especially in relation to how criminal legal contact shaped their bodies and their health.

Visible and Invisible

The cover of *If Tomorrow Comes*, the debut album of Brooklyn rapper Maino, is an image of his shoulders facing forward and head slightly turned to the left, prominently showing various tattoos on his upper torso. Less obvious but still clearly visible is the large scar running across the right side of his face, a common result of a prison fight. Known as a "buck fifty," this wound is given its slang name because of the approximate hundred and fifty stitches needed to repair one's face because of such an assault.[59] Before his career as a hip-hop artist, Maino was imprisoned for a decade for a drug-related kidnapping and this scar proves it. Moreover, this type of injury, along with other noticeable markings across participants' faces, necks, and arms, was commonplace.

However, Russell presented the most strikingly visible representation of the buck-fifty scarification. Released after twenty-two years in state prison, Russell has a face distorted by the various scars that cross both sides of his profile. On the right side, he has a large singular keloid that runs from the middle of his cheek down to his earlobe. The left side of Russell's face has two large, jagged keloids. The first runs downward from the back of his jawline to his neck. The second starts under the left side of his chin and runs upward, crossing over the first and creating an "X" as it reaches the back of his head. Russell, who stood just shy of six feet tall, is brown skinned, has a short haircut that is graying in the front, and has a crooked nose, as the bridge is slightly off-center.

Russell distinctly recalled the age of ten being a turning point in his life. He lost his grandmother, who was the bedrock of his family, and began smoking marijuana with older kids. Shortly after, his parents separated because of his father's alcoholism.

By the time Russell was a preteen, he was getting into trouble. "I never went to middle school because between the ages of twelve to fourteen I was locked up for burglary," he said. "When I got out, they put me right into high school." Already having done what he described as "hard time," Russell did not complete the ninth grade. He began living "in the streets" and "graduated" from burglary to armed robbery.

"I don't say this to brag, but robbery became a career," he explained. "I'm not proud of it and regret a lot of it but I was unfortunately very good at it, to the point that I could call myself a professional. It didn't matter who it was, I would rob drug dealers, establishments, and basically anybody who I thought had money."

Part of Russell's professionalism meant wearing disguises such as a ski mask and gloves, never robbing the same place twice, and inflicting as little pain on a person or business as possible.

The "stickup game"[60] moved Russell around the country, eventually landing him in various Midwest prisons throughout the 1980s. Upon release, Russell returned to New Jersey and was quickly swept up by the surging crack epidemic.

"I got out of prison in '89 and introduced to crack," he said, "which wasn't a big deal before I went to prison but when I got out everyone was doing it, including me." With a growing crack addiction, Russell resumed armed robbery to make money. However, unlike his earlier days as a professional, crack made him "sloppy" and by 1990 he was back in police custody.

Russell was found guilty and given a fifty-year sentence for first-degree robbery. Although no one was injured and it came out at trial that his gun was both inoperable and had no bullets, Russell believed that he would spend the rest of his life behind bars.

Throughout our interview I never found the precise moment to ask specifically about the scars on his face. Yet our conversation painted a picture of how he came to have these permanent disfigurements. In 1991 he was sent to Trenton State prison, an environment he described as being enveloped in violence and danger. "I had plenty of incidents in prison and had to adjust quickly to survive," he said. "All I knew was violence and got into plenty of trouble for it, spending a lot of years in segregation."

At age fifty, Russell was paroled after serving twenty-two years. In effect he was given a second chance. "I'm older, wiser, and lost a lot," he said. "*I know how I look* and what life expectancy is for Black men. I got less than twenty years left on this earth, so I must make the best of it."[61]

He was speaking about his appearance, lifespan, and future possibilities. The reality of having large grisly scars on his face has the potential of being a hindrance for future opportunities and relationships. These marks tell a story, one that is riddled with violence, both as the purveyor and recipient. The buck-fifty, particularly in urban street culture, is both a warning and a badge that the wearer cannot remove. While Russell is doing reentry, his scars are frequent reminders to both him and others of a past that will shape his present and impact his future.

Style and appearance play a significant role in the reentry process, conveying a specific image and identity the wearer is trying to present.[62] Sociologist Erving Goffman describes this as dramaturgy.[63] In other words, human interaction is based on a series of learned performances that consider environment, context, and other social factors, such as the nature of the relationship between two or more individuals. Here the performer is guiding the impression the viewer might have, and at the same time the viewer is obtaining information to form an opinion about the performer. Therefore, when doing reentry, many participants are trying to either reclaim or reinvent their identity by shedding the negative connotations associated with being formerly incarcerated.

Additionally, the role of stigma[64] is apparent in the reentry process. Individuals impacted by the criminal legal system are constantly negotiating their lives and well-being based on this social blemish. This becomes part of the invisible mark inscribed on the body and mind. Often, participants described the impending uneasy conversations with potential employers and others who could either grant or deny approval on various aspects of life. Ultimately, many going through reentry must move cautiously not to avoid their criminal history but try to explain it in a manner that is comforting to those with power.

The reentry center staff understood the role of stigma for this population and spent a significant amount of time practicing how to address one's past. This was done through various exercises in which individuals would prepare résumés and statements. Typically, the rule was to not overdivulge information. In other words, put only what is necessary on the document. Likewise, do not attempt to overexplain the past but speak straightforwardly and to the point. Finally, discuss the past as positively as possible, for example, by mentioning things you learned, how you are a better person, and your future goals. This approach avoids leaving an employer with a negative impression.

During one of these exercises, Freddy blurted out, "It's all bullshit, man!" His announcement halted the training and redirected the conversation to the invisible barriers of reentry, specifically the lasting impact that being incarcerated had on his own idea of self-worth.

Freddy articulated, "I get what we are trying to do here, but it's tough because I know my past, I can't just erase that. I could put on a suit and talk 'proper,' but in the back of my mind, I'm always going to be thinking, 'Does he know?' or 'Can he tell?' It just fucks with me because all these people downtown might smile at me, shake my hand, and give me the interview, but if I don't get the job, I'm left wondering is it because I'm a felon? Some places don't even call back. Another place told me they just had so many applicants and maybe that's it, maybe someone more qualified got the job, but I'm still left thinking, was it just me?"

Others agreed with Freddy that the invisible label of "felon" was one of the largest hurdles to the entire reentry process because it sowed doubt in the very exercise of doing reentry.

Beyond employment opportunities, the invisible stigma of having a felony showed up in other forms. Gloria, a Black woman in her mid-forties who had a felony conviction for drug distribution, discussed how this label impacted her future of being a parent.

Incarcerated in New York, Gloria returned to New Jersey after she was released. She described growing up as one of seven children. Her upbringing, she said, was "tough"—two of her brothers died through violence before the age of twenty, and a third is serving a life sentence. These events caused a major disruption in her family as she and all but one of the remaining siblings had struggled with substance abuse. While engaging in sex work in New York City, she was arrested while in possession of drugs. She was charged with "intent to distribute" and served almost three years in a women's state prison.

Gloria expressed the desire to adopt a child. "I'm too old now to have my own," she said, "but I have a lot of love to give, and there are plenty of babies who need a mother." The exciting idea of being a mother was tempered with the reality that because of her conviction, Gloria was not sure whether she would be allowed to adopt. While New Jersey law dictating foster care and adoption does not explicitly exclude people with drug convictions, Gloria had been convicted in New York, where people convicted of drug-related offenses cannot adopt children.[65]

Actively working on her recovery, Gloria participated in various groups, such as Narcotics Anonymous, as well as parenting classes provided by the reentry center. Furthermore, she renewed her Christian faith and had become active in her local church, volunteering with the Sunday school program. Yet, the invisible stigma of being incarcerated permeated her thoughts.

"I'm really trying to be hopeful and praying to God that once I'm done with all this and not on parole the state adoption agency will give me a chance," she said. "I just need the opportunity. But like, I think, is the adoption board going to see me for who I am now or they going to see a criminal? I just keep my faith."

Physical and Emotional

Increasingly, I began noticing the health complaints of people participating in the group, which usually appeared in the form of passing commentary about their bodies in relation to other factors, such as changes in the weather. During colder months, Stuart carried a portable inhaler to combat asthma and Ray griped about arthritis.

I also learned of the many chronic conditions participants experienced. Although I did not conduct a formal survey, my field notes suggest that at some point nearly all the participants disclosed a medical issue or chronic illness. In some cases, several clients described having "more serious" illnesses such as heart disease and hepatitis, and one individual revealed being HIV positive. Overall, many clients expressed that their physical health was worse after leaving prison.

Often evidence of chronic conditions is not readily *seen* on the body. However, these pains are *felt* on the body, prohibiting aspects of the reentry process. For example, Ray's arthritis made participation in various reentry programming less appealing. Alex, who was in his early forties, had premature chronic pain in his legs and back. He remarked, "Prison cells are not that big. Plus, you are sharing with someone else, and that type of restriction just beats you up."

Other physical afflictions either developed or were exacerbated because of the prison environment. Louis, who was already suffering from several health ailments, described the need for reading glasses. It is likely that a combination of conditions, including his diabetes, compounded with prison led to the worsening of his eyesight. Malcolm X highlights this, writing, "I had come to prison with 20/20 vision. But when I got sent back to Charlestown [prison], I had read so much by the lights-out glow in my room at the Norfolk Prison Colony that I had astigmatism and the first pair of eyeglasses that I have worn ever since."[66]

Finally, weight issues were prominent indicators of incarceration. Clients frequently described the unpalatable prison food, which was a combination of refined sugars, carbohydrates, and sodium, along with servings of "mystery meat" and other concoctions. The 2020 report *Eating Behind Bars*, produced by Impact Justice, found that prison food is a detriment to health as institutions adhere to very low standards to decrease cost and increase efficiency.[67] "Home-cooked" prison meals from an assortment of items in commissary became the alternative option, but clients noted that these meals were not necessarily healthier.

Almir, a forty-year-old, light-skinned Black man with multiple health issues, was the largest client at the reentry center, standing six-foot-two and weighing more than 350 pounds. He described always having weight problems growing up, but said he had had a positive childhood, going to Catholic school, and coming from what he described as "a long line of hustlers," who traded in narcotics and other ventures, such as boxing promotion. He shared a fond memory of meeting heavyweight champion Mike Tyson as a child.

At sixteen, Almir dropped out of school and began selling drugs. By the time he was twenty, he was operating his own drug trafficking network "down South," where he sold cocaine and heroin. This did not last long, as local drug dealers began to "knock off" out-of-town drug distributors. "At first I was going to stay," he said, "but I heard rumors that they were looking for the 'fat nigga from Jersey,' so I closed shop and got out."

Although a hustler, Almir described having pride in his community, noting, "I never wanted to sell drugs in Newark," he said. "I know that sounds weird, but from early on, I was always trying to help my neighborhood, making sure the elders were taken of. I also never liked seeing trash in the streets, so I would pay kids a dollar for each piece of trash they picked up. Besides that, we would send the youth to water parks, trips to the beach, and have cookouts in the park."

While Almir's altruistic efforts might have garnered praise from the community, law enforcement was less impressed. In the mid-1990s, Almir served two years in state prison and by the early 2000s his criminal enterprise had gained the interest of the Federal Bureau of Investigation and the Bureau of Alcohol, Tobacco, and Firearms. Eventually, federal agents arrested Almir and a dozen coconspirators on charges ranging from drug trafficking to murder. Several members of his organization were given life sentences, and he was sentenced to 121 months in federal prison. Two of his associates were his biological brothers, who received ten- and eighteen-year sentences, respectively.

After Almir entered the federal prison system, his health issues worsened, as he was moved to various institutions all over the country because he was labeled a "public safety factor of greater severity." Ultimately, he had to be moved to a medical facility after collapsing in the prison yard due to his weight. Diagnosed with diabetes, hypertension, and asthma, Almir has chronic shoulder and lower back pain and needs a cane to walk because his knees cannot support his weight. Almir also suffered from several rashes and sores known as intertrigo between skin folds.

While at the medical facility, Almir was placed on a special diet, monitored exercise, and various pharmaceutical drugs to help treat his various chronic illnesses. But he described these steps as too little, too late. "I don't understand why all of that wasn't provided to me earlier or given to everyone in prison," he said. "If we are supposed to be rehabilitating, they got to do better by us." Now that Almir is at the halfway facility, his reentry plan is to continue to lose weight and maintain a healthy diet so that he can join his wife and children out of state.

Many participants described unwanted weight increase because of the prison environment that created idle time, stress-related eating, and poor dietary options. However, a few of their accounts described healthy weight loss in prison. Russell, for example, described joining the Nation of Islam, which provided him structure and encouraged good habits, which took the form of daily exercise.

"I'm probably in the best shape in my life," he said, "cutting out drugs and eating to live not living to eat. In prison, I became a trainer, telling guys to take pride in their body and appearance." Russell's physical appearance indicated his claims that daily exercise and regimented eating were pillars in his reentry. Additionally, he thought that his physical transformation would be helpful given his desire to work with a local mosque teaching exercise and self-defense, a position that avoided his having to explain his facial scars.

While physical issues are inscribed on the body, emotional scars are imbedded in the mind. Everyone agreed that no one could be fully prepared for prison. Stories of seeing men "freak out" and "go nuts" were routine. Melvin described committing a violent act to get out of his shared cell.

"The guy lost it," Melvin shared. "I started smelling feces in our unit and after a few days the smell got worse. I confronted him and realized he was shitting himself and making wall art. I couldn't believe it. I told the guard this guy needs help, and he started laughing and thought it was funny. I made up my mind I was getting out that cell and I walked up to the same CO, who was laughing and punched him in the face. I spent the next six months in solitary."

Another shocking story by a participant, who described this incident under the strictest of confidence, was witnessing a prison rape.

"When I first got to prison, I was told to watch out for booty bandits. Soon after arriving, I witnessed a group of guys surround this young man in the shower and attack him. I don't know if it made it worse, but he tried fighting back. Imagine seeing a group of naked guys punching, kicking, and holding someone and the water, soap, blood, and other bodily fluids mixing on the floor. Afterward, the guy was lying on the floor limp, and he had shit on himself, and blood was coming from his ass that really fucked with me. I didn't shower for months. In prison, you just got to keep pushing because if you stop and think about things too long it will fuck with you. I tried forgetting that situation but right after I got out, I had a nightmare about it. This the first time I have ever spoken about it."

Conversations about prison rape rarely came up in any group setting. Men acknowledged that it occurred, but the majority downplayed its existence, often distancing themselves from this sort of violence. They said things like, "It didn't happen at the prison I was at" or "That's not a thing that guys in Jersey do." The need to put a certain distance between masculine identity and sexual violence was apparent because being both victim and/or witness to this behavior has profound impacts on one's emotional state.

The man who told this story went on to describe feeling vulnerable and guilty. He was worried that he could be a victim of the same type of violence. He also wondered if he should have helped the victim. In this case, witnessing these types of traumatic events compounded with the inability to speak about these occurrences only exacerbate emotional turmoil.

The lack of transparency in discussing mental health was not surprising. Many clients had never talked about their feelings or emotions. Rarely did individuals discuss their own mental well-being but rather offering comments about mental stability was reserved for describing others as "crazy." Yet in the blurred moments between group meetings, interviews, and conversations, I saw how mental health was profoundly impacted by the transition from prison to reentry.

Malik described exhibiting emotional instability postincarceration. His joyriding and reckless driving conviction did not come without consequences. At age eighteen, he and two friends "borrowed" their mother's car to ride around the city. Given their age, the time of night, and location in the nation's "carjacking" capital, it did not take long for Newark police to try to pull them over. Malik, who was driving, did not have a valid driver's license and instead took the police on a car chase. In the end, the vehicle crashed after Newark cops used what is known as a "pursuit intervention technique" that caused an accident when the car hit a telephone pole.

In the end, Malik suffered serious injuries to his head and back as well as a broken pelvis. His friend in the back seat was relatively unscathed, having only cuts and bruises. Unfortunately, the passenger in the front, his best friend, was not wearing a seat belt and was thrown through the front windshield, impaled on a nearby fence, and died at the scene. "I don't remember much about the accident," Malik said, "but when they were putting me in the ambulance, the nurse just kept saying, 'Look at me,' but I already saw my friend on the fence."

The subsequent investigation determined that Newark police were at fault for the crash, and so Malik faced lesser crimes and a shorter prison sentence than he would have otherwise. At the time we spoke, he had a pending civil suit against the city. Nevertheless, Malik described various instances of stress, anxiety, and paranoia, which affected his daily life, as did his tendency to become frustrated and give up easily.

His description of troubled sleeping patterns illuminated the anxieties that extend from prison to reentry. "My mind don't turn off," he said. "Sometimes I'll just be laying on the bed the whole night staring at the ceiling and then the sun comes up."

Although much of Malik's mental trauma stems from the accident, prison only exacerbated these problems. Because of his injuries, he was in the hospital for several weeks handcuffed to his bed. He explained how the cops tried lying to him that his friend had not died as an attempt to intimidate and interrogate him. Upon release from the hospital, Malik was transferred to the county jail to await trial. Still suffering from his wounds, he described feeling vulnerable because he could not defend himself. Eventually, Malik served just shy of three years in state prison and spent most of his sentence in a special housing unit because of his injuries.

The physical suffering Malik endured from such a severe accident, compounded with the mental trauma of losing his closest friend, being chained to a hospital bed, and incarceration, has affected his sleep, physical comfort, and emotional state. When I asked Malik if he had ever spoken to a professional counselor about his ordeals, he shook his head and said, "Nah."

In the few instances when therapy occurred, it typically revolved around the negative experiences associated with counseling. Many participants believed that counselors did not really care about their mental health. Sharif said that in prison pharmaceutical drugs are "passed out like candy" to "calm guys down." Others said these medicines made guys act like "zombies."

Stuart, who was convicted of a sex offense, remarked that counseling in prison is not designed to rehabilitate. "Because of my conviction I was mandated to do counseling, which consisted of a counselor sitting outside of my cell and asking me questions," he said. "It was totally impersonal as she barely looked up at me from her notepad, checking things off. I never felt comfortable answering her questions because none of this was private or anonymous. The guys in the cell next to me could hear our whole conversation."

Conversely, Freddy said that he did enjoy the group counseling he was attending in state prison until the counselor was removed. "She was nice," he said, "and you could tell she cared about her job. I guess the institution didn't like that because she was let go. So even when people want to help us, the prison doesn't give a fuck."

Post-traumatic stress disorder (PTSD) is often associated with soldiers who have fought in war because of the high-stress-induced environment. Similarly, incarceration can have a comparable effect. PTSD can lead to depression, anxiety, and other disorders such as mood swings and anger outbursts. The impact PTSD had on relationships was exposed between Sharif and Wesley.

When Wesley arrived at the reentry center, Sharif could barely contain his joy. The two men embraced. They had a history that had been forged in prison. With a twenty-year age gap between them, Sharif treated Wesley as a son. Wesley, a Black man in his early thirties, was sentenced to ten years for charges of theft and robbery by deception in the early 2000s. By chance, Sharif was Wesley's first cellmate.

"By this time, I had already done over twenty years," Sharif explained, "so they gave me new guys to get them up to speed about prison life. It was a sort of job, I guess." Yet Wesley was different from the usual roommate, and Sharif took an immediate liking to him. In time, Wesley was transferred to another institution. Ironically, both men were released a month apart and ended up in the same halfway facility.

For a time, Sharif and Wesley were inseparable, but at some point, the relationship changed, and Wesley stopped coming to group. Privately, I asked Sharif where Wesley had been, and he told me that Wesley was struggling with his own demons. "I will support him," Sharif said, "but need to keep distance now because he doesn't know how to express himself. The brother, like all of us, got PTSD from prison." Upon further explanation, Sharif elaborated that "something" triggered Wesley at the halfway house to the point of rupturing their relationship.

I'm not sure if the two men were ever able to repair their relationship. Both eventually completed their sentence and moved on. Nevertheless, the traumas inflicted in prison often show up at inopportune times. The quarrel between Wesley and Sharif might have been avoidable given proper tools and techniques to cope with anger or anxiety. Ironically, the two men were brought together through a mutual predicament of incapacitation and revived their relationship based on nostalgia.

·   ·   ·   ·   ·

The sociology of memory, a subfield within the broader discipline, looks at social aspects of individual, collective, and cultural behaviors surrounding memory.[68] In one instance, I witnessed how two individuals remembered their time in prison differently, highlighting both memory and its loss.

Lyle, a Black man in his early fifties with a thick white beard, who was finishing a twenty-five-year federal prison sentence, frequently mentioned Melvin and their time in prison. I found this odd since Melvin was serving a sentence of similar length but in the state system. Lyle later explained that in the late 1970s, they were both in the county jail together, and Melvin helped him "out of a jam." A few days later, I asked Melvin if he remembered Lyle, but he couldn't recollect any such incident.

Melvin responded, "I been inside so long, come across so many different people, and had so many different things happen, just not enough room in my mind for it all. If he [Lyle] says anything to me, I'll go along with it because I don't want to make him feel bad, but whatever I did was important for him and not so much for me. We can't expect someone else to assume what is important to them is important to you."

The prison experience affected these two individuals in two distinct ways. Loss of memory was a double-edged sword. On the one hand, not recollecting events is a form of resistance, or better yet, a relief. On the other hand, the loss of memory is unfortunately part of the postincarceration experience. Lack of memory means lost time, as imprisonment does not have the same linear pattern as free society but is rather circular, as days, weeks, months, and years merge and become "fuzzy."[69] For Lyle, the event that occurred with Melvin was remembered as important. For Melvin, it was lost and forgotten. In sum, prison manipulates the mind.

Abstract and Tangible

Incarceration—and by extension, having a felony—is inscribed onto reentry. In other words, the loss of rights has simultaneous cerebral and corporeal meanings. In this instance, the loss of rights affects both the mind and the body, highlighting the notion of purgatory citizenship, as individuals are barred from being able to fully participate in society.

Therefore, the right to vote is both abstract and tangible. As the former, the concept of voting is a theoretical exercise surrounding notions of liberty and democracy. Often participants struggled with explaining the meaning of these terms, not fully being able to settle on explicit definitions. Thus, the idea of voting seemed *abstract*. Yet participating in voting had actionable and concrete examples attached to it, including registering to vote, going to a polling station, and *tangibly* pulling the lever for a specific candidate.

In this instance, participants were able to articulate the implication of suffrage, which almost all of them were banned from partaking in. As Jerry said of this duality, "Voting is the most important aspect of a democracy, that's why they make it so difficult. People don't vote every day, so they don't *think* about it, but going to vote is *an exercise* you must do."[70]

Parenting was another realm that informed participants of the dichotomy of abstract and tangible reentry. Many spoke about having children and the generic label of *parent*, which was abstract, whereas being able to describe oneself as a mother or father had specific, tangible obligations associated with duties toward child-rearing. In other words, to be a parent simply meant one had children, but to be a mother or father had actionable implications.

SUMMARY

This chapter highlights the various ways prison informs health inequality, as well as how transformations to the mind and body are inscribed and simply not erased upon one's exit from the carceral landscape. In fact, these discursive narratives elucidate how many of the health challenges in prison are exacerbated postrelease. Here, individuals must attempt to navigate the legal and social world around them with ongoing and persistent health issues.

There is a need to create space and community to have conversations about challenges and triumphs in reentry. The next chapter goes in depth about the specific location of the community-based reentry program, which is dedicated to assisting recently released individuals as a resource in an already difficult environment—in sum, a space to simply *be*.

5 Space

Ronald was surprised when he returned to the conference room one Wednesday morning after our weekly group meeting at the reentry center, saying, "Smiley, I didn't know you were still here."

"Yeah, just writing up my notes," I replied. "Were you looking for someone?"

After a brief pause and with an odd look on his face, he said, "No, just have to get something."

"OK," I replied. Then I went back to my notes.

When I looked up, I saw Ronald walk to the back of the room. He opened the top drawer of a gray filing cabinet and dug around for a few seconds before pulling out a cell phone. Looking at me with a slight grin, he said, "Smiley, you not gon' tell nobody about this?"

"No," I replied.

Ronald then proceeded to make two phone calls, one to ask about a grandchild's upcoming birthday and another to find out if his daughter was coming to see him. He then turned off the cell phone and placed it back in the filing cabinet.

Already knowing the answer, I asked inquisitively, "Are you allowed to have that?" He just smiled without answering and left the room.

Ronald, a fair-skinned Black man with blue eyes and a gray Afro, was completing a fifteen-year federal prison sentence for drug trafficking. Now fifty-eight years old, he had six children, fourteen grandchildren, and two great-grandchildren. He spoke about being the patriarch of his tight-knit family, about his neighborhood, and about his high rank within the "drug game."

He used two items to prove these claims. The first was an article written in the street magazine *Don Diva*,[1] which highlights various hustlers, drug dealers, and other "hood" celebrities. The article mentioned him by name, cited his connection to a particular drug syndicate, and reaffirmed his status in the streets. The second was a photo of him and Akbar Pray, a notorious Newark drug kingpin, in federal prison, indicating their close relationship. "Nobody can get that close to Akbar," he said, "but I'm certified in the streets and in prison."

Finally, he spoke about his numerous nicknames, many given by friends who had all passed "by way of violent deaths." In prison, he was given the nickname "6-O," which colloquially referred to his prison fight record. However, he was adjusting to being called "Grandpa" by his grandchildren and the new title of "Pa-Pa" used by his great-grandchildren.

My chance encounter with Ronald in the conference room revealed another layer of the reentry process, which was the hidden role of the reentry center. This space became a place where clients could keep various items that were prohibited in corrections institutions and halfway house facilities. Here, clients kept a range of items, from precious materials (e.g., cell phones, clothing, and jewelry) to day-to-day products (e.g., toiletries and food), in what I call "reentry space," to make their transition less cumbersome and more equitable. This practice underscores the complicated and fragile relationship individuals have with reentry.

In a rapidly changing world, particularly given the increasing emphasis on technology and the need for items such as cell phones, clients engaged in a certain level of *risk* behavior to remain free. In other words, individuals coming out of incarcerated settings must engage in deviance to do reentry, undermining mainstream notions of desistance to retain their freedom. Furthermore, the complex world of reentry highlights the various connections and networks formed within these reentry spaces. For instance, while staff knew that items were being stored at the reentry center, only some staff knew of certain items hidden away, while others were unaware of them.

This chapter examines how those returning to society use reentry space. First, I explore the notions of space and place, particularly applying them to systems of reentry. Second, I describe the core staff and their role, particularly how small nonprofits are often underfunded and struggle while competing with larger corporate-style reentry services. Third, I discuss the intended and unintended usages of this space by clients. Here, I investigate the manifest and latent functions of the community-based reentry organization as a physical place. Finally, this chapter acknowledges the role of the reentry center as a safe space for returning individuals who oftentimes need nothing more than a place to feel accepted and ultimately protected.

COMMUNITY, SPACE, AND REENTRY

The production of space is important to the social construction of society.[2] Within criminal justice, specific neighborhoods are designated as "hot spots," suggesting higher levels of crime and therefore the need for more intensive policing and scrutiny.[3] Such an inflammatory term is a form of colorblind racist[4] rhetoric used by law enforcement to carry out punitive force upon low-income communities of color. Sociologist Jan Haldipur's work on the New York City Police Department's use of the "stop, question, and frisk" protocol highlights the fact that overpolicing changes the social ecology of communities.[5] Furthermore, sociologist Victor Rios shows how young Black and Latinx men from specific neighborhoods in Oakland, California, are criminalized and punished simply for living where they do.[6]

The significance of space is important to the reentry process as persons cycle out of the prison system and back into neighborhoods. Criminologist Todd Clear's work suggests that frequently, persons being released are sent back to the communities where they were arrested, which still retain many of the same social and economic hardships that put those individuals in prison.[7] Further, research on space and reentry indicates that those returning to society often have weaker relationships to the neighborhoods they come back to because of issues of housing insecurity, persistent institutional racism, and various other barriers.[8] Here, I look to understand how those returning to society reimagine space and place.

Discourse surrounding space and place in the social sciences varies, particularly the definitions of and distinction between the terms.[9] In this instance, *space* is the reentry center as a concept housed in a building within the community. Alternatively, the *place(s)* is (are) the various rooms and physical settings at the reentry center that are used by the clients. For example, the conference rooms, bathroom, computer lab, and break room are places within this space that are frequented.

The reentry center as a production of space and place occupies a unique role as it straddles both the public and private sector. On the one hand, public space is theoretically accessible to everyone. On the other hand, private space has regulations regarding who can occupy it. Here, the community-based reentry center is a not-for-profit organization that occupies space in a private building, making it a private space. However, the culture of the organization is welcoming and encouraging to all residents to take advantage of their services, ultimately giving residents public access.

This sort of "open door" policy gives Newark residents, particularly those who are formerly incarcerated, a form of social capital that connects them to individual and institutional networks for the purpose of positive benefits.[10] Furthermore, this space and place has intended and unintended consequences. Often, clients utilize this *space* as a way to discuss and understand what reentry entails but use this *place* to keep and store items needed to assist in the reentry process. Therefore, this highlights that reentry is not a linear process but is rather riddled with complications that walk the line between what is deemed permissible and prohibited.

"BULLETS IN THE CHAMBER"

The reentry center employed six full-time workers—the director and founder, Dr. Ginny Hazel, and five case managers, who were formerly incarcerated individuals.

Dr. Hazel, a light-skinned Black woman in her mid-seventies, started the community-based reentry center more than thirty years ago. She was married to a prominent civil rights lawyer and got her first experience working in the criminal legal system at the women's state prison in the 1970s. In 1984, she transitioned into reentry services. "Back then we didn't even call it reentry," she said. "What we were doing didn't even have a name. My office was the trunk of my car."

"We would drive around to different neighborhoods and pass out literature with resources and phone numbers to call for assistance," she continued. "If there was ever such a thing as grassroots work in reentry, we were those roots here in Newark."

While the senior case manager, Wadi Darr, had been impressed with my educational background and pursuit of a doctoral degree, Dr. Hazel was not equally captivated. After we were introduced, she bluntly asked, "Why do you want to work here?" I explained that I was eager to volunteer. She turned to her desk, picked up a manual, and said, "Read this. It will tell you everything you need to know about the services these guys need," thus ending our first meeting.

Mr. Darr did not want Dr. Hazel's demeanor to be discouraging, saying to me, "She's tough with everyone. Just show her you are serious and committed. To do this work you have to be skeptical." This skepticism kept Dr. Hazel as the sole director of the organization, and she chose her staff carefully.

Wadi Darr, whom my father introduced me to and how I came to the reentry center, worked primarily with youth, gang-affiliated clients, and those with violent criminal records, but I quickly met the other staff members and learned about their own reentry. Interestingly, the male staff members all went by "Mr." and their last names, whereas the women went by "Ms." and their first names.

Mr. Lopez, a tall Puerto Rican man in his forties and the only bilingual counselor, always wore a suit and designer prescription glasses. "Dr. Hazel saved my life, more than once," he said. Growing up on New York City's Lower East Side, Mr. Lopez described being a witness to violence from an early age, retelling a story of walking with his older cousin and watching as he was fatally shot.

Mr. Lopez spent nearly twenty years in prison, serving time in New Jersey, New York, Pennsylvania, and Maryland. "I would do a three-year stretch, get out, be free for a year, then go back to prison for another two years," he said. In the early 1990s, he met Dr. Hazel, and she hired him to work for the reentry center.

"She had a lot of faith in me," he said, "probably more than I had in myself, and always kept me employed. Sometimes people give you second chance, but a third, fourth, or fifth, shit, at this point I have lost count." When I met Mr. Lopez, he was in his last year on parole and has gone on to finish his bachelor's degree and work in several reentry organizations in New Jersey and New York.

Mr. Thomas, a stocky, light-skinned Black man, grew up in a good family and neighborhood in a wealthier and whiter suburb south of Newark. However, he developed substance abuse problems as a young man. "Thankfully, I have never done real time in state prison," he said, "but found myself in this cycle of getting locked up in county jail for years."

Eventually he got clean, began working in reentry, and enrolled in college. He found his stride working in reentry and higher education. At the time Mr. Thomas was completing his bachelor of social work degree and preparing to apply to master of social work programs. He admitted to having feelings of "imposter syndrome" but with encouragement from Dr. Hazel and a key undergraduate professor, he pursued his graduate studies and earned his master's degree. He continues to work in the field of reentry and teaches undergraduate-level college courses.

Ms. Pearl, a light-skinned Black woman who always had a smile on her face, worked primarily with female clients. I learned that she had done five years in prison for armed robbery as a young woman and met Dr. Hazel while incarcerated. Ms. Pearl eventually got a new job working within the field of reentry, and before she left the staff gave her a surprise party. Her departure from the organization was bittersweet. She had mixed emotions about leaving because of the investment that Dr. Hazel and staff members had made in her. Yet the new position came with a better title and a significant pay increase. Through her tears at the party, Ms. Pearl thanked the staff and clients for their support throughout the years.

Finally, Ms. Rosalee was a brown-skinned Black woman in her late fifties. While she did some casework and had the fewest clients, she was the go-to staff member to make sure supplies were stocked, schedules were up to date, and rooms were organized. Ms. Rosalee did a year in prison, "over thirty years ago," and described having suffered from substance abuse. While incarcerated she met Dr. Hazel, who was working at the women's state prison.

"I made a promise to her that I would never mess up again and been clean since and haven't got in any trouble, not even a speeding ticket," Ms. Rosalee said. She believed that if she could turn her life around, anyone could, and she prided herself as being an example for clients.

Clients came to the reentry center through a variety of ways, including parole and probation, halfway facilities, and word of mouth. Each potential new client had to meet with a case manager and answer a series of questions about their background, status within the criminal legal system, and level of education. This was done to build a portfolio for clients that included a checklist and goals sheet, which helped figure out what type of assistance the reentry center could provide, such as case management, group therapy, job readiness skills, parenting classes, or anger management.

Often, the first step for new clients was getting an official state identification card so they could qualify for things like jobs, housing, and public assistance. But doing this was not always simple or straightforward. First, identification cards cost money, and many clients had no income. Second, many clients had outstanding motor vehicle fines or fees that had to be paid before they got a new identification card. Third, clients complained about the wait time at the Department of Motor Vehicles. Many of them had meetings scheduled with parole or counselors, which if missed could damage their chances of freedom. Justice studies professor John Halushka calls this "the runaround" of having to engage various agencies in the reentry process.[11] Additionally, New Jersey has a six-point identification verification program for official state ID, which includes providing a series of primary and secondary documents.[12]

Simone, a Black woman in her mid-twenties, described the difficult process of securing state identification. Imprisoned for robbery as a teenager, she was serious about her reentry. "I have been violated twice, so I served my full sentence," she said. "The first time I just wasn't where I was supposed to be, and second time, I got caught smoking weed, but I need to do better now."

Simone had a troubled youth. She grew up between Newark and Plainfield, New Jersey, as her mother struggled with addiction to alcohol and narcotics, including crack. "I remember the smell," she said. "As I got older, I hated my mother because we were always moving or getting kicked out, and I had one suitcase with all my things. I wouldn't even unpack."

At sixteen, Simone dropped out of high school and ran away, staying with boyfriends and various acquaintances. To support herself, she sold drugs and lied to prospective employers about her age. "I was living the exact same way as when I was with my mother," she said, "moving from place to place, work here and there until they fired me." At nineteen, Simone landed in the women's state prison.

Simone is no longer under criminal supervision and is, as she put it, trying to "get my life together," but this was proving difficult given her lack of official identification documents. Simone does not have a copy of her birth certificate or a Social Security card—she does not even know her Social Security number. Making matters worse was her tenuous relationship with her mother.

"I don't have any information of where I was born," she said, "and when I asked my mother, she couldn't remember. Can you believe that my own mother doesn't remember where she gave birth to me?"

.   .   .   .   .

Sitting with Mr. Darr, I heard similar stories and watched how he encouraged and inspired nervous and overwhelmed individuals as they entered the reentry center for the first time. Making use of his street swagger, Mr. Darr said, "I can communicate with these guys because I was one of these guys, so I sometimes got to talk that talk."

When meeting with new clients, Mr. Darr would call out young men on their physical appearance, as the majority wore traditional urban street wear such as a do-rag, sagging jeans, fitted baseball hats, and unlaced boots or sneakers. He enforced a respectability politics, which admonished certain styles of dress and body disposition. When a young man would arrive in Mr. Darr's office, he would scan them up and down and then say, "Young brother, tie your shoes, pull up your pants, take the rag off your head, and next time you come, wear a collared shirt." Clients would address this issue by changing outfits to either reclaim an old identity or create a new one.[13] However, many clients, particularly young folks, had visible tattoos on their hands, neck, or face. In these situations, Mr. Darr would say, "You know this is going to make getting a job harder but not impossible."

Mr. Darr's most memorable saying was the analogy he used involving a gun. He would start by looking at a young man's criminal history, commenting, "I see you like weapons. I'm going to give you one that isn't going to kill people but make you stronger." He would go on to say, "We are going to put some bullets in the chamber. We are going to get you enrolled in school, that's one bullet. We are going to get you in one of our programs, that's another bullet. Then we are going to get you some job skills training, that's another bullet. After that, we are going get you a job, one more bullet. That way, next time you go in front of the judge or your PO you gon' have all these chambers filled that they can't touch you."

He continued, "After you leave my office today, you are going to stay out of trouble, not use any narcotics or alcohol, and keep away from all the knuckleheads out here who want to see you fail. Guys in your crew know you're on paper [under criminal supervision], so anyone who asks you do anything or go someplace that's not your partner. You feel what I'm saying? Next time I see you, we going to make sure you got a suit and some dress shoes and maybe even a little American flag pin for your jacket."

At this point the young men would be looking straight ahead listening to every word and break into a small laugh with his last line. Mr. Darr had the ability to connect with them because like he said, "I been there." After the young men would leave, he would reaffirm his sentiments to me. *"You got to be tough with the young ones but not harsh,"* he said. "If I told him that shit on his face [tattoo] was stupid, he liable to get mad and leave."[14]

What he meant was that lots of folks were struggling, and the last thing they needed was someone else telling them how bad they were. The reentry center cultivated an atmosphere of encouragement that also contained a healthy dose of reality, which did call clients out and hold them accountable. Yet, it took a certain ability to toe this fine line, which was a learned technique based on years on the streets and in reentry.

THE REENTRY CENTER

The reentry center had its own share of challenges. Located in downtown Newark, the agency was affected by the many structural changes occurring in the neighborhood. This was both good and bad for the small non-

Figure 10. Clients at reentry center filling out job applications in conference room after group session, 2011. Photo courtesy of the author.

profit organization. On the one hand, as more business flocked to the area, the staff could make broader connections with local establishments and larger corporations to help clients. For example, the reentry center held a small job fair, where various businesses gave presentations to clients, passed out job applications, and answered questions about the hiring process. In addition, because of Dr. Hazel's connections within city government, the reentry center held a certain level of prestige within the community, being seen as a truly homegrown institution providing resources to residents.

Periodically, a collection of White folks in business suits would poke their heads into a group session, mostly peer in and move on. On a few occasions Dr. Hazel halted the group and introduced the visitors, who were either local politicians or business leaders, describing for them the various programs the reentry center offered in an effort to attract funding. Conversely, the reentry center had to compete for contracts with larger and more lucrative organizations, such as Community Education Centers.

The reentry center relied on several channels of funding, which included individual donations, corporate or large private donations, and state and federal grants. Private donations were often the hardest to acquire, as societal stigmas surrounding crime do not lend themselves to sympathetic donors. Therefore, much of the funding came from various grants, which often came with restrictions.

For example, the reentry center had received a large grant that Mr. Darr oversaw that sought male youth who were gang-affiliated and had a violent record. Here, the specificity of the grant dictated who could take part in this program. An additional grant specified a twelve-week jobs program that entailed community beautification and would not accept individuals with violent criminal records. Therefore, staff had to pay close attention to clients' records and not place someone into a program that they did not qualify for. Otherwise, it could jeopardize the grant at the reentry agency.

Lastly, the reentry center was challenged financially in how to attract and retain clients. For example, the center provided prepaid bus cards to clients. This incentive was highly attractive as it subsidized the cost of travel and was important to the clients living in halfway houses, which were often located in more desolate and industrial areas that made walking to the agency unsafe. Further, clients who received the prepaid bus card did not have to worry about having cash. However, this program was discontinued because of budget cuts after several government grants were not renewed. Immediately, the agency saw an overall decline in day-to-day foot traffic. Many of the center's regular clients began coming less often either because they had to save money for travel or reach out to family or friends for monetary assistance.

Clients voiced their concerns with this new policy. "Not having the bus card makes getting down here much harder," said Rickey, "because I really need this place. So I walk most days now. I can walk fast, but on cold or rainy days, I can't come." Others expressed stronger feelings. "This is some bullshit," said JR, who was sixty years old. "I'm old and got bad knees. I'm not walking down here every day. I'll come once a week for group, I only got but so much money." Others relied on family members to chip in. "My daughters make sure I have my bus pass now," said Ronald. "I know it's an added burden, but they help out."

Other perks of the reentry center began to diminish, including the assorted amount of food items in the break room, which was often filled with leftovers such as bagels, wraps, and muffins. Here, clients in between meetings with case managers or after a group would be able to enjoy a small bite.

Al, a White man who served just shy of a year on a four-year shoplifting sentence, came to group weekly for several months. He rarely spoke and typically sat in the back corner actively listening. He eventually shared a thought, stating, "This place is a big help, I get to leave the [halfway] house, stretch my legs, and grab a good cup of coffee and little something to eat." For Al, and others, the place provided a certain level of nourishment that went beyond feeding their minds with strategies of reentry, but also fed them in a much more literal sense. The budget cuts limited the number of events and parties and general communal food availability, which was felt throughout the agency, but especially by clients who relied on the space for food.

In an attempt to secure new funding streams, Dr. Hazel proposed that the reentry center expand services into more rigorous substance abuse treatment, proposing the organization open an intensive outpatient program (IOP) that would focus on bringing in clients with chemical dependencies. IOPs are a type of treatment service and support program that offer a cost-effective alternative to hospitalization or residential treatment facilities by offering a more intensive level of support while still promoting a person's living in the community.[15]

Since the case managers were certified alcohol and drug counselors (CADCs), they would be able to work with this population. Unfortunately, the IOP never happened, as the reentry center could not secure funding.

Consequently, trying to establish the IOP preoccupied a significant amount of time to no avail and put the organization in a quandary. Staff began to forgo raises and had to seek out secondary jobs. Eventually Mr. Lopez and Mr. Thomas found new employment and Mr. Darr passed away from a massive heart attack in the fall of 2015.

Because of the financial constraints, the center began to rely heavily on volunteer services, and I was asked to take over Mr. Lopez's weekly group, called Positive Change, at the beginning of 2011. This freed up time for him to see more clients, especially Spanish-speaking individuals.

With me as a new addition to the weekly operations, Mr. Darr decided to rebrand the group, changing the name from Positive Change to Breaking the Cycle. When I arrived for my first day as a group leader, Mr. Darr brought me into Ms. Rosalee's office. On her computer screen was the image of a flyer with the new name and an image of chain link breaking. Mr. Darr envisioned that this new group would not be a traditional reentry group but a learning environment, telling me to "teach them something" and "not be afraid to drop some knowledge on them." The newly made flyer was printed and posted throughout the agency.

While I was supposed to "drop knowledge," my role as facilitator was about listening and learning from clients. Many came to the reentry center hoping that simply spending time in this space would get them a job immediately or find them housing quickly. But reentry was not as straightforward as that. The more a client came to group, the more the initial yearning for a job subsided and other pertinent issues pushed forward, such as rebuilding relationships with family and friends, a need to help their community, and simply moving past their criminal past. The reentry center gave these clients the space to think about themselves in a way that allowed them to reflect on the past, discuss the present, and shape the future.

"BEING A SQUARE"

Breaking the Cycle became the most popular group of the half-dozen regularly scheduled weekly groups at the reentry center and met for two hours every Wednesday. While I initially brought materials for discussion, I learned quickly that between high turnover rates of clients and reading and comprehension limitations, I needed to modify my plan.

Organic group discussions based around broader themes that related to reentry or current events helped generate discussions. For example, the killing of Trayvon Martin and the 2012 presidential election led to lengthy debate among the group. Here, clients used this space to process ideas and come to conclusions, which often went beyond the scope of reentry services.

As the group continued to grow organically through word of mouth, Dr. Hazel seemed both delighted and surprised about this development. "How are you getting so many guys to come down?" she asked. Then she added, "Well, whatever you are doing, keep it up."

After my interaction with Dr. Hazel, I inquired to the group the following week why they consistently attended. Shane responded, "Some folks try and run groups and don't know what they are doing or don't let people talk, cut them off, and try and dictate the conversation but you let us get our thoughts across and talk about shit."

Shane was forty-one and exiting prison after serving a little more than a year for possession of a controlled dangerous substance (CDS). This was his first time in prison since 2003, when he served three years on a similar charge. In total, Shane estimated that he had served between seven and eight years of his life behind bars. A personable individual, Shane described always being employed, belonging to a construction union. However, he had been selling drugs since his teen years. He said, "I sold weed as a kid, was sent to the youth house for three months, and then started selling cocaine and heroin."

Shane described the period of his life in the late 1980s as him being a hustler, which meant flaunting money, buying jewelry, and hanging out with celebrities, particularly those in the fledging scene of hip-hop music. Yet, this lifestyle eventually caught up with him and he went from "making money" to "maintaining," as he found himself addicted. He remarked, "Remember in *Scarface* [the film], Tony [Montana] says, 'Don't get high on your own supply,' well guys started to dabble and it's just downhill from there."

·   ·   ·   ·   ·

Prison settings shut people off from various forms of physical and emotional contact. The early foundation of American prisons was based on Christian values of penitence and silence.[16] Today, many of those same restrictive principles continue in forms of administrative segregation and solitary confinement. Therefore, many people returning to society are coming from institutions that have not valued their opinion and where their feelings do not matter.

Harold was a fifty-three-year-old, six-foot-five Black man released after serving a year for a controlled substance charge. As with Shane, this was not his first time incarcerated. One of Harold's most vivid memories was witnessing the murder of both of his parents during a burglary turned homicide. "For a long time I thought it was my fault and blamed myself," he said. "I felt like this until I was probably nineteen, and a youth counselor encouraged me to write a letter to my mother in heaven."

As the second youngest of thirteen children, Harold was raised by his grandmother and his oldest sister, but he was eventually placed in foster care. He recalled growing up being tough, and at an early age he was identified as learning disabled.

"I was in the special needs class," he said. "Back then the teachers didn't help us. It was more like babysitting. We were told to just sit in our seats, keep our hands folded, and be quiet." He dropped out of high school and began selling drugs. "A guy approached me asking if I wanted to make money. I started delivering packages in brown paper bags. I knew what was in them, but never looked inside."

Despite getting involved in the drug trade, Harold found his passion working in the carnival. At age twenty, he landed a job with a regional amusement tour, where he learned the trade of building, breaking down, and operating festival rides.

A life on the road was attractive. Harold had neither a wife nor children, and his only known family was his surviving siblings. However, he only kept in touch with his oldest sister, who was now seventy-five. "She is like my mother, and when I get out of here [the halfway house] that is who I am going to stay with."

My interview with Harold was forty-five minutes long, and as my final question I asked if there was anything he thought that I missed. "Nah, you covered a lot," he replied. As he got up and reached for the doorknob, he turned around and said, "You know, you are the first person to ever ask me about my life. Nobody has ever asked me any of these types of questions. Thank you."

I sat with Harold's words for a while. What Harold and others, born into unforgiving circumstances that are a blend of institutional poverty and racism, need is to be heard. Harold's journey of reentry is unfortunately not unique, but giving him the space to tell it in his own words is. Having the outlet of the reentry center gave him the time and opportunity to express his feelings and have someone simply listen.

Finally, clients used this space to change their attitude and mindset. This is what happened with Marvin, who arrived at the center after serving fours years on a seven-year weapons charge. A thirty-three-year-old Black man, Marvin was first in trouble with the law at age thirteen. Growing up between East Orange and Newark, he started selling drugs as a teenager but was never that good at being a hustler, as was clear when he described his first adult charge at age seventeen.

Marvin recalled, "A guy pulled up asking if he could get ten for forty [drug lingo]. I got in the passenger seat to make the sale and he started saying all types of shit about me being under arrest but I could tell he wasn't a cop. So, I tried getting my shit [drugs] back and we started to fight. The actual cops saw this and pulled up and charged me with carjacking."

"I had to start telling on myself, because carjacking was holding too much time," he continued. "I'm telling the police that I was trying to sell him drugs, he was trying to take it, and I was just getting it back." Marvin explained that the most serious charges of carjacking were dropped, but he was convicted of aggravated assault and robbery. Ironically, the only thing he was not charged for was selling drugs.

Drug dealing was clearly not Marvin's strength. But his blundered drug sale and subsequent prison sentence until he was twenty-two helped him avoid serving a much longer sentence. "When I came home," he said, "everybody was under federal investigation. I got friends doing thirty, forty, and fifty years. My short sentence saved me from those shenanigans. Otherwise, this interview wouldn't be happening right now."

Over the past decade, Marvin has held a variety of jobs, such as working as a telemarketer and deliveryman. Yet he retained a presence in the streets. "When I came home," he said, "I stopped selling drugs but used my skills to 'twist shit up' if needed." This was an allusion to his role as more of an enforcer with weapons. Nevertheless, as Marvin reached his late twenties, he began to see that his behavior was leading to diminishing returns. "Going in and out of jail just wasn't cool," he said.

When Marvin was twenty-eight, his long-term girlfriend gave birth to a baby girl, and he began to move away from the street life. Unfortunately, he caught his current charge right after his daughter's birth. However, Marvin did this last bid differently, saying, "I didn't hang out with anybody. In prison, you usually associate with guys from your city. But this time, I kept my ass in the library, my head down, and nose in the books."

Before leaving prison, Marvin earned his GED, and he described having no prison violations, which aided in his early release on parole. Now that he was home, Marvin was dedicated to what he described as "being a square," elaborating, "It's OK to be a civilian. Being a gangster only going to have two outcomes—jail or death."

Marvin explained that his girlfriend had a professional job making what he described as "good money," which put less pressure on him to find a job immediately. "I'm my daughter's full-time caretaker," he said. "I missed a lot of firsts, so I'm trying to get that time back and be there for all the new firsts."

While Marvin had a seemingly good setup for reentry, his past was not lost on his present or his future. Over the next several months, Marvin described some of his reservations about being outside. "I can't be outside like that," he explained. "I did a lot of dirt and got to be careful about where I go and how I move, and just because I'm not in that lifestyle anymore, doesn't mean I'm out of harm's way. I don't know whose father, brother, cousin, or partner might be looking for revenge." Marvin concluded this statement by saying, "Like that new Rick Ross song says, 'God forgives and them triggers don't.'"[17]

In *Hurricanes: A Memoir*, hip-hop artist Rick Ross writes of his first encounter with homicide. "The incident left an everlasting impression on me. I knew then that any nigga could get it and that any nigga could give it. That nobody was exempt."[18] This code of the street was not lost on Marvin. He understood that his past could negatively impact his present and future living as a "square." For this reason his reentry was not just about changing his attitude but also about changing his environment. The reentry center gave him space to do this.

"EVERYTHING OFF LIMITS"

Sociologist Robert Merton discusses how anticipated results of an event or action include unintended consequences.[19] The reentry agency was no different and offered alternative usage beyond the services listed by the organization. The clients were able to use this space in a way that aided their reentry beyond the scope of the projected norm.

After seeing Ronald's phone, I began to notice other ways clients side-stepped the rules. For example, the computer lab was a popular place within the reentry center. Here, clients learned computer skills, typed up résumés, and applied for jobs. "OFF LIMITS" signs hung on the wall behind each computer listing prohibited websites, including XXX sites, Facebook, Twitter, MySpace, and YouTube. However, I received a friend request on Facebook from Freddy and learned that many clients did in fact use social media. "Everything is off limits," Freddy said. "We are not allowed to do anything when it comes to reentry unless a counselor approves it, but Facebook is a trip. It helps me problem solve and get better at using a computer."

Having a social media presence helped many of the clients reintegrate back into society. Where more conventional pathways to reentry held barriers, social media opened doors. For example, Jalil, a Black man in his early fifties who served twenty years for robbery and kidnapping, found Facebook more useful than more traditional routes in seeking out employment. "I did two decades and have violent crime convictions," he said. "I fill out at least ten job applications a day. It is depressing knowing I changed, but that doesn't come across on online applications and can't explain my situation."

Facebook gave Jalil the ability to connect with people he had not been in contact with for decades, among them a high school friend who operated a small business in South Jersey and who offered him a job. "When I get off parole, I'm going to move down there and work for him," Jalil said. "It gets me out of Newark and a chance to start over." In this case, using a prohibited website gave Jalil an opportunity for employment that traditional employment services did not.

In another instance, Facebook became an alternative route for a client to rebuild relationships with family members. Stefan, a fifty-year-old Black man, had been incarcerated for nearly fifteen years and was completing his sentence for robbery and weapons in a halfway facility. At the time of his arrest, he was struggling with a cocaine problem that he had hidden from his family. "Nobody really knew what was going on," he said, "and it all kind of came out when I got arrested."

At the time of his conviction, Stefan had two young daughters, ages seven and nine, and admitted that he did not try to remain in their lives, and both girls had moved out of state with their mother a decade earlier. Now in their early twenties, both daughters were college graduates. While proud of their achievements, Stefan could not resume his relationship with them, and phone calls between parent and children became hostile. But finding his daughters' Facebook profiles gave him another opportunity to reach out via the messaging app so he could apologize to them.

"I don't think any of us were ready for that phone call," he said, "but with messenger, I was able to explain myself a bit better and apologize for missing so much of their lives." The use of social media helped mend his relationship with his daughters where more traditional forms of communication had been unsuccessful.

When I asked participants what would happen if they were caught using Facebook or other banned websites, there were mixed reactions. For example, Freddy said, "I don't get caught," not remembering or rather denying I had caught him, since he friend requested me. Others like Jalil commented, "Nothing would happen as long as we were being respectful of this place."

Respect is an important term within the realms of prison and reentry. It is not taken lightly, hard to earn, and if lost, nearly impossible to get back. Therefore, respecting the places within the reentry center became vital to the use of this space.

While I was in Mr. Darr's office, Freddy came in and asked if he could "get it." When he got a nod of approval, Freddy opened the top drawer of Mr. Darr's desk and pulled out a cell phone, from a place where several other cell phones were also kept. A few minutes later, Freddy returned to the office and placed the cell phone back.

As Mr. Darr explained, "Cell phones can't hurt anybody, and everybody needs one because there are no pay phones. I let them keep their phones here if they show me respect, and I show them respect back." While Mr. Darr was technically correct that a cell phone could not hurt anybody, getting caught with a cell phone did have ramifications when it came to the reentry process.

Ned, a thirty-one-year-old biracial Black man, was caught selling cell phones inside the halfway house. This violation sent him back to state prison for four months before he returned to the halfway facility.

Incarcerated since the age of eighteen for aggravated manslaughter, Ned recalled never being able to legally vote or drink, and he missed the entire first decade of the twenty-first century. He said that his conviction was not a good representation of who he was because he had never been in trouble previously. Nevertheless, while at a convenience store, Ned's friend got into a verbal and physical altercation with a man and shot him to death. Since Ned would not cooperate with authorities, he was also charged for the crime.

When I asked him about the cell phones in the halfway house, he replied, "It was stupid, and I should have known I was going to get caught, but it was quick money. But I'm going to leave the phones alone for now." Ned had believed that the benefit outweighed the risk and consequences, as he saw an opportunity to start an illicit business supplying cell phones to people who needed them.

Ned was not the only client who was sent back to prison for having what was considered contraband. Elijah was sent back to federal prison for three months because he was caught with cigarettes, which are considered illegal in federal halfway houses. "I smoke," he said. "It helps with my nerves, so I keep my cigarettes here" at the reentry center. "Got a small hiding spot for them. I usually grab a couple at a time so I have enough for the day."

.   .   .   .   .

Beyond items deemed illegal, clients kept other precious objects at the reentry center, along with more day-to-day items. For instance, clothing and cosmetics were kept and stored in various locations.

Among those who did that was Ronald. He would typically sign into group and then change from the light gray sweats he was wearing into other clothing, such as his favorite red Adidas tracksuit and white Nike Air Force One sneakers. He explained that he did not want to be seen looking "old." However, before he left to return to the halfway facility, he would put back on his gray sweats. Another client, a Black man in his early forties named Saul, who had just been released after serving nine years in federal prison, stored a pair of designer brand suede shoes in a bottom desk drawer at the reentry center. They were a prized possession, and he was not comfortable leaving them or wearing them at the halfway facility.

One day, while Saul was standing outside after group, it began to rain. He retreated inside and reemerged with plastic shopping bags covering the suede shoes. This spectacle gave everyone a hearty laugh, and for the next several weeks, jokes were made about Saul's unusual choice of material to cover his shoes. Yet, as Saul explained, "I had these shoes since before I went in. I take care of my things, and they still look brand new. Now that I can wear them again, I feel really good."

The women of the reentry center also stored items in this space, such as cosmetics and other grooming products. Jamie kept a small makeup bag she had bought at the local drugstore, along with a razor and dry shampoo, at the reentry center. "Men can come out looking like bums," she explained, "but if I don't do my makeup, people will think I'm not trying to help myself. I got some cheap eyeliner, lipstick, and foundation, and just keep it here."

Another unintended use of the reentry center was that it became a place where clients could meet with family members and acquaintances. Often, after group, Ronald would be seen sitting on the back of a car with his daughter, eating chicken wings and fries. For him, this became a time to gossip by sharing stories, news, and other pertinent information about his community, which became an important aspect toward reentry. "The streets are always talking," Ronald explained. "Newark only but a quarter million people. If you are in the game [hustling] you know all the players. Even though I'm out, I keep my ear to the streets."

At one point, Ronald's grandson had been shot. While he was not killed, the young man was in the hospital, and the shooter had not been apprehended. Ronald, upset, explained, "This isn't what I want for my kids. I know he was out here hustling, but I lost too many friends over the years."

After group, Ronald was on his cell phone speaking to his grandson and trying to find out information about the incident, telling me, "I still got pull in the streets and I'm trying to squash this beef." He added, "I don't want this escalating because any type of retaliation only going to make things worse, I lived this life before." Without access to the reentry center or his cell phone, it would have been virtually impossible for Ronald to make contact about this incident.

Others, like Freddy, would wait outside for acquaintances to stop by. While he was smoking a cigarette, a car pulled up, and the man in the driver's seat rolled down the window and screamed his name in jubilation. The two slapped hands and exchanged brief pleasantries before the man departed. While he was walking back, I noticed something in Freddy's hand. When I asked what it was, he showed me a folded ten-dollar bill. When I asked why this guy had given him money, he said, "I'm home now. People want to make sure I'm good. They not giving me much, a few dollars here and there when they got it. It's just something people do in the 'hood, got to look out for one another."

The reentry center served an important role, allowing clients to meet friends and family they would either be limited or prohibited from seeing in a prison or halfway house. For some, this was the only way to communicate with loved ones, retain possessions, and learn about what was going on in the world. The reentry center was a space where people could feel like themselves again.

"I'M GOOD . . ."

Group sessions opened with participants introducing themselves and describing something positive that had happened during the week. Often the response was "I'm good." Other variations of this phrase were "I'm living" or "I'm here." At first, I interpreted these short sayings as a flippant way to get out of a slightly corny exercise.

However, in time, I realized how profound this short message was to many clients. The phrase "I'm good" was an indication that they had some autonomy over their lives. For many, "I'm good" was a declaration of their existence, which defied most odds for people coming from violent communities and other ferocious spaces such as prisons. The ability to wake up and come to the reentry center meant that they were not just "good" but otherwise *safe*, even if just for a brief period.

The term *safe space* is often associated with educational environments as well as women's movements.[20] Furthermore, research on prison and reentry suggests creating "safe spaces" affords opportunities that traditional carceral settings eliminate.[21] The "safe space" of the reentry organization became a *safe place* for clients.

For example, the weekly group meetings became a safe place for clients to express their thoughts and ideas in a controlled setting. Beyond this, they had the ability to vent, share, and discuss topics that were either discouraged, taboo, or prohibited within prison settings. Finally, many expressed the importance of the group to "get it off their chest."

Tony was a twenty-seven-year-old Black man who had been convicted of aggravated manslaughter and possession of a controlled dangerous substance. In part because of his age, his sentence was only ten years in prison. An active listener, he shared his thoughts about the weekly meetings: "I appreciate this group because growing up I didn't hear all these political conversations. My world was just the few blocks I hung out." He continued, "Hearing guys disagree and it not turning into a fight is new to me. And guys in prison, at least guys I know, don't want to talk about these things. All guys want to do is watch TV and talk about bullshit."

This mentorship role was not lost on the more senior clients, who expressed an interest in taking younger guys under their wing. As Sharif noted, "It's much easier to get through to the young ones here because they are separated from the noise, so they are more willing to listen."

·   ·   ·   ·   ·

The weekly groups were just one aspect of the reentry center as a safe place. Another essential place within the agency were the bathrooms. There were two facilities, for men and women, respectively. For each bathroom, a key was needed to enter, and it was affixed to a large wooden block so that it could not be stolen or lost. This security measure made these restrooms one-person occupancy. Therefore, clients had a place to relieve themselves in private, something many could not do during their incarceration.

Prison bathroom politics was an important topic of discourse that many of the clients discussed at length, as this was an experience shared by all. As Tony commented, "In prison you got to piss, shit, eat, and sleep all in the same place with your cellmate." Others explained the various ways they created privacy in their cells, for example, by hanging a curtain as a divider.

Ronald recalled how he handled bathroom politics during his fifteen years in federal custody. "You must have a conversation on the first day about how things are going to go. If someone goes to the bathroom, the other person must turn away, put on headphones, and occupy their time. It's a courtesy." He added, "Also, it might sound funny, but you and your cellmate can't just eat anything you want. Commissary sells a lot of junk food, and it might be good going in, but not great coming out. You must respect the guy you are with because if you know certain foods going to affect you, you just can't eat them. Otherwise, you are going to have problems."

Clients said most incidents with cellmates occurred because of disrespectful bathroom etiquette. Shaft recalled an incident with a cellmate, saying, "He was this young nigga with an attitude, and he pissed on the seat and didn't wipe it. Only thing I ever said to him was, 'Clean that up,' and we lived together in silence."

While the clients were no longer in traditional prisons, many still lived in halfway facilities that had their own share of issues. Freddy explained that the bathroom at the halfway facility was dangerous because it was a place where guys did two things: fight and smoke K2.[22] "Every morning it stinks because guys smoking and acting crazy," he explained. "I don't even bother. I just hold it until I get here."

Jamie also expressed her relief in having access to the bathroom in the reentry center. "I'm embarrassed to talk about this," she said, "but the entire time I been locked up, I have not sat on a toilet seat. The bathrooms in prison are disgusting. Even in our cells, it's not like they give us cleaning supplies, and you don't know who was in that cell before you. I probably got the strongest legs now because all I did was squat, and the halfway house isn't much better. Here, I can get the key, shut the door, and sit down. It's an amazing feeling."

·   ·   ·   ·   ·

Finally, the reentry center space served as a place of security. The central heating and cooling system provided relief from the changing seasons, and the break room—where a water cooler, sink, coffee pot, and refrigerator were located—provided nourishment. On cold days clients could have a hot cup of coffee and in warmer months a cold cup of water.

Alvin, a fifty-five-year-old Black man, would often fill up a small plastic water bottle he received at the reentry center's job fair. Alvin had been born in New York City and was raised in a middle-class neighborhood in Bergen County, New Jersey. At thirteen, his parents got divorced, and he split his time between his mother in New Jersey and his father in Queens. "My parents put me in a military academy," he said, "and I started to lose myself. In Queens, I got involved with a gang called the Seven Crowns and part of my initiation, I snatched a women's purse. I ended up getting busted and spent about four months at Spofford," a notorious juvenile detention center in the Bronx that was closed in 2011.

After being released, Alvin lived with his mother. But they began to quarrel over his use of marijuana and selling other drugs. During one argument, she struck him, and he responded by grabbing a kitchen knife and stabbing her several times. "I almost killed her," he said. "After the incident, I was in such a daze I still went to school in the same bloody clothing. I was arrested and spent the next five years in prison."

As an incarcerated youth, Alvin underwent various psychiatric evaluations that indicated that he suffered from a mood disorder as well as bouts of depression. After he was released, he stayed away from his family. During that time, he found a job and got engaged. When he finally reunited with his family, during a Mother's Day event, his mother and grandmother both said they forgave him. "I was nervous about how my grandmother was going to respond," he admitted. "I had done this horrible thing to her daughter. But she just hugged me."

Despite the reunion, Alvin continued to engage in criminal acts, particularly robbery, which was fueled by a growing cocaine habit that he shared with his fiancée. Despite wanting to get sober, his partner became pregnant, but the baby died after a premature birth. His life began spiraling out of control, and he eventually landed in federal prison after being convicted for a string of bank robberies.

Upon his release, Alvin was living at a shelter and frequented the reentry center. On a hot summer afternoon, he showed up sweating profusely. I accompanied him to the break room, where he filled his water bottle to the brim and drank most of the contents in one large gulp. I asked him if everything was OK. It took him a moment to catch his breath.

"Nothing is working," he finally replied, "and being outside is unforgiving. I'm an addict, and the dealers know who uses and who doesn't, and they know which category I fall into. I just needed to get off the streets for a bit." We hung out, engaging in small tasks such as taking out the garbage and sweeping the floor. Before leaving, he told me, "I'm good now."

At a pivotal moment in his life, Alvin began coming to the reentry center less and less. By the beginning of the fall, he was no longer a regular client. Several months later, in early 2013, I learned through a Google search that he had been arrested for bank robbery and sent back to prison, to be released in spring 2021.

After reading about Alvin's arrest, I revisited the topic of "the streets ain't safe" with the group. Freddy summed up the situation: "People out there don't give a fuck that you just came home and trying to do right. I see guys out there hollering my name, 'Hey, Fred!' I just give them a wave and a smile and keep it moving. Half these jokers don't know me. Everyone got their own agenda, but nobody can get mad if I smile at them and keep it moving. I want to say, 'Fuck you,' but that will only end badly. If a guy tries stopping me to hear that bullshit, I just tell him I got a meeting down here [the reentry center]. Nobody questions that. Every time I'm out, I just tell folks, 'Running late, got to be downtown,' and they leave me alone."

SUMMARY

This chapter explores the various ways persons returning to society interact with a particular community-based reentry center. This space and place gave men and women traditional reentry services, allowed individuals to store items, and protected clients from an unforgiving outside world.

The dilemma of reentry is that there is no single formula to address individual and social needs. Therefore, it must be understood that the reintegration process is not a one size fits all model, but rather a delicate and unpredictable pattern of positive and negative outcomes. Reentry must take an intersectional approach that factors in many variables surrounding the human condition. In the next and final chapter, I argue that reentry must position itself as an abolitionist movement. Instead of focusing on mainstream policy reform efforts, reentry must think radically in its approach to create systems and channels that not only nurture positive change and break the cycle, but also reimagine a world without prisons to eradicate the need for reentry altogether.

6 Abolition

In early March 2012, as clients settled into the conference room, Melvin held out a copy of the *New York Times* newspaper, which had a photograph of the slain Trayvon Martin, a seventeen-year-old high school student, in his gray hooded sweatshirt.

"Smiley, I don't know what you have planned for today," Melvin said, "but can we talk about this instead?"

The month prior, Martin had been walking home in Florida and was killed by a self-appointed neighborhood watchman named George Zimmerman. Despite the fact that the 911 operators had instructed Zimmerman not to pursue Martin, he followed, assaulted, shot, and killed him. Ultimately, Zimmerman was found not guilty under the controversial statute commonly known as "Stand Your Ground." Yet between the execution and the verdict, international debate and discussion surrounding race, place, and crime was revived in several ways.

First, there was considerable discussion of Martin's location at the time of the confrontation with Zimmerman, particularly the idea of his being in the wrong place as a Black youth. Sociologist Loïc Wacquant describes how Blackness is perceived to be "out of place" in White neighborhoods, raising suspicion of criminality.[1] At the same time, the sociologist Elijah

Anderson describes what he calls "the White Space," referring to areas that were created, designated, and designed solely for White communities but that have been penetrated by Black people in a post–civil rights era.[2]

Second, the issue of neighborhood surveillance and law enforcement procedures became hotly contested. In the weeks after the shooting, the chief of police of the city of Sanford, Florida, resigned amid public pressure regarding the mishandling of the Martin case.[3] Pundits and guests on television talk shows argued about the politicization of clothing, particularly the fact that Martin's hooded sweatshirt, commonly called a "hoodie," became criminalized to justify his demise.[4] Similarly, debates and discussions about this event became a pivotal point for participants in their reentry.

The death of Trayvon Martin occurred at a critical moment in contemporary American history. In 2010, Michelle Alexander's book *The New Jim Crow: Mass Incarceration in the Age of Colorblindness* became a *New York Times* bestseller, sparking conversations about mass incarceration across the country. In 2011, the Occupy Wall Street movement began to address the issue of economic inequality, specifically capitalism and neoliberalism, producing terms such as the *99 percent* versus the *1 percent*. In New York City, members of the movement set up camp at Zuccotti Park in Lower Manhattan for two months before being forcibly removed by the police.[5] Finally, the death of Trayvon Martin is seen as the spark that ignited the Black Lives Matter movement, which has grown into an international effort to combat police violence and settler colonialism, and call for abolition.

In the early days of March 2012, it became important to hold space and make time in our meetings to discuss and grieve this murder, which reverberated powerfully in the Black community. Not surprisingly, these conversations led to discussions about activism—more specifically, the issue of mobility or the lack thereof. While clients expressed a willingness to participate in protest movements, many were hesitant because of their own precarious situation within the legal system. Simply put, if they were arrested, they could lose their freedom.

In fact, one of the more sinister aspects of the reentry process is being violated, or sent back to prison, for "fraternizing with other known felons." The ironic contradiction is that participants of the reentry center, like many other formerly incarcerated folks, are constantly in violation of this stipulation, whether living in a halfway facility, visiting the reentry center, or simply walking down the street in Newark. The threat of losing one's freedom is a constant in the realm of reentry, especially in urban low-income communities. Even more grotesque is the fact that these types of stipulations undermine the right of assembly guaranteed by the First Amendment by limiting, altering, and ultimately taking away the right to move freely.[6]

During our weekly meetings, conversations about activism evolved organically, moving from the tragedy of death to dialogues on punishment. In the end, these discussions tried to make sense of the concept of justice. In other words, *What would justice look like for seventeen-year-old Trayvon Martin, the unarmed Florida youth who was fatally shot by the "neighborhood watchman" George Zimmerman, in 2012?*

"What if this guy didn't go to prison?" Melvin said to the broader group. "We know jailing someone doesn't work. That's the easy way out." Although this idea initially drew criticism, it sparked a larger discussion of alternative forms of justice. It was at this intersection of reentry, punishment, and justice that a blossoming consideration of abolition took hold. Moreover, it became a catalyst to discuss and capture concepts beyond contemporary modalities of punishment and look toward accountability that eased pain and suffering but sought public safety through care and community.

This chapter contextualizes the notion of abolition through the lived experiences of individuals exiting incarceration settings. To discuss this growing movement, it is important to address the following issues. First, I examine the role of reform in New Jersey as well as provide a brief historical outline of the abolition movement. Second, I delve into the various ways abolition is expressed by those actively doing reentry. Here, participants critically work through and toward abolition, moving from theoretical exercises to concrete solutions. Further, it is important to keep in mind that these individuals were in the early moments of their reentry, thinking through the concepts, ideas, and actions as a starting point to abolition and *not the end*. Therefore, the principles below might not fit neatly into an abolitionist toolkit but are from the perspectives of the lived experiences of those who had been through the criminal legal system and brainstormed abolitionist principles. Finally, this chapter concludes by making the case for abolition as a pragmatic and attainable goal to upend current systems of inequality and exclusion, to be replaced by frameworks of equity and inclusion.

On a cold Martin Luther King Jr. Day in 2020, New Jersey Governor Phil Murphy, a Democrat, signed laws that he claimed would expand democracy in the Garden State. These laws included online voter registration, counting incarcerated individuals based on where they are from rather than where they reside for redistricting purposes, and creating a transparent system that compiles state voting data.[7] These laws came a month after he signed Bill A5823 in December 2019, restoring voting rights to more than eighty thousand New Jersey residents who were previously disenfranchised.[8] However, it should be noted that this right extended only to individuals on parole and probation, not those incarcerated, thus highlighting the arbitrary and subjective nature of who is disenfranchised.

Nonetheless, Murphy's policies did not occur in a vacuum but followed other reform efforts by previous state administrations. In 2007, Democratic Governor John Corzine abolished the death penalty; instead, individuals were resentenced to life without possibility of parole, a sort of extended form of capital punishment. Corzine's successor, Republican Chris Christie, became an advocate for drug addiction intervention programs as opposed to punitive responses.

While there have been bipartisan efforts to reform criminal justice in the state over the past two decades, these changes do not represent fundamental shifts in ideology but rather are measures influenced by financial pressures and racism on the part of state officials. For instance, Corzine abolished capital punishment after the New Jersey Death Penalty Study Commission Report estimated that doing so would save the state $1.46 million per year.[9] Conversely, many have criticized Christie's stance on drug intervention as reflecting the perceived racial and class demographic shift in perceived drug use, moving from low-income minorities to middle-class Whites. Historically, illicit drugs in the United States have been linked to racial groups, which assisted in the passage of drug laws and creating criminalized minority groups.[10]

Despite new legislation and policy changes, Black New Jersey residents are still systematically marginalized, underscoring the fact that reform efforts often shrink the numbers of those incarcerated but do little to change the structural inequality that is a defining aspect of the state's criminal legal system. According to the New Jersey Department of Corrections, from 2011 to 2021 the number of incarcerated individuals within the state prison system shrunk from 25,139 to 12,808.[11] However, while the state cut the prison population in half, other factors have remained the same. For instance, during that same period of time, Essex County, in which Newark is located, continued to have the highest level of commitment to the state prison system, making up roughly 15 percent of the total prison population.[12]

Also, while Black New Jersey residents make up just shy of 14 percent of the state's population, over the same ten-year span Black incarcerated individuals were consistently 60 percent of all persons imprisoned.[13] The Sentencing Project, a research and advocacy center dealing with issues of incarceration and race, highlights that New Jersey has a twelve-to-one Black-to-White disparity when it comes to incarceration, the highest in the nation.[14] When it comes to imprisonment, Black residents clearly remain disproportionately and overwhelmingly disadvantaged in New Jersey, regardless of the strides in so-called reform efforts.

And while the state, in 2017, overhauled its parole and bail systems, critics caution that the reform replacements, which use various algorithms, continue to enhance bias and discrimination against Black and other racialized populations.[15] Finally, although New Jersey released more than twenty-five hundred incarcerated individuals during the COVID-19 pandemic,[16] eighty-four-year-old Sundiata Acoli, a former Black Panther who had been incarcerated since 1973, was not extended that same amnesty because of his political affiliations and activism within the Black Power movement. He was kept imprisoned for nearly a half century, despite international calls for reprieve and compassionate release for elders.[17] In the end, the New Jersey Supreme Court intervened and ordered that he become eligible for parole, and he was released in May 2022.[18]

In short, the state has shown that reform has limits. While scores of New Jersey residents are no longer in prisons, simply shortening sentences or using other forms of criminal supervision, including expanding parole, or alternative sentences, such as probation, do not acknowledge deeper inequalities that can be traced to the need for equitable housing, universal health care, and quality education. More shocking is the growing proliferation of technology and devices used to surveil individuals, among them GPS monitors, ankle bracelets, and facial recognition software, or what Michelle Alexander calls "e-incarceration."[19]

Beyond this, it has become evident that the criminal legal system as an institution is greatly resistant to change. Police are defiant to any sort of accountability actions, the courts are slow moving, and corrections are a hellscape that breeds violence. Therefore, a deeper discussion is warranted to shift away from retributive models that use reform as a way to maintain and extend the status quo and instead implement abolition praxis to undo historic and structural disparities to create a better future.

·   ·   ·   ·   ·

Abolition represents a call for radical change, and such change is described in various ways. Media and culture studies professor Dylan Rodriguez writes, "Abolition seeks . . . a radical reconfiguration of justice, subjectivity, and social formation that does not depend on the existence of either the carceral state . . . or carceral power as such."[20] Activist and human rights lawyer Derecka Purnell argues in her book *Becoming Abolitionists: Police, Protests, and the Pursuit of Freedom*, "Abolition . . . is a bigger idea than firing cops and closing prisons; it includes eliminating the reasons people think they need cops and prisons in the first place."[21]

Writer and community organizer Mariame Kaba states, "Prison-industrial complex abolition is a political vision, a structural analysis of oppression, and a practical organizing strategy."[22] Scholar and former political prisoner Angela Y. Davis notes, "An abolitionist approach . . . would require us to imagine a constellation of alternative strategies and institutions, with the ultimate aim of removing the prison from the social and ideological landscapes of our society."[23] Or more simply put by the title of professor Ruthie Wilson Gilmore's book, *Change Everything*.[24]

The call for abolition has grown dramatically in the past decade. The proliferation of Black Lives Matter activism, social media, and video recordings of individuals being harassed, brutalized, and killed by law enforcement officers has strengthened this position. However, the call for abolition is not new but has a deep legacy in grassroots organizing around leftist liberation efforts.

The first abolition movement was birthed out of the call for emancipation against the institution of American slavery. Enslaved people resisted their captors in various ways, ranging from sabotage to mutiny. In his 1903 book *The Souls of Black Folk: Essays and Sketches*, W. E. B. Du Bois traces the history of Black resistance, noting various rebellions by enslaved Africans such as the successful Haitian Revolution.[25]

Du Bois highlights that these early forms of abolition were steeped in notions of self-defense and liberation. Furthermore, in the nineteenth century, the abolition movement sought to end formal chattel slavery by radically changing and transforming the institutions, policies, and cultural dynamics that governed systems of racial hierarchy and exploited labor, based on ideas of racial inferiority. Today, the abolition movement seeks to do the same. As Angela Y. Davis writes, "The prison is considered so 'natural' that it is extremely hard to imagine life without it."[26] Historian Barbara Jeanne Fields writes that ideology is reinforced through the repetitive nature of social routines and becomes "custom, so immemorial that it looks like nature."[27] In other words, it is difficult to see beyond the current condition and reimagine an alternative reality. Yet this is exactly what abolitionists set out to do, challenging the status quo and demanding innovation in the way justice is perceived. While the short-sighted dismissal of abolition is a common argument by reactionary voices, abolition is about reimagining society, which takes both effort and time.

The United States, and arguably the Western world and possibly the globe, teach that police are the "good guys," protecting citizens from the "bad guys." When seeing a person pulled over or being questioned by police, the first thought is usually, "I wonder what that person did wrong?" This is influenced by media and other various depictions of law enforcement in our everyday lives.[28] This is not by accident but by design. The criminal legal system has created a precarious situation that often vilifies citizens and noncitizens, which sensationalizes crime to create a fear and panic surrounding the "other."

In this case, the "other" refers to those who have been criminalized and incarcerated. Reality crime television programs create frenzy among viewers that champion the need for retribution that can only be done by police, courts, and corrections. However, abolition not only seeks alternatives to this position but also argues that the current systems do not prevent crime but in fact exacerbate criminality and fracture communities. Ultimately, Ruthie Wilson Gilmore argues, abolition is invested in resolving inequalities and providing resources to communities before acts of crime and violence can occur.[29] Therefore, abolition calls for several goals, including elimination, investment, anticapitalism, and reimagination as well as other short- and long-term goals.

First, abolition advocates for the *elimination* of state violence in communities—in other words, the elimination of police, courts, and correctional institutions, particularly in their current form, as well as the use of surveillance technologies to monitor communities. Historically, the Black community has been subject to both state and mob violence. The Federal Bureau of Investigation has a long history of infiltrating and disrupting Black communities and organizations, principally in the form of the COINTELPRO operation. Furthermore, events such as the Red Summer of 1919 and the 1921 Tulsa Riots are examples of White mob violence inflicted on the Black community.

As a result of these events, there is a robust history of Black community resistance. For example, in the early twentieth century various organizations, including the Universal Negro Improvement Association, the African Blood Brotherhood, and the Nation of Islam, advocated for varying aspects of Black nationalism regarding self-reliance, economic independence, and self-defense against White supremacist structures.

Moreover, in 1966, Huey P. Newton and Bobby Seale founded the Black Panther Party for Self-Defense in Oakland, California, an organization that embraced notions of Black nationalism but incorporated Black liberation with Marxist teachings. For example, the Black Panther Party established a Ten-Point Platform, which is an abolitionist guide. Points one through five directly address social inequalities, such as the need for employment, housing, and education. Points six through nine address the violence of American militarism, police brutality, and the call for the release of Black people from jails and prisons.

The tenth point sums up the party's philosophy: *"We want land, bread, housing, education, clothing, justice, and peace."*[30] The final word, "peace," is important. Abolition is about eliminating violence. For instance, I wrote in the American Society of Criminology's Division of Critical Criminology and Social Justice newsletter, "One can embrace both abolitionism and public safety, as these are not dueling or competing ideas. Abolitionism, at its core, is guided by the fundamental principles of keeping communities safe."[31] Eradicating institutions defined by violence, such as police and prisons, allows space to replace them with institutions of reconciliation and harmony.

Second, abolition advocates for *investment* in both individuals and communities. The 1970s became a crucial moment in the abolition movement. In 1971, during what became known as the Attica Prison rebellion in upstate New York, incarcerated individuals took control of the prison and demanded better food and health services, the recruiting of minority correction officers, and an expansion of vocational and academic training.[32] In the end, National Guard members and state police officers killed forty-three individuals, most of them prisoners, in the retaking of the institution.

In the eyes of many, the Attica uprising was seen as a turning point in America's prison history. Prophetically stated by former ABC news reporter John Johnson, "Whatever happens after the situation here at Attica, the penal system here in the United States and the people who are kept inside of them will never be the same."[33]

Two years later, in 1973, Walpole Prison in Massachusetts was the site of a similar rebellion. However, unlike what happened at Attica, Walpole correction officers went on strike, with the hopes of sparking violence throughout the unsupervised prison. Unexpectedly, this did not occur. In fact, prisoners established an organization called the National Prisoners Reform Association, a representative body that became a voice for prisoners' rights to engage in collective bargaining to obtain better wages, health care, food, and other services.[34] In this instance, their resistance highlighted that abolition was possible and the need for intensive, intrusive, and punitive supervision was not a requirement for rehabilitation.

Moreover, these early rebellions called attention to efforts to use state tax dollars for other programs and social services. Those incarcerated understood the need for community investment and became radicalized, connecting their imprisonment to a larger global context of colonialism and imperialism that was exploiting them under capitalism.

Third, abolition is fiercely *anticapitalist.* The criminal legal system exploits incarcerated persons in various ways. Specifically, racial capitalism articulates how social and economic (and political) value is extracted from racially oppressed populations for the purposes of supporting white supremacy.[35] In this case, capitalism is intimately interwoven with various forms of violence and oppression. Jackie Wang, an African American studies scholar, writes in her book *Carceral Capitalism* that various techniques are used by the state and work together with global capitalism, which manifests in predatory lending and parasitic governance.[36]

In some instances, private entities such as private prisons, halfway facilities, or other institutions profit from imprisoned labor. However, most incarcerated individuals are warehoused in state-operated facilities. Here, Ruthie Wilson Gilmore makes the distinction between profit and revenue. The latter refers to money allocated in state budgets, money for which many agencies must compete. As she states in an interview, "If you follow the money, you don't have to find the company that's profiting. . . . You can find all the people who are dependent on wages paid out by the Department of Corrections."[37]

George Jackson highlighted the intersection of capitalism and incarceration. In 1961, he was imprisoned for stealing seventy dollars and given an indeterminate sentence of one year to life in prison. A decade later, in 1971, he was killed in San Quentin prison in California, by guards. Yet during his incarceration, he became an advocate for the abolition of prisons and a symbol of carceral resistance. Letters written by Jackson were compiled and published, in 1970, in a book titled *Soledad Brother.* Readers glean insight into his experiences and philosophies and how prisons are intimately tethered to larger oppressive economic and historic systems of capitalism and slavery. As Jackson writes, "The pig [police] is an instrument of neoslavery [prison] to be hated and avoided. . . . They're protecting the unnatural right of a few men to own the means of all of our subsistence."[38]

Jackson articulates how law enforcement is an extension of the state's ability to carry out violence on behalf of the ruling class. Furthermore, he emphasizes the fact that "our principal enemy must be isolated and identi-fied as *capitalism*."[39]

Other revolutionary activists have also made these connections. Former Black Panther and political prisoner Safiya Bukhari writes, "I believe nothing short of a revolution will eradicate the racism, capitalism, and imperialism that oppress me and my people. . . . [T]he capitalist system of this country has to be destroyed and replaced."[40]

Today, abolitionists continue to recognize the fight of Jackson and Bukhari against capitalism. Mariame Kaba states, "We're not going to abolish the police, if we don't abolish capitalism."[41] Furthermore, Angela Y. Davis articulates this thread of abolition through her discussion sur-rounding what she terms *abolition democracy*. She borrows this concept from W. E. B. Du Bois's book *Black Reconstruction*, which argues that slav-ery was never truly abolished because social institutions and economic means were not provided to Black people after slavery ended.

As Davis writes in extending Du Bois's idea of abolition democracy, "There is a direct connection with slavery: when slavery was abolished, black people were set free, but they lacked access to the material resources that would enable them to fashion new, free lives. Prisons have thrived over the last century precisely because of the absence of those resources and the persistence of some of the deep structures of slavery."[42] Davis, along with Du Bois, is advocating investments in alternative economic infrastructures, outside a capitalist paradigm, must occur for any type of social change.

Additionally, Davis is grappling with the notion that prisons and incar-ceration have never been designed for reentry purposes. Therefore, reen-try becomes a fallacy. Individuals sent to violent institutions are not meant to come back from these places, having been stripped of citizenship, iden-tity, and agency. The carceral continuum perpetuates this notion upon the individual's return to society as economic, political, and social aspects of life are prohibited. Thus, it creates a cycle of perpetual violence in com-munities because of the lack of resources, materials, and necessary invest-ments in individuals and neighborhoods.

Fourth, abolition is about *reimagining* society. In fact, a 1973 report by the National Advisory Commission on Criminal Justice Standards and Goals suggested, "The facts set forth earlier in this chapter lead logically to the conclusion that *no new institutions for adults should be built and existing institutions for juveniles should be closed.*[43] The report goes on to state, "The prison, the reformatory, and the jail have achieved only a shocking record of failure. There is overwhelming evidence that these institutions create crime rather than prevent it."[44] Here, right at the onset of the exponential growth of prisons and jails, there was a moment to pivot away from punitive practices that did not come to fruition.

In 1976, the Prison Research Education Action Project published *Instead of Prisons: A Handbook for Abolitionists*, which outlines the arguments for the abolition of prisons and advocates for a three-pronged approach: economic and social justice for all, concern for all victims, and instead of punishment, reconciliation in a caring community.[45]

Violent crime impacts both individuals and society. Cringe-worthy news reports evoke emotional turmoil, which could be triggering to victims, family, and friends. The knee-jerk reaction has often been to respond to violence with more violence. This is where prisons intervene. Furthermore, within prison spaces there is vengeance in the use of solitary confinement and capital punishment.

It is at this juncture that abolition advocates for reimagining justice by using accountability. For example, an organization called the Caring & Compassionate New Deal for NYC advocates for the implementation and building of an infrastructure for a caring community by replacing police and prisons with care and services that address the root causes of many social ills, notably poverty and public health concerns. The organization, which was established by Voices of Community Activists & Leaders (VOCAL-NY), advocates this approach, writing, "We must end piecemeal approaches, 'pilot programs,' and halfhearted criminal justice reforms. The solution calls for nothing short of a historic investment in the creation of housing, social services, and a 'caring and compassionate' workforce infrastructure—and a complete realignment in the way city government has previously addressed issues of homelessness, substance use, mental health issues, criminalization, and incarceration."[46]

Abolition is also about creating awareness through accountability, dignity, and respect. The implementation of consistent and transparent communication skills will allow for growth. Additionally, acceptance of failure needs to be normalized for perseverance to flourish over time. In short, people make mistakes, and we need to have policies, institutions, and public servants who are trained and equipped to intervene accordingly, in a manner that promotes positive change and does not reinforce negative behaviors.

Ultimately, abolition as a reimagined society must also look beyond the scope of human suffering. Here, abolitionist praxis must incorporate a critical nonhuman animal and environmental perspective as well to stymie violence. Research surrounding commercial animal slaughter has shown it leads to higher rates of substance abuse and domestic violence, and contributes to global warming.[47] In sum, violence begets violence. Abolitionists such as philosopher Lori Gruen have articulated the need for dignity and respect across the human-animal divide.[48] Therefore abolitionist reimagination must focus on individual growth and maturity, replacement of institutions of violence with spaces of reconciliation, and reorienting human relationships with nonhuman animals and the environment.

Fifth, abolition must have ongoing and persistent *short- and long-term goals*. Conservative and reactionary stances against abolition premise that these changes will create anarchy and chaos. Yet the reality is that many of our poorest communities are already living with these things. Throughout my fieldwork at the reentry center, clients described their neighborhoods in terms of violence, in many cases describing interpersonal as well as state-sanctioned violence in the form of police, county jail, or state and federal prison. Therefore, abolition is a long-term goal to eradicate systems of violence. As Mariame Kaba states, "This work [abolition] will take generations, and I'm not going to be alive to see the changes."[49] While the long-term goal is creating a society in which prisons and police are nonexistent, the reality is it will take many years and sacrifice for these changes to be implemented.

To achieve long-term abolition, short-term measures must be taken. In the interim, abolitionist reforms, which champion dignity and respect for those incarcerated, should be advocated as long as they do not strengthen the overall carceral system. One example is providing health care and hygiene products to incarcerated individuals. Ruthie Wilson Gilmore calls this a nonreformist reform.[50]

Abolitionism should care about the treatment of those imprisoned without trying to make the system better. For example, abolition of the death penalty calls for the end of state-sanctioned murder. However, in many instances, the alternative is mandating life without possibility of parole. For instance, Mumia Abu-Jamal spent more than thirty years on death row in Pennsylvania. Eventually, his sentence was commuted to life without possibility of parole. Now a senior citizen in poor health, Mumia is in general population and exposed to prison violence as well as other public health concerns. This is not the type of reform abolitionists seek. The abolition of the death penalty incorporates the idea that nobody should die within prison settings. Life without possibility of parole is nothing more than a nefarious way to execute someone.

In the end, a pragmatic abolition approach seeks to incorporate tools in the short-term that will eventually lead to long-term outcomes. Moreover, sociologist Reneé Byrd argues, "Prisoner reentry must be grounded in a politics of abolition if it is to undermine the conditions that make possible mass imprisonment."[51]

"ABOLITION IS SOLUTION"

Discussions about abolition were not why clients came to the reentry center. However, the death of Trayvon Martin became an impetus to begin these conversations. I delicately but explicitly cited abolitionist premises and raised the question *What would a society without prisons look like?* An immediate response was "heaven," which was met with laughs. Another reply came from Ray, who shouted, "Success!"

I asked Ray if he could elaborate because the theme of *success* came up frequently. It is a term often linked to reentry, particularly in response to recidivism rates and other statistical measurements. In the corporate and nonprofit realm of reentry services, "success" translates to funding and programming, but often lacks context. Political scientist Keesha M. Middlemass criticizes mainstream notions of success as she points out that someone is considered "successful" even if homeless, if they are outside of a prison facility. She advocates taking narratives of the formerly incarcerated into consideration and incorporating them into analyses of "success."[52]

Before Ray answered, he leaned forward in his chair, folded his hands, and exhaled a large breath. "You probably won't know that," he said of the concept of success, "until you are dead." The room fell silent. The reality was that criminal justice interaction, incapacitation, and supervision were continuing themes throughout their lives. In this case, reentry, with the various limitations on rights and amplified social stigmas, is simply a new iteration of social control.

The following week, I decided to give a presentation about abolition. I defined the theory, discussed the history of the term, and connected individuals such as Angela Y. Davis and Geronimo Pratt, who had been falsely imprisoned and became known as political prisoners because of their involvement in leftist organizing and various social movements such as Black Power. The lecture lasted about thirty minutes, and no one asked any questions. Clients typically participated in discussions, but outside of a few coughs and "can you say that again" remarks, it was virtually a hushed room.

I feared I had alienated myself, or worse, expressed an opinion that was not equally shared. Then Ray asked a question. "So you mean get rid of *all* the prisons?"

"Theoretically, yes," I replied. "That's the goal."

"Shit, abolition is [the] solution," he countered. Immediately, a jolt of adrenaline rushed through me. In that tiny conference room in Newark, New Jersey, we were going to discuss, debate, and decide what a future without prisons looked like.

"Take It to Trial": Disrupting the Carceral Machine

"Let's go to trial, we guilty 'til prove innocent" is part of the chorus in the 2017 song "Dead Presidents" by Rick Ross, featuring Yo Gotti, Jeezy, and Future.[53] While the song boasts about the benefits of having wealth and money (i.e., dead presidents), this line reflects the economic disparity within the American legal system. In this case, the artists can afford to stand trial, but this is often the exception, not the rule. While television legal dramas portray courtrooms with judges, lawyers, and juries, most criminal cases end in a plea agreement.[54] In fact, 95 percent of all cases in the United States end in this manner.[55]

Clients referred to this as "copping out," which meant taking a deal offered by a prosecutor to avoid a jury trial. Furthermore, clients insisted that "copping out" was not the same as "snitching" but rather just an admission of guilt in the legal sense.

Prosecutors rely on the coercive nature of pressuring the accused to take a plea deal in order to continue shuttling defendants through the legal process and avoid the possibility of long and expensive trials. In some cases, it has been estimated that "prosecuting and convicting a single drug offender may cost up to $70,000, while plea bargaining could reduce that number to $4,200."[56] The Brennan Center for Justice, a law and public policy institute, has highlighted the fact that criminal courts impose fines and fees on defendants, money that is used to fund the court systems and other government operations, as an added incentive to take a plea agreement.[57] Moreover, the Vera Institute of Justice reports on the possibility of a "plea discount" versus a "trial penalty," finding a 64 percent increase in length of sentence for defendants who go to trial.[58]

Therefore, prosecutors often overcharge defendants as a scare tactic to produce a favorable outcome for the state.[59] While discussing plea agreements, many of the clients admitted to taking this option.

Shane suggested that there really is not another option, stating, "Everybody cops out at some point. You ain't got no other choice." He went on to further elaborate, "I remember the prosecutor told me I was looking at fifteen years if I took my case to trial, or I could take the deal and get a three flat [years] with time served in the county. You would have to be stupid not to take that deal. What's funny is on the streets everybody jokes around like they tough and wouldn't take a deal, but when you are looking at a lot of time, you start to see things differently."

"I kept asking for a lawyer, and it's not like on TV," Regina explained. She took a plea deal partly out of ignorance, not understanding the technical details of her case. She continued, "The first time I met my lawyer was in the courtroom. Before that, these two big ass cops were screaming in my face and because I'm a female they had this lady cop in the room too, but she ain't say shit. Then they sent me to county [jail], so by the time I had the opportunity to make a deal, I think I took the first one they offered. I didn't really understand all the legal stuff they were saying, but I understood 'Sign this and you can go home.'"

The criminal legal system thrives on intimidation and fear, and operates through an adversarial model that must have a winner and a loser. Ultimately, this system is obsessed with clearance rates and convictions, not justice.

Among the clients, there was an age divide about plea agreements. The older generation of baby boomers decidedly expressed resentment toward taking a plea. For instance, Melvin's story, as told in the introduction to this book, outlined how he declined to "snitch" for a shorter sentence. Sharif's narrative in chapter 2 explained how he refused to take a plea. Ronald, in chapter 5, bragged about still having street credentials for not cooperating with federal agencies. Finally, Lyle explained, "You just don't. It's a street thing. Also, why make it easy for them? I can do time, but they are going to have to spend money to lock me up because I'm not going to help them out." While older men prided themselves for not taking deals, they understood younger clients' reasons, admitting that prison was no place to spend one's life. Yet the notion of taking a case to trial became a point of discussion as an abolitionist strategy to upend the system.

The concept of "taking it to trial" allowed clients to ponder what would happen to the system if literally *all* people charged with crimes took their case to adjudication. As Sharif said poignantly, "It would bring their whole system to a standstill." The Bail Project, a national nonprofit organization that pays bail for people in need, reported that nearly 40 percent of all cases in which they posted bond were entirely dismissed.[60] The criminal legal system's predatory pretrial detainment is designed to force plea agreements. Without this leverage, prosecutors are forced to choose between costly trials or dropping cases.

Lastly, clients acknowledged that "taking it to trial" could lead to retaliation by prosecutors, who would exact revenge and make examples out of those who resisted plea agreements. Therefore, it is vital to create an abolitionist praxis that does not forget folks "behind enemy lines."[61]

In this circumstance, I became the resident photographer, which enabled clients to send pictures to folks still "down." These images became part of a larger form of resistance and were also intended to communicate and inspire those still imprisoned. Moreover, clients continued to think through this exercise of taking it to trial and enjoyed this vision of seeing the gears of the machine grind to a screeching halt.

"Separation Not Segregation": Power, Punishment, and
Accountability

While conversations surrounding abolition occurred, I dreaded the inevitable question: *What about . . . ?*

It is common in the realm of abolition to be confronted by opposition citing extreme cases and examples, particularly acts of violence used to negate or misdirect the larger abolitionist framework of seeking alternative institutions and paradigms for community safety. However, my previous activism and organizing around the death penalty gave me some strategies in how to answer these questions.

When the *What about . . . ?* question came up, I used it as a moment to be transparent with the clients about my own bias. In other words, these approaches are not mutually exclusive; one can both be an abolitionist and struggle with the idea of certain criminal acts. From here, we discussed crime and abolition as seen through the notions of power, punishment, and accountability. First, we looked at the concept that "crime" itself is a social construct, determined by those with power, that disproportionately affects low-income communities. Second, we grew understanding that sending people to jails and prisons as a punishment does not work to rehabilitate but only further marginalizes people. Finally, we thought through accountability as an abolitionist tool, as this is a constant process requiring self-reflection, healing, and learning.

During these conversations, I revisited the notion of alternatives to incarceration, asking clients to think through this process with the concept of *What about . . . ?* in mind. Often, it is easy to think of strategies when empathy is applied. It becomes more challenging when prejudice is present. After several minutes, Ronald put forth an idea, saying, "What about separation not segregation?" He went on to elaborate, "Prison segregates people from society, but if we were to separate people and give them some time to cool out, that might help everyone." To that, Tony responded, "Yeah, replace 'street justice' with 'street healing.'"

Clients began to unpack this idea of "separation versus segregation" through the concept of "removal" to avoid further harm. We developed distinctions between the two words.

First, separation is about short-term removal but does not involve taking someone away from the community. Conversely, segregation is currently used and is a form of long-term removal, taking folks out of the community. Second, separation removes people from harmful situations so they cannot hurt themselves or others and replaces negative energy with care, counseling, and alternative outlets. Conversely, segregation is used as a form of isolation, which cuts people off from family, friends, and society, thus inhibiting forms of communication. Finally, separation explores sympathy and empathy as active learning. By contrast, segregation breeds hostility and animosity. Jerry best summarized the debate and discussion surrounding "removal" by saying, "There are certain crimes I will never understand, horrible things, unthinkable acts but we must give second chances. It doesn't mean we forget, but we must learn to forgive."

Furthermore, clients expressed their own bitterness toward the system, describing their experiences and explaining their feeling that prison had not helped them in any meaningful way. Interestingly, even those who expressed being a better person than before being incarcerated did not ascribe that change to the physical institution and the people in charge. Instead, credit and praise were bestowed upon fellow comrades, counselors, and volunteers, who took the time to get to know them and showed interest in their lives.

In sum, the discussion surrounding separation and segregation argued that segregation and being confined to a small cell did not make people better—quite the opposite. Segregation is the catchall of our penal system and is used to limit contact and enforce punitive distress. By contrast, separation seeks accountability, as clients believed various offenses need numerous remedies and treatments and not a one-size-fits-all solution. As Sharif put it, "You can't fit a round peg into a square hole and expect it to fit."

Lastly, we talked about environmental and international crime. Regarding the former, clients mentioned the BP oil spill in the Gulf of Mexico in 2010 that led to the death of several people because of corporate greed and a subsequent cover-up. Regarding the latter, clients considered American military prison camps such as Abu Ghraib in Iraq. Ironically, the military leader of these torture facilities was a Pennsylvania prison guard known for his sadistic treatment of prisoners.[62]

Clients expressed frustration about the fact that these types of crimes were often downplayed and the perpetrators were rarely held accountable for their actions. Yet, in the end, clients held that prisons do not offer solutions and that better ways of handling crime should be practiced. There was, however, a consensus that one person should go to prison: President George W. Bush.

"Gotta Stop the Money": Ending For-Profit Justice

The hashtag #DefundThePolice was popularized in 2020 in the wake of multiple high-profile shootings involving the police that left several Black Americans dead or paralyzed.[63] Within the ongoing Black Lives Matter movement, which focuses attention on police brutality, this phrase drew attention to the bloated law enforcement budgets throughout the United States and sparked growing support for shrinking these expenditures. For example, the budget in New York City for law enforcement, courts, and corrections is more than $14 billion a year.[64] Furthermore, the defund movement is not simply about taking money away from police but rather *divesting* from militarized and punitive assaults on communities and *reinvesting* in community care with the long-term goal of abolition.

While the hashtag and divest/reinvest effort are being debated, organizing around these issues has been a tenet in the abolition movement. The prison industrial complex and prison reentry industry highlight neoliberal policies that support austerity and deregulation within carceral logics. Moreover, while the private prison industry is relatively small, it has expanded in the twenty-first century. According to The Sentencing Project, "From 2000 to 2016 the number of people housed in private prisons increased five times faster than the total prison population. Over a similar time frame, the proportion of people detained in private immigration facilities increased by 442 percent."[65] Additionally, enterprises such as GEO Group and Core Civic, the two largest private prison enterprises, collectively control more than half of all private prison contracts in the United States.[66]

Beyond private prisons, the larger looming and more complex issue is how private companies operate within state-operated facilities. For instance, communication within prisons is limited, and phone calls are essential to keep in contact with family, friends, and attorneys. Private phone companies often hold a monopoly within carceral settings and charge premium prices to those incarcerated. As one report noted, "States that contract with these providers tend to choose the contractor that provides not the lowest price, but the *highest* commission rate for the state."[67]

Moreover, private, third-party contractors who claim that they can save states money by providing services at cheaper rates facilitate many aspects of life in prison. For example, state prisons have contracts with private companies that offer a wide array of services in the areas of health care, food, transportation, financial assistance, and communications.[68] Finally, private companies are invested in reentry services, such as operating electronic monitoring devices.[69] Simply put, in the world of incarceration, there is a moral and ethical conflict between human services and profiteering that must be eradicated.

Clients were aware of their position within this carceral continuum. As Sharif put it, "Only way this all ends is you gotta stop the money." He was referring to the flow of income and revenue generated both directly within corrections institutions and indirectly from companies that rely on corrections. Therefore, eradicating both prisons and "community corrections" becomes another abolitionist strategy.

Clients were critical of the idea that police were needed in communities to be "problem solvers" and referred to law enforcement agents as outside occupiers. Therefore, discussions about their own role in the community became important. Many described wanting to pursue a certified alcohol and drug counselor certificate and felt that they could serve the community and help others "coming up behind them."

Ned expressed an interest in becoming an emergency medical services paramedic. "I'm pretty calm and not grossed out by blood," he said. "I have been looking into courses and hope that I will be able to work in the medical field. I think responding to emergencies is something I would be good at." Others showed a passion for mentoring, among them Ronald, who aspired to do community work as a violence interrupter, credible messenger, or gang liaison.

Clients also described the overall need to provide an abundance of social services to the community in the form of mental health and drug counselors, social workers, and teachers. One of the most active discussions was about providing outreach specialists to work in homeless services. Many discussed the overlap of drug addiction, mental illness, and arrest as a primary reason for homelessness.

Furthermore, research has shown that literally giving individuals housing is much more cost-effective than cycling them in and out of jails.
Studies and pilot programs across the country, including in Florida, Utah,
and New York, have shown that money could be saved through the creation of permanent housing infrastructure.[70] In 2008, New York City initi-
ated a pilot program that gave permanent housing with support services,
and after two years there had been a 40 percent decrease in the amount
of days participants spent in jail.[71] More recently, New York has begun
a new housing program, which costs the city $16,000 less per person
annually than allowing individuals to cycle between jail and shelter
systems.[72]

In early 2020, Newark Mayor Ras Baraka announced a partnership
with a California-based company and other nonprofit groups that convert
shipping containers into housing and provide bathrooms, showers, and
meals as well as mental health and substance abuse services.[73] However,
the mayor recognized that this is the start, not the end goal, for Newark's
vulnerable population that grapples with housing instability. Sociologist
Matthew Desmond's work highlights how housing eviction disproportionately impacts people of color and Black women, specifically, leading to
contact with the criminal legal system in a variety of ways.[74]

Based on research and other data, the steps going forward are clear.
America must invest in affordable, clean, and safe permanent housing;
universal health care that addresses physical, mental, and public health
concerns, such as decriminalizing and legalizing drug use and sex
work; and equitable, comprehensive education with access to up-to-date
resources and technologies. To do any of this, we need to invest in what
political scientist Michael Lipsky calls "street-level bureaucrats," who are
public servants invested in the community.[75]

People in these jobs need to be compensated at higher rates and given
training at no cost to the individual pursuing these fields. Currently, many
social service careers require higher education, with people pursuing these
jobs facing low salaries and massive debt. We need to eliminate all forms
of debt for college and other training, especially for public servants.

Finally, we need to see what is happening around the world and curb
American exceptionalism. For instance, Ecuador has legalized gangs and
the state has met with gang leaders, who have opened businesses, and the

biggest consequence is that murder rates have plummeted.[76] In Central America, El Salvador's presidential administration has met with gang leaders of MS-13. These meetings, rather than a "war on gangs," have produced improved prison conditions and gang war truces, curbing homicide rates by 60 percent.[77]

"Make Us Whole:" Reentry, Citizenship, and Justice

The most obvious and immediate abolitionist strategy included restoring all forms of political participation, employment possibilities, social welfare opportunities, and access to social and cultural capital. Abolition explicitly rejects archaic political ideologies and arguments of liberalism and republicanism, which defend the preservation of civil death.[78]

During discussions about the loss of rights, it was clear that clients understood that they had "lost something." Yet, these instances of loss were not necessarily all felt at once or even uniformly among members of the group. However, clients knew that they were at a disadvantage. Moreover, Jerry said, "In order for reentry to truly work, they [the state] need to make us whole." He was referring to the loss of political, economic, and social rights.

Furthermore, his use of the term *whole* is reminiscent of the longer legacy of Black exclusion in American history. For example, the Three-Fifths Compromise in the U.S. Constitution treated Black people as fractions, disaggregating humanity for the purposes of a white supremacist agenda. Today, perpetual punishment continues to exacerbate this incompleteness for those returning to society.

Further, the lack of inclusion preserves and extends purgatory citizenship, marginalizing formerly incarcerated folks to the fringes of society. Conversely, abolition is invested in the completeness and wholeness of humanity. If we truly want to live in a world with diminished harm, we cannot arrest and imprison our way out of social problems. It will only happen through long-term healing, understanding, and accountability that seek restorative and transformative paradigm shifts in society.

While not interchangeable, restorative and transformative justice are complementary in addressing harm. Restorative justice seeks to make amends by working with victims and offenders to heal from criminal acts and violations of a person. Transformative justice looks beyond individual damages to address social, political, and economic injustices that create environments for harm to occur.[79] To that end, I am advocating that theoretical and practitioner-based models be used as the starting point rather than the end. Ultimately, beyond my lifetime, I expect innovative frameworks to take abolition even further.

For clients, restorative justice assisted in addressing regret, wrongdoing, and self-reflection. For instance, Elijah spoke about holding on to a lot of pain and "not knowing how to let go." Others wished they had the chance to address past behaviors and said they would have if given the opportunity. Furthermore, transformative justice would take a more holistic approach to tackling structural problems such as poverty and the need for housing, education, health care, jobs, therapeutic services, and recreational outlets.

·   ·   ·   ·   ·

During the annual Lincoln Park Music Festival, located in Newark, New Jersey, the three-day summer event featured hip-hop, house, jazz, and gospel music and was attended by more than fifty thousand people. The reentry center rented a booth to advertise their services to the community. This particular year, Mr. Darr chose bright yellow T-shirts, saying, "Everybody in the crowd is going to see us."

I, along with Mr. Darr and several clients, volunteered for the Saturday schedule, which showcased house music, a local favorite as "garage house" originated in Newark's Club Zanzibar, developed by legendary DJs such as Tony Humphries in the early 1980s. Songs like "Follow Me" by Aly-Us kept everyone dancing and in good spirits despite the burning midday sun.

Darren was one of the volunteers. By summer's end, he would no longer be living in the halfway house and he was looking forward to being "free" for the first time in more than fifteen years. At one point in the afternoon, Darren and I were standing in front of our table talking when he cut me off midsentence, saying, "Excuse me, Smiley, I'll be right back." I watched Darren briskly weave through the crowd and approach a Black man a few years his senior. Because of the music, I could not hear them, but I noticed

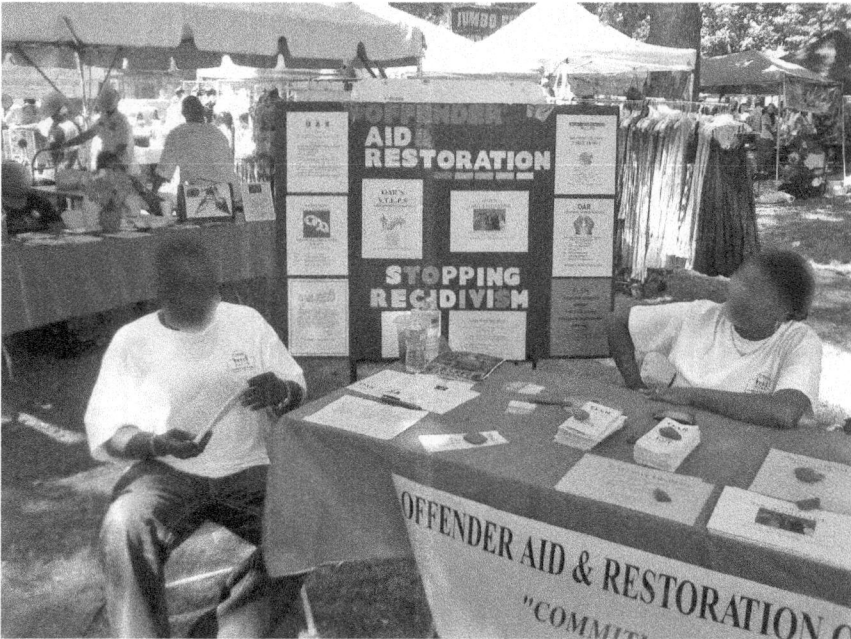

Figure 11. Reentry center table at Lincoln Park Music Festival at Lincoln Park, Newark, 2012. Photo courtesy of the author.

a serious expression on Darren's face. A minute later a reserved smile appeared, and the two men embraced.

"That was an old friend," Darren explained when he returned. Later, he recanted his previous statement and admitted, "That guy I spoke to was someone from my past. He was someone I had robbed."

"Really?" I asked, incredulous.

"Yeah, when I was out here doing dirt [crime] I robbed him and his brother," Darren explained. "We were all from the same neighborhood, committing crimes and what have you. I probably haven't seen him in over twenty years but recently learned his brother passed away. I couldn't let him walk by without extending my condolences and asking for forgiveness. I told him I'm a changed man now and needed to look him in the eyes and apologize."

"Did he accept your apology?" I asked.

"Yeah, yeah, he did," Darren replied.

CONCLUSION: THE IMPERATIVE FOR ABOLITION

To make abolition a reality, we must be expansive, comprehensive, and imaginative. To do this, there must be an entire overhaul of systems of justice, one that seeks to upend current structures and replace them with utopian visions. While some say a utopia is unattainable and naive, what is the harm in striving for it? The more we collectively work together, build bridges, break down borders, and communicate our problems to find solutions, the closer we come to being a society that diminishes harm, reduces violence, and propagates love and understanding.

Abolition seeks to end the need for reentry. Without prisons and cages of confinement, the reeducating, retraining, and reintegrating of folks back into society is unnecessary, thus putting the reentry industry out of business. Under an abolitionist model, the money allotted to reentry services would go toward stopping problems before they can fester. Therefore, abolition praxis strives for several outcomes.

First, we must humanize and decarcerate. The stories told in this book make clear that people change and are often victims of their circumstances and environments. Second, we must devise innovative strategies that address violence and harm and create healing. This needs to be done through forms of compassion and learning, which eliminate humiliation and vengeance. Third, we must invest in people through various forms of therapies, trainings, and other services. Finally, we must commit to investment in community resources like housing, education, health care, the arts, athletics, and other programs. We can no longer continue to perpetuate liberalist myths of individualism that promote success and failure based on singular choices.

This struggle will be neither quick nor easy, but it is imperative to establish an abolitionist tool kit. Here, I am reminded of the words of the political prisoner Mumia Abu-Jamal:

> Violence violates the self.
> Yet that's exactly what the system believes in, what the system preaches, what the system practices: violence. Certainly, I believe in the necessity of fighting the system, and in the necessity of self-defense, but I'm *not* going to employ the same tactics and methods the system uses every day. Why replace the system with the same thing?

Figure 12. Illustration anonymously left by a participant after a reentry group meeting, 2010. Photo courtesy of the author.

We need a *new* system, one where people are free of the violence of the system. I may not be a pacifist, but I still hope for a day when there are no bombs, no guns—no weapons whatsoever—no war, poverty, or other injustices; no social and class hatreds; no crime and no prisons.

I reject the tools and weapons of violence.[80]

Mumia's words continue to resonate. The proliferation of reforms such as community complaint review boards, implicit bias and de-escalation training, diversifying law enforcement personnel, and the use of body-worn cameras have done nothing but perpetuate state violence. In the spring of 2021, while I was writing these words, Daunte Wright, Adam Toledo, Ma'Khia Bryant, Andrew Brown Jr., Mario Gonzalez, and others were killed by law enforcement officers.

In sum, the goal is nothing less than abolition if we want to end the cycle of violence of doing reentry and creating purgatory citizenship status for individuals in society. Otherwise, we continue to be let down, exploited, and trampled by state-sanctioned violence that manifests in the form of cops in our neighborhoods, courts that are stacked against us, and prisons that remove people from communities.

Notes

INTRODUCTION

1. All names in this book are pseudonyms to protect the identity of participants, staff, and others.

2. For purposes of confidentiality, no specific name is given to the organization in this book. Throughout, I use interchangeable terms such as *center* or *organization*.

3. In December 2019, New Jersey legislation changed this law. See chapter 6 for details. See also Jeff Manza & Christopher Uggen, *Locked Out: Felon Disenfranchisement and American Democracy* (New York: Oxford University Press, 2008).

4. Shedd, 2011.

5. *Stir Crazy*, 1980.

6. Sabol, West, & Cooper, 2009.

7. Pew Center on the States, 2009; Bryant, 2021.

8. Guerino, Harrison, & Sabol, 2011.

9. Durose, Cooper, & Snyder, 2014.

10. Austin, 2001; Lynch & Sabol, 2001; Travis & Petersilia, 2001; Seiter & Kadela, 2003; Petersilia, 2004; Wormith et al., 2007; Solomon et al., 2008.

11. See Nikki Jones, *The Chosen Ones: Black Men and the Politics of Redemption* (Berkeley: University of California Press, 2018); Marieke Liem, *After Life Imprisonment: Reentry in the Era of Mass Incarceration* (New York: NYU Press,

2016); Liam Martin, *Halfway House: Prisoner Reentry and the Shadow of Carceral Care* (New York: NYU Press, 2021); Keesha M. Middlemass, *Convicted and Condemned: The Politics and Policies of Prisoner Reentry* (New York: NYU Press, 2017); Reuben Miller, *Halfway Home: Race, Punishment, and the After-life of Mass Incarceration* (New York: Little, Brown, 2021); Bruce Western, *Homeward: Life in the Year After Prison* (New York: Russell Sage Foundation, 2018); and Andrea Leverentz, *The Ex-prisoner's Dilemma: How Women Negoti-ate Competing Narratives of Reentry and Desistance* (New Brunswick, NJ: Rutgers University Press, 2014).

12. Alexander, 2010; Lerman & Weaver, 2014; Miller & Stuart, 2017; Sered, 2021; Smith & Kinzel, 2021.

13. Bucerius, 2013.

14. Tolnay, 2003.

15. Refers to "original gangster," a compliment earned by elders in the community.

16. Middlemass & Smiley, 2019.

17. Middlemass & Smiley, 2019, 4.

18. Driving under the influence (DUI), intensive outpatient (IOP), controlled dangerous substance (CDS), domestic violence (DV), and housing and urban development (HUD).

19. See Jabri Asim, *The N Word: Who Can Say It, Who Shouldn't, and Why* (Boston: Houghton Mifflin Harcourt, 2007); Randall Kennedy, *Nigger: The Strange Career of a Troublesome Word* (New York: Knopf Doubleday, 2003).

20. Within the discipline of criminology there is a debate surrounding these terms, for example, the use of the word *convict* or the idea of the word *prisoner* before reentry, as this emphasizes an individual's past rather than highlighting their present and future postimprisonment. It is my desire not to contribute to the harm of hurtful and stigmatizing language in this book. However, there are places where terms that might be currently disapproving are used, whether in a direct quote or to describe a situation. See J. M. Ortiz, A. Cox, D. R. Kavish, & G. Tietjen, 2022, "Let the Convicts Speak: A Critical Conversation of the Ongoing Language Debate in Convict Criminology," *Criminal Justice Studies*, 35(3), 255–73.

CHAPTER 1. UNDERDEVELOPMENT

1. Anti-Car Theft Act of 1992, H.R. 4542.

2. Caldwell Epps, 2010, 86–88.

3. Curvin, 2014, 330–31, fn 2.

4. Anderson, 1999.

5. Rodney, 1972, 13.

6. Rodney, 1972, 14.

7. Marable, 2000, 3.

8. Riot and rebellion have been used interchangeably to describe the events of July 12–17, 1967. For further reading on the Newark rebellion, please see *Report for Action* (Governor's Select Commission on Civil Disorders: State of New Jersey, February 1968); *Report of the National Advisory Commission on Civil Disorders* (New York: Bantam Books, 1968); Tom Hayden, *Rebellion in Newark* (New York: Vintage Books, 1967); Robert Curvin, *Inside Newark: Decline, Rebellion, and the Search for Transformation* (New Brunswick, NJ: Rutgers University Press, 2014); and Linda Caldwell Epps, *From Zion to Brick City: What's Going On? Newark and the Legacy of the Sixties* (ProQuest Dissertations and Theses, 2010).

9. Brady, 1970.

10. Caldwell Epps, 2010.

11. Massey & Denton, 1993, 45.

12. Curvin, 2014, 114.

13. *Report of the National Advisory Commission on Civil Disorders*, 1968, 31.

14. The Detroit rebellion, which occurred July 23–28, 1967, was also sparked by police violence, and had more deaths and total amount of damage to property.

15. Lilley, 1968.

16. Curvin, 2014; Cohen, 2007.

17. *Report of the National Advisory Commission on Civil Disorders*, 1968, 5.

18. *Report of the National Advisory Commission on Civil Disorders*, 1968, 1.

19. Parks, 2008.

20. Foner, 1972.

21. Ramirez, 2013.

22. Murakawa, 2014.

23. Hinton, 2016, 13.

24. Baum, 2016.

25. Butterfield, 2008.

26. Gilmore, 2007.

27. Hallinan, 2003; Perkinson, 2010.

28. Ditton & Wilson, 1999.

29. Austin et al., 2000; Emert, 2003.

30. Alexander, 2010, 73.

31. Lennard, 2019; Bruggeman, Dwyer, & Ebbs, 2022.

32. Pew Center on the States, 2009.

33. See Douglas Blackmon, *Slavery by Another Name: The Re-enslavement of Black Americans from the Civil War to World War II* (New York: Anchor Books, 2008); David Oshinsky, *Worse than Slavery: Parchman Farm and the Ordeal of*

Jim Crow Justice (New York: Free Press, 1997); and Calvin John Smiley, "Citizen to Convict: The Consumption of the Body in the Age of Prisoner Reentry" (In *The Body in History, Culture, and the Arts*, 130–145. New York: Routledge).

34. Western, Kleykamp, & Rosenfeld, 2006.

35. Pettit & Western, 2004.

36. Hinton, Henderson, & Reed, 2018.

37. Zecker, 2008.

38. Fried, 1996.

39. Cave, 2006.

40. Browne, 2015; Eubanks, 2017.

41. Ofer & Rosemarin, 2014; Huffington Post Black Voices, 2014.

42. Jones-Brown et al., 2013.

43. Haldipur, 2019.

44. McCrea, 2014; Perez-Pena, 2011.

45. Coleman, 2016.

46. Lockhart, 2019.

47. U.S. Department of Justice, 2017.

48. Taylor, 2016, 127.

49. Cagnassola, 2020.

50. Cagnassola, 2020.

51. Wacquant, 2001.

52. Schwirtz, 2017; Durkin, 2016.

53. VanNostrand, 2013.

54. Zimmerman & Hunter, 2018.

55. Gonnerman, 2015.

56. Alexander, 2010.

57. DePalma, 1985; Smiley, 2016.

58. Lambros, 2011.

59. Jacobs, 1961, 68.

60. Beck, 2020; Beck & Goldstein, 2018; Laniyonu, 2018; Maharawal, 2017.

61. Smiley, 2016.

62. Curvin, 2014, 10.

63. Anderson, 2022.

64. Kiefer, 2020.

CHAPTER 2. PURGATORY

1. For the complete 2012 New Jersey presidential results, see *Politico*, "2012 New Jersey Presidential Results," last updated November 19, 2012, https://www.politico.com/2012-election/results/president/new-jersey/.

2. ACLU, 2021.

3. Uggen, Manza, & Behrens, 2003, 51. (Note: Only Black men received the right to vote under the 15th Amendment.)

4. New Jersey Institute for Social Justice, n.d.

5. Brotherton & Kretsedemas, 2008; Brotherton & Barrios, 2011; Brotherton, Stageman, & Leyro, 2013.

6. Shklar, 1991; Marshall, 1992 [1950].

7. Carrigan, 1999; Stampp, 1989 [1956].

8. Garland, 2010; Wacquant, 2004.

9. Alexander, 2010; Western, 2006.

10. Lerman & Weaver, 2014.

11. Miller & Stuart, 2017.

12. Sered, 2021.

13. Wacquant, 2005, 135.

14. Du Bois, 2003 [1903], 8.

15. Du Bois, 2003 [1903].

16. Ellison, 1980, 507.

17. Gwaltney, 1980, 29.

18. Jay-Z, 2013.

19. Pettit & Western, 2004.

20. Davis, 2018, 1128 (emphasis added).

21. See Thomas Hobbes, *The Leviathan* (1651); John Locke, *Second Treatise of Government* (1689); and Jean-Jacques Rousseau, *The Social Contract* (1762).

22. Torpey, 1997, 841 (emphasis added).

23. Glenn, 2011, 3.

24. Glenn, 2002.

25. For further reading, see Eric Williams, *Capitalism and Slavery*, 3rd ed. (Chapel Hill: University of North Carolina, 2021); Jerrold M. Packard, *American Nightmare: The History of Jim Crow* (New York: St. Martin's Griffin, 2003); *Scott v. Sanford* decision (https://supreme.justia.com/cases/federal/us/60/393/); and *Plessy v. Ferguson* decision (https://supreme.justia.com/cases/federal/us/163/537/).

26. Alexander, 2010, 57.

27. Freudenberg et al., 2005; Roman & Travis, 2006; LeBel, 2017.

28. Gonnerman, 2005.

29. Gonnerman, 2005; Wacquant, 2005.

30. Middlemass, 2017.

31. Kim, 2015.

32. Comfort, 2008.

33. Zgoba et al., 2008.

34. Western, 2006; Hattery & Smith, 2010.

35. Department of Labor and Workforce Development, 2015. (Note: This legislation passed after most fieldwork for this study had occurred.)

36. Pager, 2008.

37. Davis, 1998.

38. Thompkins, 2010.

39. Maher, 1997; Venkatesh, 2008; Sullivan, 2010; Human Rights Watch, 2012.

40. As of 2012, it is known as the Division of Child Protection and Permanency.

41. Sokoloff, 2003; Glaze & Bonczar, 2010.

42. Roberts, 2011.

CHAPTER 3. HALFWAY

1. Thompkins, 2010.

2. Dolnick, 2012b.

3. Dolnick, 2012b.

4. Dolnick, 2012b.

5. "John Clancy" (obituary), 2016.

6. This is from the now defunct CEC website (accessed June 2012).

7. Paez, 2017.

8. Meehan, 2019.

9. WPA, 2020.

10. Flannery & Glickman, 1996.

11. Meehan, 2019.

12. Meehan, 2019.

13. Martinson, 1974.

14. West, Sabol, & Greenman, 2010; Petersilia, 2011; Wagner & Sakala, 2014.

15. Dolnick, 2012a.

16. Thompkins, Curtis, & Wendel, 2010, 428.

17. Ortiz & Jackey, 2019.

18. Schlosser, 1998, 54.

19. Davis, 2016.

20. Eisen, 2017.

21. Wacquant, 2010.

22. Fang, 2017.

23. Carola, 2019.

24. Mays, 2018; Carola, 2019.

25. Du Bois, 1992 [1935], 698.

26. Du Bois, 1992 [1935], 698.

27. Blackmon, 2009.

28. Du Bois, 1992 [1935], 506 (emphasis added).

29. McKim, 2008.

30. Skarbek, 2014.
31. Knight, 2013.
32. Ortiz & Jackey, 2019.
33. FAMM, 2012.
34. Ravenelle, 2019.
35. Middlemass & Smiley, 2016a.
36. O'Keefe, 2008; Guenther, 2013; Carson, 2019.
37. West & Zimmerman, 1987.
38. West & Fenstermaker, 1995.
39. Durose, Cooper, & Snyder, 2014.
40. Durkheim, 1995 [1912].
41. Greenwald, 1973, 166 (emphasis added).
42. Daly, 1978.
43. Leverentz, 2010.
44. Ikeler & Smiley, 2020; Brenner & Theodore, 2002.
45. Brenner & Theodore, 2002; Duggan, 2003.
46. Harvey, 2015.
47. Kaufman, 2019a, 2019b.
48. Yates & Lakes, 2010.
49. De Giorgi, 2017.
50. De Giorgi, 2017, 94.
51. FAMM, 2012.

CHAPTER 4. BODY

1. Direct quote from a participant.
2. Drucker, 2013.
3. Maruschak, Berzofsky, & Unangst, 2015.
4. Bronson et al., 2017.
5. Bronson, Maruschak, & Berzofsky, 2015.
6. Brown, Bell, & Patterson, 2016; Patterson, Talbert, & Brown, 2021.
7. Lee et al., 2014.
8. Lee et al., 2014; Patterson, Talbert, & Brown, 2021.
9. Jacobs & Annese, 2016.
10. Geller et al., 2009; Arditti & Savla, 2015.
11. Phillips & Zhao, 2010.
12. Boch & Ford, 2015.
13. Miller, 2007.
14. Sewell & Jefferson, 2016.
15. Kerrison & Sewell, 2020.
16. Patterson, 2010.

17. Wang et al., 2009.

18. Western et al., 2015.

19. Wacquant, 2001.

20. Eze, 1997, 5 (emphasis in original).

21. Jefferson, 1999 [1785].

22. Smiley, 2021.

23. Browne, 2015.

24. Benjamin, 2019.

25. Li, 2020.

26. Smiley and Fakunle, 2016; Colburn & Melander, 2018.

27. Brodhead, 1988.

28. History Link 101, 2019.

29. Douglass, 2002 [1845].

30. Davis, 2003.

31. Weld, 1839.

32. Fields, 1990.

33. Lussana, 2010.

34. Woodard, 2014.

35. U.S. Constitution amendment XIII, § 1.

36. Uggen, Manza, & Behrens, 2003, 51.

37. Lacey, 1953; Myrdal, 1962 [1944].

38. Blackmon, 2009, 71.

39. Reed, 2016, 1.

40. Reed, 2016, xxxii.

41. Lightweis-Goff, 2007.

42. Holden-Smith, 1996.

43. Lightweis-Goff, 2007.

44. The Sentencing Project, 2021.

45. John, 2013.

46. Gillespie, 2018; Ikeler & Smiley, 2020.

47. Oshinsky, 1997.

48. Smiley & Middlemass, 2016.

49. Trimbur, 2009.

50. de la Tierra, 2019.

51. See Coss Marte, *Conbody: The Revolutionary Bodyweight Prison Boot Camp* (New York: St. Martin's Griffin, 2018). The Conbody website lists the trainers as having mug shots; see Conbody, "Meet Our Instructors," n.d., accessed October 12, 2022, https://conbody.com/meet-our-instructors/.

52. Moran, 2012.

53. DeVeaux, 2013.

54. Mualimm-ak, 2013.

55. Whitman, 2003.

56. Foucault, 2003.

57. Roberts, 2008, 247.

58. Fearnow, 2020.

59. Tong, McIntyre, & Silmon, 1997.

60. See Randol Contreras, *The Stickup Kids: Race, Drugs, Violence, and the American Dream* (Oakland: University of California Press, 2013).

61. Emphasis added.

62. Middlemass & Smiley, 2016b; Smiley & Middlemass, 2016.

63. Goffman, 1959.

64. Goffman, 1986 [1963].

65. For more information on New Jersey and New York adoption rules, see Adoption Network, "Criminal Background Checks for Adoption by State," n.d., accessed October 12, 2022, https://adoptionnetwork.com/adoption-laws-by -state/criminal-background-checks/.

66. X & Haley, 1992 [1965], 218.

67. Soble, Stroud, & Weinstein, 2020.

68. Jedlowski, 2001.

69. Middlemass & Smiley, 2016a.

70. Emphasis added.

CHAPTER 5. SPACE

1. See www.dondivamag.com.

2. Lefebvre, 1991.

3. Sherman, 1995; Braga, 2001; Eck et al., 2005.

4. Bonilla-Silva, 2006.

5. Haldipur, 2019.

6. Rios, 2011.

7. Clear, 2009.

8. Simes, 2019; Leverentz, 2020.

9. Gieryn, 2000; Goonewardena et al., 2008.

10. Bourdieu, 2011 [1986].

11. Halushka, 2020.

12. For detailed information about the documents required, see New Jersey Motor Vehicle Commission, *6 Point ID Verification Program*, n.d., accessed October 12, 2022, https://www.state.nj.us/corrections/pdf/OTS/FRARA /MotorVehicle/6_Pt_ID_Brochure.pdf.

13. Smiley & Middlemass, 2016.

14. Emphasis added.

15. Smith, Ruiz-Sancho, & Gunderson, 2001.

16. Rubin & Reiter, 2018.

17. Ross, 2012.

18. Ross, 2019, 57.

19. Merton, 1936.

20. Rom, 1998; Holley & Steiner, 2005; Roestone Collective, 2014.

21. Szifris, Fox, & Bradbury, 2018; Middlemass, 2017.

22. Rose et al., 2015.

CHAPTER 6. ABOLITION

1. Wacquant, 2005, 129.

2. Anderson, 2015.

3. McVeigh, 2012.

4. Smiley, 2019.

5. Del Signore, 2011.

6. Smiley, 2019.

7. State of New Jersey, 2020.

8. Romo, 2019.

9. William Howard Jr., 2007.

10. Musto, 1991; Muhammad, 2010.

11. State of New Jersey Department of Corrections, 2021.

12. State of New Jersey Department of Corrections, 2021.

13. State of New Jersey Department of Corrections, 2021.

14. Nellis, 2016.

15. Angwin et al., 2016; Benjamin, 2019; Kofman, 2019.

16. Wong, 2020.

17. Lennard, 2021.

18. Funk, 2022.

19. Alexander, 2018; Eubanks, 2017.

20. Rodriguez, 2018, 1576.

21. Purnell, 2021, 6.

22. Kaba, 2021, 2.

23. Davis, 2003, 107.

24. Gilmore, 2022.

25. Du Bois, 2003 [1903].

26. Davis, 2003, 10.

27. Fields, 1990, 106.

28. Olurin, 2021.

29. Kushner, 2019.

30. Foner, 1995 [1970], 3 (emphasis in original).

31. Smiley, 2020, 11.

32. Thompson, 2016.

33. Hampton, 1987.

34. Bissonette, 2008.

35. Robinson, 1983.

36. Wang, 2018, 69.

37. Kushner, 2019.

38. Jackson, 1994 [1970], 253.

39. Jackson, 1994 [1970], 236 (emphasis added).

40. Bukhari, 2010, 48.

41. Kaba & Duda, 2017.

42. Davis, 2005, 96.

43. National Advisory Commission on Criminal Justice Standards and Goals, 1973, 358 (emphasis added).

44. National Advisory Commission on Criminal Justice Standards and Goals, 1973, 597.

45. Morris, 1976.

46. VOCAL-NY, 2021, 5.

47. Fitzgerald, Kalof, & Dietz, 2009; Nordgren, 2012; Jacques, 2015.

48. Gruen, 2014.

49. Kushner, 2019.

50. Gilmore, 2007.

51. Byrd, 2016, 1.

52. Middlemass, 2017.

53. Ross, 2017.

54. Canon, 2022.

55. Zimmerman & Hunter, 2018.

56. Revanur, 2019.

57. Menendez et al., 2019.

58. Subramanian et al., 2020.

59. Covey, 2008; Graham, 2014.

60. The Bail Project, 2020.

61. A reference to prisons.

62. Abu-Jamal, 2009.

63. Breonna Taylor killed in Louisville, Kentucky, March 2020; George Floyd killed in Minneapolis, Minnesota, May 2020; Jacob Blake shot and paralyzed in Kenosha, Wisconsin, August 2020.

64. VOCAL-NY, 2021.

65. Gotsch & Basti, 2018, 5.

66. Gotsch & Basti, 2018.

67. Thomhave, 2017 (emphasis added).

68. Armstrong, 2019.

69. Chen, 2018.

70. Shank, 2013; Thompson, 2017; Yglesias, 2019; Peiffer, 2020.

71. Thompson, 2017.

72. Thompson, 2017.

73. Panico, 2021.

74. Desmond, 2016.

75. Lipsky, 2010, 25. (Note: I am fully aware Lipsky includes police. I am explicitly stating we should remove them.)

76. Samuel, 2019.

77. Farah, 2012.

78. Ewald, 2002.

79. Nocella & Anthony, 2011.

80. Abu-Jamal, 1996, 100 (emphasis in original).

Bibliography

Abu-Jamal, M. 1996. *Death Blossoms: Reflections from a Prisoner of Conscience*. San Francisco: City Lights Books.

———. 2009. *Jailhouse Lawyers: Prisoners Defending Prisoners v. the USA*. San Francisco: City Lights Books.

ACLU. 2021. "Felony Disenfranchisement Laws (Map)." American Civil Liberties Union. https://www.aclu.org/issues/voting-rights/voter-restoration/felony-disenfranchisement-laws-map.

Alexander, M. 2010. *The New Jim Crow: Mass Incarceration in the Age of Colorblindness*. New York: New Press.

———. 2018. "The Newest Jim Crow: Recent Criminal Justice Reforms Contain the Seeds of a Frightening System of 'E-carceration.'" *New York Times*, November 8, 2018. https://www.nytimes.com/2018/11/08/opinion/sunday/criminal-justice-reforms-race-technology.html.

Anderson, E. 1999. *Code of the Street: Decency, Violence, and the Moral Life of the Inner City*. New York: W. W. Norton.

———. 2015. "The White Space." *Sociology of Race and Ethnicity, 1*(1), 10–21.

———. 2022. *Black in White Space: The Enduring Impact of Color in Everyday Life*. Chicago: University of Chicago Press.

Angwin, J., Larson, J., Mattu, S., & Kirchner, L. 2016. "Machine Bias: There's Software Used across the Country to Predict Future Criminals. And It's Biased against Blacks." *ProPublica*, May 23, 2016. https://www.propublica.org/article/machine-bias-risk-assessments-in-criminal-sentencing.

Anti-Car Theft Act of 1992, H.R. 4542, 102nd Cong. 1992. https://www
.congress.gov/bill/102nd-congress/house-bill/4542.

Arditti, J. A., & Savla, J. 2015. "Parental Incarceration and Child Trauma
Symptoms in Single Caregiver Homes." *Journal of Child and Family Studies*,
24(3), 551–61.

Armstrong, M. 2019. "Here's Why Abolishing Private Prisons Isn't a Silver Bullet."
The Marshall Project, September 12, 2019. https://www.themarshallproject
.org/2019/09/12/here-s-why-abolishing-private-prisons-isn-t-a-silver
-bullet.

Austin, J. 2001. "Prisoner Reentry: Current Trends, Practices, and Issues."
Crime & Delinquency, *47*(3), 314–34.

Austin, J., Clark, J., Hardyman, P., & Henry, D. A. 2000. *Three Strikes and
You're Out: The Implementation and Impact of Strike Laws*. Research report
submitted to the U.S. Department of Justice. https://www.ojp.gov/pdffiles1
/nij/grants/181297.pdf.

Baum, D. 2016. "Legalize It All." *Harper's Magazine*, *24*, 21–32. https://
harpers.org/archive/2016/04/legalize-it-all/.

Beck, B. 2020. "Policing Gentrification: Stops and Low-Level Arrests during
Demographic Change and Real Estate Reinvestment." *City & Community*,
19(1), 245–72.

Beck, B., & Goldstein, A. 2018. "Governing through Police? Housing Market
Reliance, Welfare Retrenchment, and Police Budgeting in an Era of Declin-
ing Crime." *Social Forces*, *96*(3), 1183–1210.

Benjamin, R. 2019. *Race After Technology: Abolitionist Tools for the New Jim
Code*. Medford, MA: Polity Press.

Bissonette, J. 2008. *When the Prisoners Ran Walpole: A True Story in the
Movement for Prison Abolition*. Cambridge, MA: South End Press.

Blackmon, D. A. 2009. *Slavery by Another Name: The Re-enslavement of Black
Americans from the Civil War to World War II*. New York: Anchor.

Boch, S. J., & Ford, J. L. 2015. "C-reactive Protein Levels among US Adults
Exposed to Parental Incarceration." *Biological Research for Nursing*, *17*(5),
574–84.

Bonilla-Silva, E. 2006. *Racism without Racists: Color-Blind Racism and the
Persistence of Racial Inequality in the United States*. New York: Rowman &
Littlefield.

Bourdieu, P. 2011 [1986]. "The Forms of Capital." *Cultural Theory: An
Anthology*, *1*, 81–93.

Brady, T. F. 1970. "Addonizio Is Linked to Dummy Account." *New York Times*,
June 6, 1970. https://www.nytimes.com/1970/06/06/archives/addonizio-is
-linked-to-dummy-account-dummmy-account-tied-to.html.

Braga, A. A. 2001. "The Effects of Hot Spots Policing on Crime." *The Annals of
the American Academy of Political and Social Science*, *578*(1), 104–25.

Brenner, N., & Theodore, N. 2002. "Cities and the Geographies of 'Actually Existing Neoliberalism.'" *Antipode, 34*(3), 349–79.

Brodhead, R. H. 1988. "Sparing the Rod: Discipline and Fiction in Antebellum America." *Representations, 21,* 67–96.

Bronson, J., Maruschak, L. M., & Berzofsky, M. 2015. *Disabilities among Prison and Jail Inmates, 2011-12.* Washington, DC: U.S. Department of Justice, Office of Justice Programs, Bureau of Justice Statistics.

Bronson, J., Stroop, J., Zimmer, S., & Berzofsky, M. 2017. *Drug Use, Dependence, and Abuse among State Prisoners and Jail Inmates, 2007-2009.* Washington, DC: U.S. Department of Justice, Office of Juvenile Justice and Delinquency Prevention.

Brotherton, D. C., & Barrios, L. 2011. *Banished to the Homeland: Dominican Deportees and Their Stories of Exile.* New York: Columbia University Press.

Brotherton, D. C., & Kretsedemas, P., eds. 2008. *Keeping Out the Other: A Critical Introduction to Immigration Enforcement Today.* New York: Columbia University Press.

Brotherton, D. C., Stageman, D., & Leyro, S., eds. 2013. *Outside of Justice: Immigration and the Criminalizing Impact of Changing Policy and Practice.* New York: Springer.

Brown, T. N., Bell, M. L., & Patterson, E. J. 2016. "Imprisoned by Empathy: Familial Incarceration and Psychological Distress among African American Men in the National Survey of American Life." *Journal of Health and Social Behavior, 57*(2), 240–56.

Browne, S. 2015. *Dark Matters: On the Surveillance of Blackness.* Durham, NC: Duke University Press.

Bruggeman, L., Dwyer, D., & Ebbs, S. 2022. "Climate Activist's Fight against 'Terrorism' Sentence Could Impact the Future of Protests." *ABC News,* April 28, 2022. https://abcnews.go.com/US/climate-activists-fight-terrorism-sentence-impact-future-protests/story?id=84345514.

Bryant, E. 2021. "Why We Say 'Criminal Legal System,' Not 'Criminal Justice System.'" Vera Institute of Justice, December 1, 2021. https://www.vera.org/blog/why-we-say-criminal-legal-system-not-criminal-justice-system.

Bucerius, S. M. 2013. "Becoming a 'Trusted Outsider': Gender, Ethnicity, and Inequality in Ethnographic Research." *Journal of Contemporary Ethnography, 42*(6), 690–721.

Bukhari, S. 2010. *The War Before: The True Life Story of Becoming a Black Panther, Keeping the Faith in Prison & Fighting for Those Left Behind.* New York: Feminist Press.

Butterfield, F. 2008. *All God's Children: The Bosket Family and the American Tradition of Violence.* New York: Vintage.

Byrd, R. R. 2016. "'Punishment's Twin': Theorizing Prisoner Reentry for a Politics of Abolition." *Social Justice, 43*(1), 1–22.

Cagnassola, M. E. 2020. "Newark Council Approves Ordinance Redirecting Police Budget to Anti-Violence Initiatives." *Tap into Newark*, June 10, 2020. https://www.tapinto.net/towns/newark/sections/police-and-fire/articles/newark-council-approves-ordinance-redirecting-police-budget-to-anti-violence-initiatives.

Caldwell Epps, L. 2010. *From Zion to Brick City: What's Going On? Newark and the Legacy of the Sixties*. Available from ProQuest Dissertations & Theses A&I (304710883). http://proxy.wexler.hunter.cuny.edu/login.

Canon, D. 2022. *Pleading Out: How Plea Bargaining Creates a Permanent Criminal Class*. New York: Basic Books.

Carola, C. 2019. "3 State Prisons on Chopping Block Under Cuomo Budget Changes." *U.S. News*, February 15, 2019. https://www.usnews.com/news/best-states/new-york/articles/2019-02-15/3-state-prisons-on-chopping-block-under-cuomo-budget-changes.

Carrigan, W. D. 1999. "Slavery on the Frontier: The Peculiar Institution in Central Texas." *Slavery and Abolition*, 20(2), 63–96.

Carson, L. 2019. "Release from Long-Term Restrictive Housing." In *Prisoner Reentry in the 21st Century*, edited by K. M. Middlemass & C. J. Smiley, 96–106. New York: Routledge.

Cave, D. 2006. "In a Debate of Newark Mayoral Candidates, Some Agreement and a Lot of Discord." *New York Times*, May 4, 2006. http://www.nytimes.com/2006/05/04/nyregion/04newark.html.

Chen, M. 2018. "Who Profits from Our Prisons System?" *The Nation*, August 9, 2018. https://www.thenation.com/article/archive/profits-prison-system/.

Clear, T. R. 2009. *Imprisoning Communities: How Mass Incarceration Makes Disadvantaged Neighborhoods Worse*. New York: Oxford University Press.

Cohen, D. 2007. "Lilley Commission's Prescient Report." *NJ.com*, October 30, 2007. https://www.nj.com/njv_guest_blog/2007/10/history_matters_because_it_can.html.

Colburn, A., & Melander, L. A. 2018. "Beyond Black and White: An Analysis of Newspaper Representations of Alleged Criminal Offenders Based on Race and Ethnicity." *Journal of Contemporary Criminal Justice*, 34(4), 383–98.

Coleman, V. 2016. "Newark Council Approves Police Oversight Board, Union Vows to Sue." *NJ.com*, March 17, 2016. https://www.nj.com/essex/2016/03/newark_municipal_council_citizen_police_overight_b.html.

Comfort, M. 2008. *Doing Time Together: Love and Family in the Shadow of the Prison*. Chicago: University of Chicago Press.

Covey, R. D. 2008. "Fixed Justice: Reforming Plea Bargaining with Plea-Based Ceiling." *Tulane Law Review*, 82(4), 1237–90.

Curvin, R. 2014. *Inside Newark: Decline, Rebellion, and the Search for Transformation*. New Brunswick, NJ: Rutgers University Press.

Daly, M. 1978. *Gyn/Ecology: The Metaethics of Radical Feminism*. Boston: Beacon Press.

Davis, A. 1998. "Race and Criminalization: Black Americans and the Punishment Industry." In *The Angela Y. Davis Reader*, edited by J. James, 61–73. New York: Blackwell.

———. 2003. *Are Prisons Obsolete?* New York: Seven Stories Press.

———. 2005. *Abolition Democracy: Beyond Empire, Prisons, and Torture*. New York: Seven Stories Press.

———. 2016. *Freedom Is a Constant Struggle: Ferguson, Palestine, and the Foundations of a Movement*. Chicago: Haymarket Books.

Davis, J., III. 2018. "Law, Prison, and Double-Double Consciousness: A Phenomenological View of the Black Prisoner's Experience." *Yale Law Journal*, *128*, 1126–44.

De Giorgi, A. 2017. "Back to Nothing: Prisoner Reentry and Neoliberal Neglect." *Social Justice*, *44*(1), 83–120.

de la Tierra, A. 2019. "Carceral Calisthenics: (Body) Building a Resilient Self and Transformative Reentry Movement 1." In *Prisoner Reentry in the 21st Century*, edited by K. M. Middlemass & C. J. Smiley, 129–40. New York: Routledge.

Del Signore, J. 2011. "[Updates] NYPD Evicts Occupy Wall Street, Clearing Zuccotti Park." *Gothamist*, November 15, 2011. https://gothamist.com /news/updates-nypd-evicts-occupy-wall-street-clearing-zuccotti-park.

DePalma, A. 1985. "In New Jersey: Success Breeds Fourth Newark Gateway." *New York Times*, October 13, 1985. https://www.nytimes.com/1985/10 /13/realestate/in-new-jersey-success-breeds-fourth-newark-gateway .html.

Department of Labor and Workforce Development. 2015. "Opportunity to Compete Act Takes Effect March 1." State of New Jersey, February 27, 2015. https://nj.gov/labor/lwdhome/press/2015/20150227_OpportunitytoCompete .html.

Desmond, M. 2016. *Evicted: Poverty and Profit in the American City*. New York: Crown.

DeVeaux, M. 2013. "The Trauma of the Incarceration Experience." *Harvard Civil Rights-Civil Lib Law Review*, *48*(1), 257–77.

Ditton, P. M., & Wilson, D. J. 1999. *Truth in Sentencing in State Prisons*. Washington, DC: U.S. Department of Justice, Bureau of Justice Statistics. https://bjs.ojp.gov/content/pub/pdf/tssp.pdf.

Dolnick, S. 2012a. "At a Halfway House, Bedlam Reigns." *New York Times*, June 18, 2012. http://www.nytimes.com/2012/06/18/nyregion/at-bo-robinson-a-halfway-house-in-new-jersey-bedlam-reigns.html?ref=unlocked.

———. 2012b. "Unlocked." *New York Times*, June 2012. https://longform.org /posts/unlocked.

Douglass, F. 2002 [1845]. "Narrative of the Life of Frederick Douglass." In *The Classic Slave Narratives*, edited by H. L. Gates Jr., 323–436. New York: Signet Classic Printing.

Drucker, E. 2013. *A Plague of Prisons: The Epidemiology of Mass Incarceration*. New York: New Press.

Du Bois, W. E. B. 1992 [1935]. *Black Reconstruction in America: 1860–1880*. Edited by D. L. Lewis. New York: Free Press.

———. 2003 [1903]. *The Souls of Black Folk: Essays and Sketches*. Edited by F. J. Griffin. New York: Barnes & Noble Classics.

Duggan, L. 2003. *The Twilight of Equality: Neoliberalism, Cultural Politics and the Attack on Democracy*. Boston: Beacon Press.

Durkheim, E. 1995 [1912]. *The Elementary Forms of the Religious Life*. Translation and introduction by K. E. Fields. New York: New Press.

Durkin, E. 2016. "Kalief Browder's Brother Rips Mayor de Blasio's Justice Reboot Program for Failing to Speed Up Cases on Rikers Inmates Awaiting Trial." *Daily News*, October 25, 2016. https://www.nydailynews.com/new-york/rikers-island-inmates-waiting-long-trials-article-1.2844859.

Durose, M. R., Cooper, A. D., & Snyder, H. N. 2014. *Recidivism of Prisoners Released in 30 States in 2005: Patterns from 2005 to 2010* (Vol. 28). Washington, DC: U.S. Department of Justice, Office of Justice Programs, Bureau of Justice Statistics.

Eck, J. E., Chainey, S. P., Cameron, J. G., Leitner, M., & Wilson, R. E. 2005. *Mapping Crime: Understanding Hot Spots*. Washington, DC: National Institute of Justice. https://discovery.ucl.ac.uk/id/eprint/11291/1/11291.pdf.

Eisen, L. B. 2017. *Inside Private Prisons: An American Dilemma in the Age of Mass Incarceration*. New York: Columbia University Press.

Ellison, R. 1980. *Invisible Man*. New York: Vintage International.

Emert, P. R. 2003. "Three Strikes and You're Out." *The Legal Eagle*, 7(3). https://njsbf.org/wp-content/uploads/2017/03/LE-Spring-2003.pdf.

Eubanks, V. 2017. *Automating Inequality: How High-Tech Tools Profile, Police, and Punish the Poor*. New York: St. Martin's Press.

Ewald, A. C. 2002. "'Civil Death': The Ideological Paradox of Criminal Disenfranchisement Law in the United States." *University of Wisconsin Law Review*, 5(5), 1045–1137.

Eze, E. C., ed. 1997. *Race and Enlightenment: A Reader*. Oxford: Blackwell.

FAMM. 2012. *Frequently Asked Questions about Federal Halfway Houses & Home Confinement*. Washington, DC: Families Against Mandatory Minimums. https://famm.org/wp-content/uploads/FAQ-Halfway-House-4.24.pdf.

Fang, C. 2017. "The California Inmates Fighting the Wine Country Wildfires." *The Marshall Project*, October 23, 2017. https://www.themarshallproject.org/2017/10/23/the-california-inmates-fighting-the-wine-country-wildfires.

Farah, D. 2012. *The Transformation of El Salvador's Gangs into Political Actors*. Center for Strategic & International Studies, June 21, 2012. https://csis-website-prod.s3.amazonaws.com/s3fs-public/legacy_files/files /publication/120621_Farah_Gangs_HemFocus.pdf.

Fearnow, B. 2020. "White Bystanders Appear to Re-enact George Floyd Killing with Trump Signs in Background as Protesters March." *Newsweek*, June 9, 2020. https://www.newsweek.com/white-bystanders-appear-re-enact-george-floyd-killing-trump-signs-background-protesters-march-1509689.

Fields, B. J. 1990. "Slavery, Race and Ideology in the United States of America." *New Left Review*, *181*(1), 95–118.

Fitzgerald, A. J., Kalof, L., & Dietz, T. 2009. "Slaughterhouses and Increased Crime Rates: An Empirical Analysis of the Spillover from 'the Jungle' into the Surrounding Community." *Organization & Environment*, *22*(2), 158–84.

Flannery, M., & Glickman, M. 1996. *Fountain House: Portraits of Lives Reclaimed from Mental Illness*. Center City, MN: Hazeldon Information & Educational Services.

Foner, P., ed. 1972. *The Voice of Black America: Major Speeches by Negroes in the United States 1797–1971*. New York: Simon & Schuster.

———, ed. 1995 [1970]. *The Black Panthers Speak*. Cambridge, MA: Da Capo Press.

Foucault, M. 2003. *Society Must Be Defended: Lectures at the College de France 1975–1976*. New York: Picador.

Freudenberg, N., Daniels, J., Crum, M., Perkins, T., & Richie, B. E. 2005. "Coming Home from Jail: The Social and Health Consequences of Community Reentry for Women, Male Adolescents, and Their Families and Communities." *American Journal of Public Health*, *95*(10), 1725–36.

Fried, C. 1996. "America's Safest City: Amherst, N.Y.; the Most Dangerous: Newark, N.J." *Money*, November 27, 1996. https://money.cnn.com/magazines /moneymag/moneymag_archive/1996/11/27/225088/index.htm.

Funk, L. 2022. "NJ Supreme Court Orders Sundiata Acoli Eligible for Parole; Killed State Trooper in 1973." *Fox5 New York*, May 10, 2022. https://www .fox5ny.com/news/sundiata-acoli-bla-parole-nj.

Garland, D. 2010. *Peculiar Institution: America's Death Penalty in an Age of Abolition*. New York: Oxford University Press.

Geller, A., Garfinkel, I., Cooper, C. E., & Mincy, R. B. 2009. "Parental Incarceration and Child Well-being: Implications for Urban Families." *Social Science Quarterly*, *90*(5), 1186–1202.

Gieryn, T. F. 2000. "A Space for Place in Sociology." *Annual Review of Sociology*, *26*(1), 463–96.

Gillespie, K. 2018. "Placing Angola: Racialisation, Anthropocentrism, and Settler Colonialism at the Louisiana State Penitentiary's Angola Rodeo." *Antipode*, *50*(5), 1267–89.

Gilmore, R. W. 2007. *Golden Gulag: Prisons, Surplus, Crisis, and Opposition in Globalizing California.* Berkeley: University of California Press.

———. 2022. *Change Everything: Racial Capitalism and the Case for Abolition.* Chicago: Haymarket Books.

Glaze, L. E., & Bonczar, T. P. 2010. *Parents in Prison and Their Minor Children.* Report NCJ 222984. Washington, DC: Bureau of Justice Statistics. https://bjs.ojp.gov/content/pub/pdf/pptmc.pdf.

Glenn, E. N. 2002. *Unequal Freedom: How Race and Gender Shaped American Citizenship and Labor.* Cambridge, MA: Harvard University Press.

———. 2011. "Constructing Citizenship: Exclusion, Subordination and Resistance." *American Sociological Review, 76*(1), 1–24.

Goffman, E. 1959. *Presentation of Self in Everyday Life.* New York: Anchor Books.

———. 1986 [1963]. *Stigma: Notes on the Management of Spoiled Identity.* New York: Touchstone.

Gonnerman, J. 2005. *Life on the Outside: The Prison Odyssey of Elaine Bartlett.* New York: Picador.

———. 2015. "Kalief Browder, 1993–2015." *New Yorker,* June 7, 2015. https://www.newyorker.com/news/news-desk/kalief-browder-1993-2015.

Goonewardena, K., Kipfer, S., Milgrom, R., & Schmid, C., eds. 2008. *Space, Difference, Everyday Life: Reading Henri Lefebvre.* New York: Routledge.

Gotsch, K., & Basti, V. 2018. *Capitalizing on Mass Incarceration: U.S. Growth in Private Prisons.* Washington, DC: The Sentencing Project.

Graham, K. 2014. "Overcharging." *Ohio State Journal of Criminal Law, 11*(2), 701–24.

Greenwald, D. E. 1973. "Durkheim on Society, Thought and Ritual." *Sociological Analysis, 34*(3), 157–68.

Gruen, L., ed. 2014. *The Ethics of Captivity.* New York: Oxford University Press.

Guenther, L. 2013. *Solitary Confinement: Social Death and Its Afterlives.* Minneapolis: University of Minnesota Press.

Guerino, P., Harrison, P. M., & Sabol, W. J. 2011. *Prisoners in 2010.* Washington, DC: Bureau of Justice Statistics.

Gwaltney, J. L. 1980. *Drylongso: A Self-Portrait of Black America.* New York: Vintage.

Haldipur, J. 2019. *No Place on the Corner: The Costs of Aggressive Policing.* New York: NYU Press.

Hallinan, J. T. 2003. *Going Up the River: Travels in a Prison Nation.* New York: Random House.

Halushka, J. M. 2020. "The Runaround: Punishment, Welfare, and Poverty Survival after Prison." *Social Problems, 67*(2), 233–50.

Hampton, H. 1987. "A Nation of Law? 1968–1971." *Eyes on the Prize* (transcript). Boston: Blackside.

Harvey, D. 2015. *Seventeen Contradictions and the End of Capitalism*. New York: Oxford University Press.

Hattery, A. J., & Smith, E. 2010. *Prisoner Reentry and Social Capital: The Long Road to Reintegration*. Lanham, MD: Lexington Books.

Hinton, E. 2016. *From the War on Poverty to the War on Crime: The Making of Mass Incarceration in America*. Cambridge, MA: Harvard University Press.

Hinton, E., Henderson, L., & Reed, C. 2018. *An Unjust Burden: The Disparate Treatment of Black Americans in the Criminal Justice System*. New York: Vera Institute of Justice. https://www.issuelab.org/resources/30758/30758 .pdf.

History Link 101. 2019. "Ten Days from Today I Left the Plantation." History Link 101. https://historylink101.com/bw/American_Image/slides/4-j-IMG_ 1583.html.

Holden-Smith, B. 1996. "Lynching, Federalism, and the Intersection of Race and Gender in the Progressive Era." *Yale Journal of Law & Feminism, 8*, 31–78.

Holley, L. C., & Steiner, S. 2005. "Safe Space: Student Perspectives on Classroom Environment." *Journal of Social Work Education, 41*(1), 49–64.

Huffington Post Black Voices. 2014. "Stop and Frisk Much More Likely in Newark Than New York City." *HuffPost*, February 25, 2014. https://www .huffpost.com/entry/stop-and-frisk-newark_n_4853367.

Human Rights Watch. 2012. *Sex Workers at Risk: Condoms as Evidence of Prostitution in Four US Cities*. New York: Human Rights Watch. https:// www.hrw.org/report/2012/07/19/sex-workers-risk/condoms-evidence-prostitution-four-us-cities.

Ikeler, P., & Smiley, C. 2020. "The Racial Economics of Mass Incarceration." *Spectre Journal, 1*(2), 78–99.

Jackson, G. 1994 [1970]. *Soledad Brother: The Prison Letters of George Jackson*. Chicago: Lawrence Hill Books.

Jacobs, J. 1961. *The Death and Life of Great American Cities*. New York: Vintage.

Jacobs, S., & Annese, J. 2016. "Mom Dies of 'Broken Heart' after Son Kalief Browder Killed Himself Last Year." *Daily News*, October 16, 2016. https:// www.nydailynews.com/new-york/bronx/exclusive-mom-late-kalief-browder-dies-broken-heart-article-1.2833023.

Jacques, J. R. 2015. "The Slaughterhouse, Social Disorganization, and Violent Crime in Rural Communities." *Society and Animals, 23*(6), 594–612.

Jay-Z. 2013. "F.U.T.W." *Genius*. https://genius.com/Jay-z-futw-lyrics.

Jedlowski, P. 2001. "Memory and Sociology: Themes and Issues." *Time & Society, 10*(1), 29–44.

Jefferson, T. 1999 [1785]. *Notes on the State of Virginia*. New York: Penguin.

"John Clancy." (obituary). 2016. *Star-Ledger*. https://obits.nj.com/obituaries
/starledger/obituary-print.aspx?n=john-clancy&pid=180015352.

John, P. S. 2013. "Inmates End California Prison Hunger Strike." *Los Angeles
Times*, September 5, 2013. https://www.latimes.com/local/la-xpm-2013-
sep-05-la-me-ff-prison-strike-20130906-story.html.

Jones-Brown, D., Stoudt, B., Johnston, B., & Moran, K. 2013. *Stop, Question
and Frisk Policing Practices in New York City: A Primer (Revised)*. Center on
Race, Crime and Justice; John Jay College of Criminal Justice, July 2013.
http://www.atlanticphilanthropies.org/wp-content/uploads/2015/09/SQF_
Primer_July_2013.pdf.

Kaba, M. 2021. *We Do This 'Til We Free Us: Abolitionist Organizing and
Transforming Justice*. Chicago: Haymarket Books.

Kaba, M., & Duda, J. 2017. "Towards the Horizon of Abolition: A Conversation
with Mariama Kaba." The Next System Project, November 9, 2017. https://
thenextsystem.org/learn/stories/towards-horizon-abolition-conversation-
mariame-kaba.

Kaufman, N. 2019a. "Nongovernmental Organizations and Postprison Life:
Examining the Role of Religion." *Punishment & Society*, *21*(4), 393–416.

———. 2019b. "The State's Accomplices? Organizations and the Penal State." In
Prisoner Reentry in the 21st Century: Critical Perspectives of Returning Home,
edited by K. M. Middlemass & C. J. Smiley, 39–52. New York: Routledge.

Kerrison, E. M., & Sewell, A. A. 2020. "Negative Illness Feedbacks: High-Frisk
Policing Reduces Civilian Reliance on ED Services." *Health Services Research*,
55, 787–96.

Kiefer, E. 2020. "Newark Reaches Big Turning Point with Its Lead Water Crisis."
Patch, July 6, 2020. https://patch.com/new-jersey/newarknj/amp/28837541
/newark-reaches-big-turning-point-with-its-lead-water-crisis.

Kim, C. J. 2015. *Dangerous Crossings: Race, Species, and Nature in a Multicul-
tural Age*. Cambridge: Cambridge University Press.

Knight, M. M. 2013. *The Five Percenters: Islam, Hip-Hop and the Gods of New
York*. New York: Simon & Schuster.

Kofman, A. 2019. "Digital Jail: How Electronic Monitoring Drives Defendants
into Debt." *ProPublica*, July 3, 2019. https://www.propublica.org/article
/digital-jail-how-electronic-monitoring-drives-defendants-into-debt.

Kushner, R. 2019. "Is Prison Necessary? Ruth Wilson Gilmore Might Change
Your Mind." *New York Times*, April 17, 2019. https://www.nytimes
.com/2019/04/17/magazine/prison-abolition-ruth-wilson-gilmore.html.

Lacey, F. W. 1953. "Vagrancy and Other Crimes of Personal Condition." *Harvard
Law Review*, *66*(7), 1203–26.

Lambros, M. 2011. "The Newark Paramount Theatre." *After the Final Curtain*.
September 28, 2011. https://afterthefinalcurtain.net/2011/09/28/the-newark-
paramount-theatre/.

Laniyonu, A. 2018. "Coffee Shops and Street Stops: Policing Practices in Gentrifying Neighborhoods." *Urban Affairs Review, 54*(5), 898–930.

LeBel, T. P. 2017. "Housing as the Tip of the Iceberg in Successfully Navigating Prisoner Reentry." *Criminology & Public Policy, 16*(3), 889–908.

Lee, H., Wildeman, C., Wang, E. A., Matusko, N., & Jackson, J. S. 2014. "A Heavy Burden: The Cardiovascular Health Consequences of Having a Family Member Incarcerated." *American Journal of Public Health, 104*(3), 421–27.

Lefebvre, H. 1991. *The Production of Space.* Translated by D. Nicholson-Smith. Oxford: Blackwell.

Lennard, N. 2019. "How the Prosecution of Animal Rights Activists as Terrorists Foretold Today's Criminalization of Dissent." *The Intercept*, December 12, 2019. https://theintercept.com/2019/12/12/animal-people-documentary-shac-protest-terrorism/.

———. 2021. "After Half Century in Prison, Elderly Black Panther Should Not Be Left to Die." *The Intercept*, March 28, 2021. https://theintercept.com/2021/03/28/elderly-prisoner-black-panther-parole/.

Lerman, A. E., & Weaver, V. 2014. *Arresting Citizenship: The Democratic Consequences of American Crime Control.* Chicago: University of Chicago Press.

Leverentz, A. 2010. "People, Places, and Things: How Female Ex-prisoners Negotiate Their Neighborhood Context." *Journal of Contemporary Ethnography, 39*(6), 646–81.

———. 2020. "Beyond Neighborhoods: Activity Spaces of Returning Prisoners." *Social Problems, 67*(1), 150–70.

Li, D. K. 2020. "Black Man in New Jersey Misidentified by Facial Recognition Tech and Falsely Jailed, Lawsuit Claims." *NBC News*, December 29, 2020. https://www.nbcnews.com/news/us-news/black-man-new-jersey-misidentified-facial-recognition-tech-falsely-jailed-n1252489.

Lightweis-Goff, J. 2007. "'Blood at the Root': Lynching, Memory, and Freudian Group Psychology." *Psychoanalysis, Culture & Society, 12*(3), 288–95.

Lilley, R. 1968. *Report for Action: Governor's Select Commission on Civil Disorder, State of New Jersey.* NCJRS 69748. February 1968. https://www.ojp.gov/pdffiles1/Digitization/69748NCJRS.pdf.

Lipsky, M. 2010. *Street-Level Bureaucracy: Dilemmas of the Individual in Public Service.* New York: Russell Sage Foundation.

Lockhart, P. R. 2019. "Meek Mill's Decade-Long Probation Showed How Broken America's Justice System Is." *Vox*, updated August 27, 2019. https://www.vox.com/identities/2018/6/28/17487850/meek-mill-charges-dropped-brinkley-probation-reform-criminal-justice.

Lussana, S. 2010. "To See Who Was Best on the Plantation: Enslaved Fighting Contests and Masculinity in the Antebellum Plantation South." *Journal of Southern History, 76*(4), 901–22.

Lynch, J. P., & Sabol, W. J. 2001. *Prisoner Reentry in Perspective.* Crime Policy Report, Vol. 3, September 2001. Washington, DC: Urban Institute. http://webarchive.urban.org/UploadedPDF/410213_reentry.PDF.

Maharawal, M. M. 2017. "Black Lives Matter, Gentrification and the Security State in the San Francisco Bay Area." *Anthropological Theory, 17*(3), 338–64.

Maher, L. 1997. *Sexed Work: Gender, Race and Resistance in a Brooklyn Drug Market.* New York: Oxford University Press.

Marable, M. 2000. *How Capitalism Underdeveloped Black America: Problems in Race, Political Economy, and Society.* Cambridge, MA: South End Press.

Marshall, T. H. 1992 [1950]. *Citizenship and Social Class.* London: Pluto.

Martinson, R. 1974. "What Works? Questions and Answers about Prison Reform." *Public Interest, 35*(2), 22–54.

Maruschak, L. M., Berzofsky, M., & Unangst, J. 2015. *Medical Problems of State and Federal Prisoners and Jail Inmates, 2011–12.* Washington, DC: U.S. Department of Justice, Office of Justice Programs, Bureau of Justice Statistics.

Massey, D., & Denton, N. 1993. *American Apartheid: Segregation and the Making of the Underclass.* Cambridge, MA: Harvard University Press.

Mays, J. C. 2018. "For Sale, Must See: Former Prison in Upstate New York." *New York Times,* May 6, 2018. https://www.nytimes.com/2018/05/06/nyregion/prison-auction-new-york.html.

McCrea, J. 2014. "Newark Police to Be Monitored by Federal Watchdog, Sources Say." *Star-Ledger,* February 9, 2014. https://www.nj.com/essex/2014/02/justice_department_will_place_federal_monitor_over_newark_police_sources_say.html.

McKim, A. 2008. "'Getting Gut-Level' Punishment, Gender, and Therapeutic Governance." *Gender & Society, 22*(3), 303–23.

McVeigh, K. 2012. "Trayvon Martin Death: Sanford Police Chief Bill Lee to Quit." *Guardian,* April 23, 2012. https://www.theguardian.com/world/2012/apr/23/trayvon-martin-sanford-bill-lee.

Meehan, K. 2019. "Halfway House." *Britannica.* https://www.britannica.com/topic/halfway-house.

Menendez, M., Crowley, M. F., Eisen, L. B., & Atchison, N. 2019. *The Steep Costs of Criminal Justice Fees and Fines.* New York: Brennan Center for Justice at NYU Law School. https://static1.squarespace.com/static/5daf53015bc9a966f3ea3674/t/5e5ea1aba90e4344f8a51dd4/1583260083452/2019_10_Fees%26Fines_Final5.pdf.

Merton, R. K. 1936. "The Unanticipated Consequences of Purposive Social Action." *American Sociological Review, 1*(6), 894–904.

Middlemass, K. 2017. *Convicted and Condemned: The Politics and Policies of Prisoner Reentry.* New York: NYU Press.

Middlemass, K. M., & Smiley, C. 2016a. "Doing a Bid: The Construction of Time as Punishment." *Prison Journal, 96*(6), 793–813.

———. 2016b. "Jumpsuit to Button-Down: Clothing Used as Resistance in Prisoner Reentry." *Journal of Criminal Justice and Law Review*, 5(1–2), 63–80.

———, eds. 2019. *Prisoner Reentry in the 21st Century: Critical Perspectives of Returning Home*. New York: Routledge.

Miller, K. M. 2007. "Risk and Resilience among African American Children of Incarcerated Parents." *Journal of Human Behavior in the Social Environment*, 15(2–3), 25–37.

Miller, R. J., & Stuart, F. 2017. "Carceral Citizenship: Race, Rights and Responsibility in the Age of Mass Supervision." *Theoretical Criminology*, 21(4), 532–48.

Moran, D. 2012. "Prisoner Reintegration and the Stigma of Prison Time Inscribed on the Body." *Punishment & Society*, 14(5), 564–83.

Morris, M. 1976. *Instead of Prisons: A Handbook for Abolitionists*. Syracuse, NY: Prison Research Education Action Project.

Mualimm-ak, F. O. 2013. "Solitary Confinement's Invisible Scars." *Guardian*, October 30, 2013. https://www.theguardian.com/commentisfree/2013/oct/30/solitary-confinement-invisible-scars.

Muhammad, K. 2010. *The Condemnation of Blackness: Race, Crime, and the Making of Modern Urban America*. Cambridge, MA: Harvard University Press.

Murakawa, N. 2014. *The First Civil Right: How Liberals Built Prison America*. New York: Oxford University Press.

Musto, D. F. 1991. "Opium, Cocaine, and Marijuana in American History." *Scientific American*, 265(1), 40–47.

Myrdal, G. 1962 [1944]. *An American Dilemma: The Negro Problem and Modern Democracy*. New York: Harper and Row.

National Advisory Commission on Criminal Justice Standards and Goals. 1973. *Corrections*. Washington, DC: U.S. Government Printing Office.

Nellis, A. 2016. *The Color of Justice: Racial and Ethnic Disparity in State Prisons*. Washington, DC: The Sentencing Project. https://www.sentencingproject.org/wp-content/uploads/2016/06/The-Color-of-Justice-Racial-and-Ethnic-Disparity-in-State-Prisons.pdf.

New Jersey Institute for Social Justice. n.d. "1844 No More." Accessed March 16, 2020. https://www.njisj.org/1844nomorereport2017.

Nocella, A. J., & Anthony, J. 2011. "An Overview of the History and Theory of Transformative Justice." *Peace & Conflict Review*, 6(1), 1–10.

Nordgren, A. 2012. "Meat and Global Warming: Impact Models, Mitigation Approaches and Ethical Aspects." *Environmental Values*, 21(4), 437–57.

Ofer, U., & Rosemarin, A. 2014. "Stop-and-Frisk: A First Look at Six Months of Data on Stop-and-Frisk Practices in Newark." *ACLU New Jersey*, February

25, 2014. https://www.aclu-nj.org/files/8113/9333/6064/2014_02_25_
nwksnf.pdf.

O'Keefe, M. L. 2008. "Administrative Segregation from Within: A Corrections
Perspective." *Prison Journal*, *88*(1), 123–43.

Olurin, O. 2021. "*Law & Order* Taught Americans to Root for the Police." *Teen
Vogue*, December 8, 2021. https://www.teenvogue.com/story/law-and-order-
policing-media.

Ortiz, J. M., & Jackey, H. 2019. "The System Is Not Broken, It Is Intentional:
The Prisoner Reentry Industry as Deliberate Structural Violence." *Prison
Journal*, *99*(4), 484–503.

Oshinsky, D. M. 1997. *Worse than Slavery: Parchman Farm and the Ordeal of
Jim Crow Justice*. New York: Simon & Schuster.

Paez, P. E. 2017. "The GEO Group Announces $360 Million Acquisition of
Community Education Centers." *Business Wire*, February 22, 2017. https://
www.businesswire.com/news/home/20170222005729/en/The-GEO-Group-
Announces-360-Million-Acquisition-of-Community-Education-Centers.

Pager, D. 2008. *Marked: Race, Crime, and Finding Work in an Era of Mass
Incarceration*. Chicago: University of Chicago Press.

Panico, R. 2021. "Converted Shipping Containers to House Homeless Who
Frequent Newark Penn Station." *NJ.com*, January 16, 2021. https://www
.nj.com/essex/2021/01/converted-shipping-containers-to-house-homeless-
who-frequent-newark-penn-station.html.

Parks, B. 2008. "In Final Days, King Left Imprint on New Jersey." *NJ.com*,
January 21, 2008. https://www.nj.com/njv_guest_blog/2008/01/in_final_
days_king_left_imprin_1.html.

Patterson, E. J. 2010. "Incarcerating Death: Mortality in US State Correctional
Facilities, 1985–1998." *Demography*, *47*(3), 587–607.

Patterson, E. J., Talbert, R. D., & Brown, T. N. 2021. "Familial Incarceration,
Social Role Combinations, and Mental Health among African American
Women." *Journal of Marriage and Family*, *83*(1), 86–101.

Peiffer, E. 2020. "Five Charts That Explain the Homelessness-Jail Cycle—and
How to Break It." *Urban Institute*, September 16, 2020. https://www.urban
.org/features/five-charts-explain-homelessness-jail-cycle-and-how-
break-it.

Perez-Pena, R. 2011. "Police Department in Newark Is Facing U.S. Inquiry." *New
York Times*, May 10, 2011. https://www.nytimes.com/2011/05/10/nyregion
/justice-department-investigates-newark-police.html.

Perkinson, R. 2010. *Texas Tough: The Rise of America's Prison Empire*. New
York: Metropolitan Books.

Petersilia, J. 2004. "What Works in Reentry?" *Federal Probation*, *68*, 4–8.

———. 2011. "Beyond the Prison Bubble." *Wilson Quarterly (1976-)*, *35*(1), 50–55.

Pettit, B., & Western, B. 2004. "Mass Imprisonment and the Life Course: Race and Class Inequality in U.S. Incarceration." *American Sociological Review*, *69*(2), 151–69.

Pew Center on the States. 2009. *One in 31: The Long Reach of American Corrections*. Washington, DC: Pew Center on the States.

Phillips, S. D., & Zhao, J. 2010. "The Relationship between Witnessing Arrests and Elevated Symptoms of Posttraumatic Stress: Findings from a National Study of Children Involved in the Child Welfare System." *Children and Youth Services Review*, *32*(10), 1246–54.

Purnell, D. 2021. *Becoming Abolitionists: Police, Protests, and the Pursuit of Freedom*. New York: Astra House.

Ramirez, M. D. 2013. "Punitive Sentiment." *Criminology*, *51*(2), 329–64.

Ravenelle, A. J. 2019. *Hustle and Gig: Struggling and Surviving in the Sharing Economy*. Oakland: University of California Press.

Reed, A. 2016. *The Life and the Adventures of a Haunted Convict*. Edited by C. Smith. New York: Random House.

Report of the National Advisory Commission on Civil Disorders. 1968. New York: Bantam Books.

Revanur, S. 2019. "Examining the Costs and Benefits of Plea Bargaining in the United States." *Medium*, April 13, 2019. https://sneharevanur.medium.com /examining-the-costs-and-benefits-of-plea-bargaining-in-the-united-states-b744545e3f36.

Rios, V. M. 2011. *Punished: Policing the Lives of Black and Latino Boys*. New York: New York University Press.

Roberts, D. 2008. "Torture and the Biopolitics of Race." *University of Miami Law Review*, *62*(2), 229–47.

———. 2011. "Prison, Foster Care, and the Systemic Punishment of Black Mothers." *UCLA Law Review*, *59*, 1474–1501.

Robinson, C. J. 1983. *Black Marxism: The Making of the Black Radical Tradition*. London: Zed Press.

Rodney, W. 1972. *How Europe Underdeveloped Africa*. Washington, DC: Howard University Press.

Rodriguez, D. 2018. "Abolition as Praxis of Human Being: A Foreword." *Harvard Law Review*, *132*(6), 1575–1612.

Roestone Collective. 2014. "Safe Space: Towards a Reconceptualization." *Antipode*, *46*(5), 1346–65.

Rom, R. B. 1998. "'Safe Spaces': Reflections on an Educational Metaphor." *Journal of Curriculum Studies*, *30*(4), 397–408.

Roman, C. G., & Travis, J. 2006. "Where Will I Sleep Tomorrow? Housing, Homelessness, and the Returning Prisoner." *Housing Policy Debate*, *17*(2), 389–418. https://doi.org/10.1080/10511482.2006.9521574.

Romo, V. 2019. "New Jersey Governor Signs Bills Restoring Voting Rights to More Than 80,000 People." NPR, December 18, 2019. https://www.npr.org /2019/12/18/789538148/new-jersey-governor-signs-bills-restoring-voting-rights-to-more-than-80–000-peop.

Rose, D. Z., Guerrero, W. R., Mokin, M. V., Gooch, C. L., Bozeman, A. C., Pearson, J. M., & Burgin, W. S. 2015. "Hemorrhagic Stroke following Use of the Synthetic Marijuana 'Spice.'" *Neurology*, *85*(13), 1177–79.

Ross, R. 2012. "Ice Cold." *God Forgives, I Don't* (album). https://genius.com /Rick-ross-ice-cold-lyrics.

———. 2017. "Dead Presidents." *Rather You Than Me* (album). https://genius .com/Rick-ross-dead-presidents-lyrics.

———. 2019. *Hurricanes: A Memoir*. With Neil Martinez-Belkin. Toronto: Hanover Square Press.

Rubin, A. T., & Reiter, K. 2018. "Continuity in the Face of Penal Innovation: Revisiting the History of American Solitary Confinement." *Law & Social Inquiry*, *43*(4), 1604–32.

Sabol, W. J., West, H. C., & Cooper, M. 2009. "Prisoners in 2008." *Bureau of Justice Statistics Bulletin*, *228417*, 1–45.

Samuel, S. 2019. "Ecuador Legalized Gangs. Murder Rates Plummeted." *Vox*, March 26, 2019. https://www.vox.com/future-perfect/2019/3/26/18281325 /ecuador-legalize-gangs.

Schlosser, E. 1998. "The Prison-Industrial Complex." *Atlantic Monthly*, *282*, 51–77.

Schwirtz, M. 2017. "What Is Rikers Island?" *New York Times*, April 5, 2017. https://www.nytimes.com/2017/04/05/nyregion/rikers-island-prison-new -york.html#:~:text=On.

Seiter, R. P., & Kadela, K. R. 2003. "Prisoner Reentry: What Works, What Does Not, and What Is Promising." *Crime & Delinquency*, *49*(3), 360–88.

Sered, S. S. 2021. "Diminished Citizenship in the Era of Mass Incarceration." *Punishment & Society*, *23*(2), 218–40.

Sewell, A. A., & Jefferson, K. A. 2016. "Collateral Damage: The Health Effects of Invasive Police Encounters in New York City." *Journal of Urban Health*, *93*(1), 42–67.

Shank, J. 2013. "Utah Is on Track to End Homelessness by 2015 with This One Simple Idea." *Nation Swell*. https://nationswell.com/one-state-track-become-first-end-homelessness-2015/.

Shedd, C. 2011. "Countering the Carceral Continuum: The Legacy of Mass Incarceration." *Criminology & Public Policy*, *10*(3), 865–71.

Sherman, L. W. 1995. "Hot Spots of Crime and Criminal Careers of Places." *Crime and Place*, *4*, 35–52.

Shklar, J. N. 1991. *American Citizenship: The Quest for Inclusion*. Cambridge, MA: Harvard University Press.

Simes, J. T. 2019. "Place after Prison: Neighborhood Attainment and Attachment during Reentry." *Journal of Urban Affairs*, *41*(4), 443–63.

Skarbek, D. 2014. *The Social Order of the Underworld: How Prison Gangs Govern the American Penal System*. New York: Oxford University Press.

Smiley, C. 2016. "Can I Sit? The Use of Public Space and the 'Other.'" *Tijdschrift over Cultuur & Criminaliteit*, *6*(1), 66–81. https://doi.org/10.5553/TCC/221195072016006001005.

———. 2019. "Release in the Era of BLM: The Nexus of Black Lives Matter and Prisoner Reentry." *Prison Journal*, *99*(4), 396–419.

———. 2020. "Reform Is Never Enough: Embracing the Defund and Abolition Movement." *Critical Criminologist: Spotlight*, *28*(2), 10–12. https://divisiononcriticalcriminology.com/wp-content/uploads/ASC-DCCSJ-Fall-Newsletter-2020.pdf.

———. 2021. "Display, Performance, and Re-imagining the Black Body." In *The Black Index*, edited by B. Cooks & S. Watson, 62–73. Munich: Hirmer.

Smiley, C., & Fakunle, D. 2016. "From 'Brute' to 'Thug': The Demonization and Criminalization of Unarmed Black Male Victims in America." *Journal of Human Behavior in the Social Environment*, *26*(3–4), 350–66.

Smiley, C., & Middlemass, K. M. 2016. "Clothing Makes the Man: Impression Management and Prisoner Reentry." *Punishment & Society*, *18*(2), 220–43.

Smith, G. W., Ruiz-Sancho, A., & Gunderson, J. G. 2001. "An Intensive Outpatient Program for Patients with Borderline Personality Disorder." *Psychiatric Services*, *52*(4), 532–33.

Smith, J. M., & Kinzel, A. 2021. "Carceral Citizenship as Strength: Formerly Incarcerated Activists, Civic Engagement and Criminal Justice Transformation." *Critical Criminology*, *29*(1), 93–110.

Soble, L., Stroud, K., & Weinstein, M. 2020. *Eating Behind Bars: Ending the Hidden Punishment of Food in Prison*. Impact Justice. https://impactjustice.org/wp-content/uploads/IJ-Eating-Behind-Bars.pdf.

Sokoloff, N. 2003. "The Impact of the Prison Industrial Complex on African American Women." *Souls*, *5*(4), 31–46.

Solomon, A. L., Osborne, J. W. L., Winterfield, L., Elderbroom, B., Burke, P., Stroker, R. P., & Burrell, W. D. 2008. *Putting Public Safety First: 13 Parole Supervision Strategies to Enhance Reentry Outcomes*. Washington, DC: Urban Institute.

Stampp, K. M. 1989 [1956]. *Peculiar Institution: Slavery in the Ante-bellum South*. New York: Vintage Books.

State of New Jersey. 2020. "Governor Murphy Signs Legislation to Expand Access to and Strengthen Democracy." Official Site of the State of New Jersey, January 21, 2020. https://www.nj.gov/governor/news/news/562020/approved/20200121j.shtml.

State of New Jersey Department of Corrections. 2021. "Offender Statistics." Official Site of the State of New Jersey. https://www.state.nj.us/corrections /pages/OffenderInformation.html#OffenderStats.

Stir Crazy. 1980. Directed by S. Poitier. Written by B. J. Friedman. Columbia Pictures.

Subramanian, R., Digard, L., Washington, M., II, & Sorage, S. 2020. *In the Shadows: A Review of the Research on Plea Bargaining.* Vera Institute of Justice, September 2020. https://www.vera.org/downloads/publications /in-the-shadows-plea-bargaining.pdf.

Sullivan, B. 2010. "When (Some) Prostitution Is Legal: The Impact of Law Reform on Sex Work in Australia." *Journal of Law and Society*, 37(1), 85–104.

Szifris, K., Fox, C., & Bradbury, A. 2018. "A Realist Model of Prison Education, Growth, and Desistance: A New Theory." *Journal of Prison Education and Reentry*, 5(1), 41–62.

Taylor, K. Y. 2016. *From Black Lives Matter to Black Liberation.* Chicago: Haymarket Books.

The Bail Project. 2020. *Annual Report 2020.* https://bailproject.org/wp-content/uploads/2020/12/the_bail_project_annual_report_2020_5x8_ Portrait_50pp_v5_WEB.pdf.

The Sentencing Project. 2021. *Trends in U.S. Corrections.* May 17, 2021. https://www.sentencingproject.org/publications/trends-in-u-s-corrections/.

Thomhave, K. 2017. "How the Prison Phone Industry Further Isolates Prisoners." *American Prospect*, October 12, 2017. https://prospect.org/economy /prison-phone-industry-isolates-prisoners/.

Thompkins, D. E. 2010. "The Expanding Prisoner Reentry Industry." *Dialectical Anthropology*, 34(4), 589–604.

Thompkins, D. E., Curtis, R., & Wendel, T. 2010. "Forum: The Prison Reentry Industry." *Dialectical Anthropology*, 34(4), 427–29.

Thompson, C. 2017. "A Fresh Take on Ending the Jail-to-Street-to-Jail Cycle." *Marshall Project*, May 10, 2017. https://www.themarshallproject.org/2017 /05/10/a-fresh-take-on-ending-the-jail-to-street-to-jail-cycle.

Thompson, H. A. 2016. *Blood in the Water: The Attica Prison Uprising of 1971 and Its Legacy.* New York: Vintage Books.

Tolnay, S. E. 2003. "The African American 'Great Migration' and Beyond." *Annual Review of Sociology*, 29, 209–32.

Tong, V., McIntyre, T., & Silmon, H. 1997. "What's the Flavor? Understanding Inmate Slang Usage in Correctional Education Settings." *Journal of Correctional Education*, 48(4), 192–97.

Torpey, J. 1997. "Revolutions and Freedom of Movement: An Analysis of Passport Controls in the French, Russian, and Chinese Revolutions." *Theory and Society*, 26, 837–68.

Travis, J., & Petersilia, J. 2001. "Reentry Reconsidered: A New Look at an Old Question." *Crime & Delinquency, 47*(3), 291–313.

Trimbur, L. 2009. "'Me and the Law Is Not Friends': How Former Prisoners Make Sense of Reentry." *Qualitative Sociology, 32*(3), 259–77.

Uggen, C., Manza, J., & Behrens, A. 2003. "Felony Voting Rights and the Disenfranchisement of African Americans." *Souls, 5*(3), 48–57.

U.S. Department of Justice. 2017. *Federal Reports on Police Killings: Ferguson, Cleveland, Baltimore, and Chicago.* Brooklyn, NY: Melville House.

VanNostrand, M. 2013. *New Jersey Jail Population Analysis: Identifying Opportunities to Safely and Responsibly Reduce the Jail Population.* U.S. Department of Justice, Office of Justice Programs, March 2013. https://www.ojp.gov/ncjrs/virtual-library/abstracts/new-jersey-jail-population-analysis-identifying-opportunities.

Venkatesh, S. A. 2008. *Off the Books.* Cambridge, MA: Harvard University Press.

VOCAL-NY. 2021. *Why a Caring & Compassionate New Deal for New York City.* March 16, 2021. https://static1.squarespace.com/static/5edbd1827536f464a00c32de/t/608c1e7f2fc3804381d9458c/1619795584284/ccnewdeal_April21.pdf.

Wacquant, L. 2001. "Deadly Symbiosis: When Ghetto and Prison Meet and Mesh." *Punishment & Society, 3*(1), 95–133.

———. 2004. "The New 'Peculiar Institution': On the Prison as Surrogate Ghetto." In *Violence in War and Peace*, edited by N. Scheper-Hughes & P. Bourgois, 318–23. Malden, MA: Blackwell.

———. 2005. "Race as Civic Felony." *International Social Science Journal, 57*(183), 127–42.

———. 2010. "Prisoner Reentry as Myth and Ceremony." *Dialectical Anthropology, 34*(4), 605–20.

Wagner, P., & Sakala, L. 2014. "Mass Incarceration: The Whole Pie—A Prison Policy Initiative Briefing." *Prison Policy Initiative*, March 12, 2014. https://www.prisonpolicy.org/reports/pie.html.

Wang, E. A., Pletcher, M., Lin, F., Vittinghoff, E., Kertesz, S. G., Kiefe, C. I., & Bibbins-Domingo, K. 2009. "Incarceration, Incident Hypertension, and Access to Health Care: Findings from the Coronary Artery Risk Development in Young Adults (CARDIA) Study." *Archives of Internal Medicine, 169*(7), 687–93.

Wang, J. 2018. *Carceral Capitalism.* South Pasadena, CA: Semiotext(e).

Weld, T. D., ed. 1839. *American Slavery As It Is: Testimony of a Thousand Witnesses.* New York: American Anti-Slavery Society.

West, C., & Fenstermaker, S. 1995. "Doing Difference." *Gender & Society, 9*(1), 8–37.

West, C., & Zimmerman, D. H. 1987. "Doing Gender." *Gender & Society, 1*(2), 125–51.

West, H. C., Sabol, W. J., & Greenman, S. J. 2010. *Prisoners in 2009*. Washington, DC: Bureau of Justice Statistics.

Western, B. 2006. *Punishment and Inequality in America*. New York: Russell Sage.

Western, B., Braga, A. A., Davis, J., & Sirois, C. 2015. "Stress and Hardship after Prison." *American Journal of Sociology, 120*(5), 1512–47.

Western, B., Kleykamp, M., & Rosenfeld, J. 2006. "Did Falling Wages and Employment Increase US Imprisonment?" *Social Forces, 84*(4), 2291–2311.

Whitman, J. Q. 2003. *Harsh Justice: Criminal Punishment and the Widening Divide between America and Europe*. New York: Oxford University Press.

William Howard, M., Jr. 2007. *New Jersey Death Penalty Study Commission Report*. January 2007. http://www.njleg.state.nj.us/committees/dpsc_final.pdf.

Wong, W. 2020. "More Than 2,000 New Jersey Inmates Released to Slow Spread of Coronavirus in Prisons." *NBC News*, November 4, 2020. https://www.nbcnews.com/news/us-news/more-2-000-new-jersey-inmates-released-slow-spread-coronavirus-n1246388.

Woodard, V. 2014. *The Delectable Negro: Human Consumption and Homoeroticism within U.S. Slave Culture*. New York: New York University Press.

Wormith, J. S., Althouse, R., Simpson, M., Reitzel, L. R., Fagan, T. J., & Morgan, R. D. 2007. "The Rehabilitation and Reintegration of Offenders: The Current Landscape and Some Future Directions for Correctional Psychology." *Criminal Justice and Behavior, 34*(7), 879–92.

WPA. 2020. "Historic Mission." Women's Prison Association. https://www.wpaonline.org/historic-mission/.

X, M., & Haley, A. 1992 [1965]. *The Autobiography of Malcolm X as Told by Alex Haley*. New York: Ballantine Books.

Yates, M. T., & Lakes, R. D. 2010. "After Pell Grants: The Neoliberal Assault on Prisoners." *Policy Futures in Education, 8*(1), 61–70.

Yglesias, M. 2019. "The Most Cost-Effective Way to Help the Homeless Is to Give Them Homes." *Vox*, May 30, 2014. https://www.vox.com/2014/5/30/5764096/homeless-shelter-housing-help-solutions.

Zecker, R. M. 2008. "'We Never Locked Our Doors at Night': Newark on the 'Net, Minus the Mob." *Journal of American Culture, 31*(4), 361–72.

Zgoba, K., Witt, P., Dalessandro, M., & Veysey, B. 2008. *Megan's Law: Assessing the Practical and Monetary Efficacy*. Washington, DC: U.S. Department of Justice.

Zimmerman, D. M., & Hunter, S. 2018. "Factors Affecting False Guilty Pleas in a Mock Plea Bargaining Scenario." *Legal and Criminological Psychology, 23*(1), 53–67.

Index

Page numbers followed by "*fig.*" indicate a figure.

Founded in 1893,
UNIVERSITY OF CALIFORNIA PRESS
publishes bold, progressive books and journals
on topics in the arts, humanities, social sciences,
and natural sciences—with a focus on social
justice issues—that inspire thought and action
among readers worldwide.

The UC PRESS FOUNDATION
raises funds to uphold the press's vital role
as an independent, nonprofit publisher, and
receives philanthropic support from a wide
range of individuals and institutions—and from
committed readers like you. To learn more, visit
ucpress.edu/supportus.